Praise for "When the Moon is Dark You Can See the Stars"

"As suffering propelled Pamela Prime down her ancient wisdom path, she instinctively began stretching boundaries that were cramping her spiritual growth. ...When the Moon Is Dark belongs to a genre of spiritual literature written by mystics like St. Teresa of Avila, St. Therese of Lisieux, and Blessed Julian of Norwich... it is a fresh questioning of how we look at God and what God is about in our rapidly changing world."

— *Robert Lentz, OFM, renowned Iconographer, co-author, "Christ in the Margins from the Preface"*

"The absolute honesty and ruthless authenticity of this book, written by an emerging female theologian, integrates the personal experience of profound transformation, social vision and revelation. It challenges the assumptions of what it means to be a woman, a mother and a scholar, and offers the allegiance to the experience of living as a litmus test of the degrees of intimacy with God. Reading this book will benefit laity, theologians and spiritual guides alike, and raise the consciousness of the reader regardless of gender or age."

— *Olga Louchakova, MD, PhD. Professor at the Institute of Transpersonal Psychology*

"This book has it all: provocative prophetic stories of transformation of grief into joy, a journey of deepening faith through deep inner listening, transformational theological inquiry into a more central place of the feminine in spirituality and creative wisdom and healing issuing forth from initial tragedies. Prime lures us into thinking more deeply, sensing more acutely and seeing more clearly the spiritual choices available to us as we make meaning out of life's vicissitudes. A must-read for anyone who is curious about merging her or his spirituality with everyday life to form a fuller pattern of living."

— *Rev. Suzanne Fageol Episcopal Priest, Spiritual Director & Educator*

"Pamela Prime writes with the authority of one who has gone to both the edge and the center of her faith. Her compelling journey invites us to engage our own beginnings, stirrings, shatterings, and awakenings....It invites us to enter our own inner terrain of transformation. This is the story of a woman's radical spiritual quest, filled with honesty, courage, vulnerability, and power."

— *Clare Ronzanni, MA Theology, Director of Spiritual Formation,*
Franciscan School of Theology, Berkeley, CA

"In recent years Narrative Spirituality has become prominent in the literature of spirituality. The genre uses personal experience--autobiography—to discover and communicate the mystery of the God who enters our personal human experience. In When the Moon is Dark We Can See the Stars, Pamela Prime gives us an extraordinary example of Narrative Spirituality.

In this work she explores the mystery of her own life. She deftly searches for the God for whom she longed through most of her young adult years. By honestly examining her joy and her sadness, her tears and her laughter, her loves and her losses, she discovers a new face of God, the God who has brought her peace and deep joy.

This is a book that will delight and invite the reader to explore the mystery within and behind his or her own life. It will provoke laughter, joy, and even tears. It will inspire, encourage, and empower the reader to the same kind of personal exploration that it describes. I recommend it to anyone who is serious about the quest for the living God."

— *Frank Houdek S.J. PhD Spiritual Director, author "Guided By The Spirit"*

I

"Pamela Prime has shown us a way to move into the mystical....to find the light in the darkness. This is a brilliant book for all women...a must read."

— *Laura Bushnell, author of "Life Magic"*

"The persistent search for Truth in continued deepening relationship with the mystery of God revealed in Pamela's reflections on her life, spirituality, and motherhood challenges each of us to seriously engage in a similar quest. Our twenty-first century consumer culture does not encourage such honest self-reflection and self-revelation. This book reveals her intimate struggle to follow Jesus, to know God's unconditional love for us all, to do her best to really see, and to live her life with integrity."

— *Patricia N. Benson, OP, PhD*

As Pamela Prime courageously delves into the darkest areas of her being in When the Moon Is Dark We See the Stars , she miraculously becomes more and more transparent like the light of the stars themselves illuminating her very soul. This is her story, her journey, but the way she uncovers the profound love that is her true self somehow pulls the reader into his or her own authentic discovery. While accompanying Pamela on her journey, one hears a clear invitation to open to one's own deep life with the benefit of knowing the light is there for each one of us, if we are willing to venture into the challenging dark places of our own journeys.

— *Sharon Anderson, M.A. Transpersonal Psychology, Spiritual Director*

"Listening to [Pamela's] heart as she moves through the loss of her children reopened mine to the loss of my own. Her words articulate the experience of a spiritual journey that opens the door to a realm beyond the limits of defined theology."

— *Linda Emerson, Writer and Business Entrepreneur*

"After reading When the Moon is Dark We can See the Stars, I exclaimed...Pamela Prime is Sophia. Her wisdom is a way to light the awareness of our connection with all humanity and with the divine. My gratitude has no words as my heart floods with joy."

— *Kimberly Pierce, Outreach Worker, Teacher, and Case Manager, Family Support Services*

To Kelly,
Blessings as you read
this book. See you in San Francisco.
With love
Pamela Prime

When the Moon is Dark
You Can See the Stars

An Awakening of the Spirit Within

—

Pamela Prime

Published by: The Printed Voice
                     1755 Novato Blvd. #C5
                     Novato, CA 94947

The author gratefully acknowledges Hallie Iglehart Austen for permission to use the photograph of Theotokos from her book, *The Heart of the Goddess*.

Cover design, black and white illustrations and book typography design by Mop Prime, Smith-Felver & Prime, Ltd.

ISBN: 0-9637891-9-8

First Printing, December, 2008

Printed in the U.S.A.

10 9 8 7 6 5 4 3 2 1

Dedicated to:
Wisdom — Sophia,
The Mother God,
to
Mary,
The Mother of God,
and
to
All Mothers,
Especially mothers whose children have died,
because
Children are the Light of the World
and
Our best teachers.

In Gratitude

This book has been in my heart for many years and is possible because of the people I love and who love me, many of whom are described in these pages. I could never have written it without the love, support, effort and companionship of my present husband, Dave. He has heard every word I have written over the past months. He has laughed with me, cried with me, and felt anger with me as I read the words I wrote each day. Dave has typed this and retyped it. His patience and persistence has been extraordinary. The emotions that this book brought to the surface would have been too much for me to have held alone. I am sure that I am writing now, finally, after years of talking about it, because Dave is at my side and tends my heart. I am blessed.

I am also grateful for my children, Mark, Katie, and Annie who read the very first, very awkward draft with encouragement and a number of suggestions. And I am delighted by my older grandchildren, Bella, Rosie, and Virginia, who are excited that their grandma has written a book. The youngest grandchild, Ezra, will most likely join the girls in their enthusiasm, although it will be awhile before any of the grandchildren read it.

Many of my friends and two of my sisters have read for me with excellent feedback. So, thank you: Sharon and Neil Anderson, Pat Benson O.P. PhD, Bernie Owens S.J. PhD, Judy Perry, Kim Pierce, Vickie Noble, Clare Ronzanni, Bruce Lescher PhD, Robert Lentz O.F.M., Rev. Suzanne Fageol, Frank Houdek S.J. PhD, Mop Prime, and Nina DeNigris. I also wish to thank several artists for sharing their creative gifts: my sister Mop Prime, and my niece Amanda Bertele, for the book design and Lexie Proietti for her developing my website, www.whenthemoonisdark.com.

This book has come a long way over the years with the help of my first editor, Ron Pickup, a gentle, supportive guide who said it was a wild child when he first read it, and with subsequent editors, Vinita Wright, Hal Bennett, and lastly, Leslie Keenan, who has been a great support as editor and publisher.

I thank all of you, and many others, for your affirmation along the way that made this possible.

I am most especially grateful to God. This book is a story of my faith, a faith that held me close as I emerged from the darkness, remade me in the image of the Mother God with her love and Spirit within me. It is the story of a faith that held me in the face of tragedies and triumphs; a faith that is alive, continuously transforming me into my fullest self, a self that now knows there is no such thing as separation from the love of God.

Table of Contents

Beginnings

Stirrings

Shatterings

Awakenings

Preface

By Robert Lentz, O.F.M.

We are in a time of profound cultural change. Like massive tectonic plates that lie beneath continents, plates that are always shifting and which occasionally move very suddenly as earthquakes, world views we once found satisfying are now shifting violently. Everything they formerly supported is beginning to crack and sway. Some historians say we have not experienced such change since the rise of Christendom in the fourth century. Others describe this as the greatest cultural change in thousands of years. Because old answers often seem too small now for questions we face in our lives, sensitive people at one end of the cultural spectrum are beginning to search for new answers, or new ways to rephrase the old. Most people, who fall somewhere in the middle of the spectrum, feel unsettled, without fully realizing the extent of the changes they face. Sometimes they scratch their heads or grumble about shifting gender roles and challenges Third World cultures are posing to "the way things have always been." They read about scientific and technological breakthroughs, incorporating them in their lives when appropriate, but never reflecting on the challenges these breakthroughs make to their traditional worldview. Basically they try to continue living, more or less successfully, in time-honored ways, often numbed by the pace of modern life. On the extreme opposite end of the cultural spectrum, a small portion of humanity is turning to religious fundamentalism as a violent defense of what has passed. Because these things have indeed passed, their frustration becomes increasingly violent, denying the reality of change that confronts them on every side.

This book will terrify fundamentalists, even as it inspires men and women who are searching anew. Pamela shows how she moved from a rigid, enculturated mindset to the edge of possibilities, and she invites the reader to join her. Her book belongs to a genre of spiritual literature written by mystics like St. Teresa of Avila, St. Therese of Lisieux, and Blessed Julian of Norwich. Men have also authored such books, but it has more often been women who have set down their spiritual experiences in an effort to make sense of what they feel God has been doing in their lives. In a male-dominated religion like Christianity, women have had to search much harder than men to find ways their unique experiences as women fit into the general religious matrix. Though written from a feminine perspective, their autobiographies end up speaking to countless men, as well. Perhaps there is something feminine about the human soul. This book ought to take its place among the spiritual classics that precede it. Only time will tell whether it will. As we enter the 21st century, it is a fresh questioning of how we look at God and what God is about in our rapidly changing world.

This book is an account of a modern woman's efforts to rediscover her ancient Christian wisdom path. Christianity is before all else a wisdom path, even though Christians often tend to reduce it to a series of dogmas, rituals, and moral precepts. Wisdom paths require hard work and commitment. They are not for the faint of heart. Perhaps it was inevitable that the Christian path to wisdom would eventually demand simplification. When the Roman Empire embraced Christianity in the fourth century, hundreds of thousand of new converts began filling Christian churches. The challenge to accommodate such numbers demanded immediate simplification for mass consumption, and this simplification came at a great price. In time, boundaries defining the path to wisdom became more important than the path itself, distracting travelers from what was beneath their feet. Hermits, monks and nuns fled into the wilderness in order to keep wisdom in sight. Edifying stories about their efforts to travel the path slowly replaced actually traveling the path, and Christianity became a second-hand experience.

No wisdom path is meant to be a second-hand experience. When a religion loses sight of its wisdom path, when it sacrifices its wisdom path for simpler external observances, it can maintain its hold on human society only through fear. When it can no longer inspire fear, it slowly dies. Christianity is in danger of dying today, in this time of profound cultural change. *When the Moon is Dark* is an inspiration for those who seek the wisdom path and has the capacity to be an inspiration to the church as well.

Christianity is an oriental religion, profoundly mystical in character, despites its western trappings. Early Christians referred to their faith simply as "the Way." There is no need for Christianity to die in our time, provided that Christians rediscover their wisdom path. If Christians were to return to the mysteries lying beneath their dogmas, rituals, and morality— which is to say, if they would learn again how to pray, how to listen to God's voice beneath the din of modern life, as Pamela has—Christianity would be reborn. Most Christian leaders continue to reinforce boundaries, however, rather than teaching their flocks how to pray, hoping that the boundaries in and of themselves will keep their flock headed in the right direction. And much of the flock simply mills around between the boundaries, lost.

Pamela began her life, like most Christians, in awe of ecclesiastical fences and unsure of what they were protecting. From childhood on, she had psychic experiences that would have made sense in a traditional shamanic culture but, in the twentieth century, challenged ecclesiastical fences or boundaries she had learned to respect. These experiences, coupled with intense suffering that ripped her life from the normal moorings that should have held it secure, gradually pulled her attention away from time-honored fences, leaving her gazing forward into the unknown. With nowhere else to go, and unwilling to mill around in circles or turn back, she walked forward into the darkness, one step at a time, discovering the path the fences had always defined.

Just as each of us experiences the material world in a unique way, determined by our personality, culture, and life history, so, too, do we experience God uniquely. Religious authorities do violence to souls when they challenge the validity of individual spiritual experience. Christian history is bloody with the persecution of fellow Christians whose experience of God differed from the accepted norm. The accepted norm has always had a strongly masculine character. It fits comfortably within the ecclesiastical boundaries of dogma and ritual, both of which are largely products of masculine thought and experience. Add to this the fact that those who formed these norms came from a small number of related subcultures in a small geographic area, and the result is a box much too tiny to confine the divine.

When Moses approached the burning bush, as told in the book of Exodus, he heard a voice warn him to take off his shoes because he was standing on holy ground. St. Gregory of Nyssa tells us that we would discover all ground was holy if only we would take off our shoes. By shoes he means anything we put between God and ourselves.

Christians believe that God is love. In the Hebrew Scriptures there is a growing awareness that God's love is universal. Throughout the Bible and Christian tradition God is described as lover and spouse. God's self-revelation began with the first moment of creation, but it is most eloquent in the depths of each human heart. God has spoken to human beings throughout history and in every human culture.

The Christian wisdom path is not tied to any time or culture, nor is it specifically masculine or feminine. At the same time, it must be incarnated in individual human lives, all of which are culturally determined, if it is to be anything more than an abstract concept. A thin line divides these two truths, and we have no choice but to walk this tightrope. As with any tightrope, falling off on either side is a constant danger.

"Show me your icons," declared St. John of Damascus, "and I will show you your faith." He said this almost thirteen centuries ago, when the Christian world was bitterly torn between those who maintained that Christ and the saints could be depicted visually and those who felt this was idolatry. The Seventh Ecumenical Council settled the dispute in favor of visual images. It said that images were a necessary part of Christian faith, as a witness to the completeness of Christ's incarnation.

Images are not idols. They can never replace the reality for which they stand. They are windows to that reality, but windows as limited as the vision of those who created them. From most ancient times humans have tried to describe their experiences of God through art. Cave paintings, bone statues, and petroglyphs speak eloquently of our ancestors' religious experiences. Artistic images and metaphors have been our most useful means to share what we have "seen" of God. Because an encounter with God is always intensely personal, images and metaphors differ widely. Many religious traditions welcome these images in all their variety. They thus honor the individual experience and acknowledge that the divine is too vast for any set of images to contain. Unfortunately, official Christianity has not often shared this tolerant view. But Pamela, in her desire to reclaim her spirituality, has discovered and re-animated some important ancient images.

Male clerics and theologians from European cultures have carefully controlled religious imagery for all other Christians. Councils of these men established strict guidelines that Byzantine iconographers still follow. Canonizing specific images is a risky business, however, for it is a short step afterwards to condemn those that in any way differ from the norm. Such condemnation is in reality a denial of individual, personal encounters with God. It is an attempt to control and define the divine mystery, a terrible sin of blasphemy.

Mystics in the Christian West lived in fear of the Inquisition when they tried to describe their experiences in poetic terms. St. Teresa of Avila and St. Rose of Lima were both investigated by the Inquisition. Sor Juana Inez del al Cruz was silenced, and the Inquisition forced her to burn all her poetry and other writings. Tens of thousands of other women were burned at the stake because their experiences of God differed from those of the men who controlled the churches.

In the fifth century, bands of crazed monks in Egypt, incited by the rhetoric of Christian bishops, ran through Alexandria and other cities, smashing pre-Christian religious imagery. Many mutilated statues we now treasure in our museums bear the marks of monastic vandalism. The destruction spread in western Europe as missionary monks spread out from the Mediterranean. Celtic, Germanic, and Slavic peoples all "learned" that their ancient religious imagery belonged to the devil. From Europe, the missionary purge spread to the Americas, Africa, and Asia. Modern Christians are left with an official set of religious images that often has very little to do with their personal lives.

Feminine images have suffered more than any other in ecclesiastical purges. The feminine has either been demonized or reduced to a sexless virginity. The feminine images we have lost could now lend new insights to Christian doctrine and spirituality. Few peoples on earth fear death as much as those from Christian cultures, despite our insistence on Christ's resurrection. Every year Hollywood produces a new crop of morbid films about demon possession, walking zombies, vampires and werewolves, all of which reflect the general populations' fear and obsession with death. We fear death, in part, because we have lost our ancient images that dealt with death. Most of these images had some feminine connection or a connection with sex and fertility.

Religious imagery should not be turned into fence posts circumscribing a wisdom path. Images instead are maps and traveling guides for how to travel that path. Like travel literature available in modern bookstores, images point out landmarks and offer encouragement to those setting out on their quest. Different individuals will find some images more useful than others. Images that are not useful will fall naturally by the way, through disuse. Those that prove useful will find their way into many lives. There is no need for religious censors armed with hammers and flames.

As suffering propelled Pamela down her ancient wisdom path, she instinctively began stretching boundaries that were cramping her spiritual growth. Ignorance of the Christian tradition and its history traps most Christians between misplaced fence posts that all but strangle their traveling the path. By returning to university studies in mid-life, Pamela learned to distinguish legitimate, ancient fence posts from those later placed willy-nilly by those the path had frightened. Some of the barriers over which she had to climb were official religious images that blocked vistas meant to feed her soul. This book is about imagery and how it has helped one woman find God.

Reading spiritual autobiographies cannot take the place of actually traveling one's wisdom path. Wisdom paths must not become second-hand, vicarious experiences. Spiritual autobiographies, like religious imagery, are merely aids in our own personal search. To encounter wisdom is to stand before a mirror in which we see ourselves as we are seen by God, for, as Pamela slowly discovered, wisdom is none other than Wisdom, the divine mystery we name God. She shares with us her journey, an intimate, personal experience. I invite you to remove your sandals, like Moses, as you step onto this sacred ground. ✳

Introduction

There were days in my life when I wondered how I could continue living. I thought the pain I was in would surely take my life. It had taken my joy more than once and any sense that I would ever wear colors again or find a smile that came from my heart. My heart was broken open again and again until I could see into the depths of my soul, and there, I found God. Much to my surprise, after each tragedy, I did continue living. And with the gift of my faith, many friends, and compassionate listeners, I found a smile that comes from the deepest depths of my heart, a smile that I had never before known. Today I am aware that the lightness and joy that is mine has come because I have been faithful to God and to myself. I have been blessed with the willingness to feel deeply and completely the pain and suffering that was mine, as an adult. I also have been blessed with the courage to return to my childhood and re-enter those dark and hidden fears which my body held for me from long ago. I learned to hold myself in love and compassion, and, as I did, entered those feelings and recalled the memories, always asking for the guidance of my God and the support of the angels and saints. I hope that as you read you will find a companion in me, and as we walk together that you also will find your deepest self and God within your heart. I have felt called by God to write for those of you who wonder if it is possible to ever truly smile again. I share my path with you in gratitude for my healing and to support your healing.

As the story unfolds, you will see a progression in my life. A movement from a young, naive woman who believed everything she learned, to a woman who began to wake up to the painful reality that life is not always what we make it up to be—that we are individuals who have a contribution to make if and when we emerge from the darkness of the cocoon in which we reside and are born anew. I believe that our stories are powerful teachers. In writing my story, it is my hope that I will give the reader who resonates with me an opportunity to recall and reflect on his or her own story, and that as this happens, the reader will naturally burst forth, more alive and more beautiful—as the butterfly who is finally free to fly. Such opportunities to 'burst forth' can be everyday experiences for us, and this book is intended to be one of those opportunities.

As you read, you may find that my perspectives are different from yours, and you may want to read no further. You may find yourself feeling upset or even angry. Although my viewpoints may be different, I do not consider them to be definitive. I only hope to open a dialogue between my point of view and yours. I have written with the intention to support healing and happiness. I know from my own experience that disturbances can be healthy when I acknowledge them as such. Someone once said that God comes to comfort the afflicted and afflict the comfortable. It is no accident that you are reading this book. I ask that you allow our differences to be a challenge to deepen your own beliefs, trusting that God uses every moment, every challenge, as an opportunity to grow in love, if we are willing.

We are all on a journey of self-discovery, which is opening the way daily to fresh understandings of God, of others, and of ourselves. My journey is not complete by any means. Writing this book has shown me that. I have written and re-written over these seven years, as my images of God and self, along with my beliefs, have expanded. Our journeys, like our stories are sacred and require us to be aware, to carefully reflect, and to pray constantly to see clearly the road upon which we walk. I am reminded of a prayer,,which I find encouraging as I walk along, often not knowing if I am on the right path, especially if the night is dark and the territory unfamiliar. I share this prayer, from Thomas Merton, a simple and holy man, a contemplative Trappist monk and friend on the journey, as encouragement for you:

> *My Lord God, I have no idea where I am going.*
> *I do not see the road ahead of me.*
> *I cannot see for certain where it will end.*
> *Nor do I really know myself, and the fact that I think*
> *That I am following your will does not mean that*
> *I am actually doing so.*
> *But I believe that the desire to please you does in fact*
> *please you.*
> *And I hope I have that desire in all that I am doing.*
> *I hope I will never do anything apart from that desire.*
> *And I know if I do you will lead me by the right road,*
> *Though I may know nothing about it.*
> *Therefore I will trust you always, though I seem to be lost*
> *And in the shadow of death.*
> *I will not fear you, for you are ever with me,*
> *And you will never leave me to face my perils alone.*

I am filled with gratitude for the happiness in my life and have felt called to share my story as a way to encourage others to hope and to trust, especially those who are in the midst of suffering. I share my triumphs and my failures, my fears and my joys, my suffering and my blessings. I share also, the movement of God in my life, as best I can, for the sole purpose of witnessing to the power of Divine Grace and God's longing to communicate with us. I wrote the first draft of this book in three weeks as a 60th birthday present to myself and it has taken the last seven years with the help of my editors, to craft and refine it. I can honestly say, this book has been a great teacher for me and has provided me with seven years of refinement.

I am more aware of who I am and more aware of my blessings and challenges because of having written and re-written this story. I cried my way through some chapters and got angry and frightened all over again through others as I revisited and relived my past. I have worked endless hours at my desk and in prayer to come to a place of forgiveness, acceptance, gratitude and peace with my life... every bit of it! I have learned through the experience of writing that our stories are Sacred. They are our most powerful teachers, first for ourselves, and then for others.

Over the years I have listened to many women and men tell their stories. Whether I was on retreat or in spiritual direction, in the classes I have taught, or in grocery stores, airports, or park benches, I have come to understand that each of us has stories in which we find ourselves in the midst of darkness and suffering. Some of us make our way to the light and grow wiser and more alive. Others become engulfed by the darkness for long periods of time; some, forever. I have written this book for those in darkness who need encouragement to walk through their suffering, trusting that a brighter light than they have ever known awaits on the other side. I have also written this book to join with those of you whose path has taken you to the light as a way of encouraging all of us to acknowledge, celebrate, and give thanks for our freedom.

I have included reflection questions at the end of each chapter to help you recall your own story and to come to a deeper understanding of the wonder of your experiences, even those which have been or are painful. You will see more clearly how you are being led...sometimes carried and sometimes pulled... toward the full and glorious realization of who you truly are and who God is for you. Take time to reflect on these questions, in a quiet place away from interruptions. Use a new journal and a special pen, and if you like, get some colored pencils or colored chalk from the art store. Sometimes color can better express your deeper feelings. Begin and end each reflection period with prayer. Take this time as a gift for yourself and let it be a mini-retreat for you, with God as your guide. If you find that your emotions are overwhelming, seek the help of a friend, a therapist, or a spiritual director (one who has the charism and the training to walk with another as a companion along the spiritual path). You may be opening your heart to healing, and you do not want to miss an opportunity for the emergence of your deeper self.

There is a wonderful little book called *The Little Bird Who Found Herself,* written by Ed McMahon. This little book, for children of all ages, is a simplified version of Bio-Spirituality, a brilliant method of noticing and nurturing all of our feelings—most especially, our physical, mental, emotional, and spiritual pain. I have found this practice to be remarkably healing over the years. Bio-Spirituality was co-created by Ed McMahon and Peter Campbell, both PhD psychotherapists. The little bird book is the story of how a little bird struggles to find her song, in spite of all the taunting and criticism of the other birds. The little bird learns how to listen to her feelings, feelings of sadness and fear, as the other birds shun her because her song is not like theirs. As the story progresses, we see that, by paying attention to those feelings, she is led naturally to the most melodious song of all. The teachings in this amazing story are for you and me. Each one of us is looking for our song and will search until we find it. When we find our song, we find our true and glorious selves, and when we find ourselves, we find our true and Glorious God. Therein lies the joy... we are one! ✷

Beginnings

1

Encountering Faith

"*Who am I?*" I ask in the quiet of the night, and a vision unfolds before my eyes:

> *A massive gray volcano appears. I watch closely and become aware of an aura of heat surrounding it. I hear the gurgling, festering sounds that precipitate explosion. Completely absorbed, I hear the violent crack, the roar of shattering rock, and see the brilliant red and yellow come to life. Fire burns. The volcano erupts. It gushes forth its once hidden interior for all the world to view . . .*
>
> *The night is again dark and finally calm. The volcano, now empty, rests. Just before dawn the rains appear and*

gently wash away the ashes and charred pebbles. The rain continues, partially filling the abyss with its soothing drink. Soon the winds come, as if from the four corners, and the breezes glide across the surface of the mountains like a hand with a soft white cloth, slowly, effortlessly patting the surface dry. And as the new day begins, the sun shines brilliantly on the mountain face, bringing it new life and sparkle.

The volcano radiates a brilliant light, and all the animals are drawn to it. They wander about peacefully, quiet and respectful of this new life.

Soon, people begin to arrive, and one at a time they ascend to the volcano's peak, to join me. As I look over the edge and into the abyss, I see a perfect reflection of myself. I leave filled with a special wonder, renewed with love, more alive and more in harmony with life.

And when one among them asks, "But where is God?" a voice answers, "Did you not look into the abyss?"

This visionary experience occurred in 1981 as I was quietly saying my nightly prayers. I felt as though I was taken to a place beyond myself and shown something extraordinary. I was left breathless! It was just months before my whole life tragically exploded before my eyes with the death of my oldest son, Sean, the second of my children to die.

There is nothing that has brought me so completely into the depths of the abyss than Sean's death (though my daughter Maggie's death, nine years earlier, and the loss of my marriage six years after Sean's death, felt utterly eruptive at the time). Nor has there been any other event that has made God's presence and love more palpable. Sean's death has been the volcanic eruption that holds the deepest suffering and, through the healing I experienced around it, the greatest joy. Although I didn't understand the vision of the volcano at the time it happened, I knew it was significant, and I received it as though it was a very special gift. I carefully wrote the vision in my journal, and I have always kept it alive in my heart. This vision has had an enormous impact on my life. It has held me through many volcanic eruptions and helped birth me into my present knowing: *When we look into the depth of our being, we see God.*

The first vision I can recall having occurred in 1972. I was married by then and had three children. I was in my car, driving home from the grocery store. The children were in school, and I was alone in the car. It was an ordinary day. My life was full — I had a lovely home, healthy children, loving husband — but suddenly, as I was driving, darkness overcame me.

> *I am being enveloped in a black cloud. There is no light. I*
> *know the car could go off the side of the road, and, if it does,*
> *I will die, but it doesn't matter. Nothing matters. Suddenly,*
> *there is nothing. There is no light; no life or death, no love,*
> *no such thing as love or God or faith. There is nothing, not*
> *even a memory of those truths.*

I remember the intensity of the moment, the sense of loss, of emptiness, of nothing to live for or die for. In retrospect, it was as if, for a brief period, the Spirit which gives me life had left me. I remember thinking that I couldn't sustain this experience for very long. For in that brief opening, nothing was real. Neither I, nor anything I knew, existed or had ever existed. It was an experience of total annihilation.

I don't recall driving home or pulling into the garage that day. I only remember coming into consciousness as I stood in my kitchen in shock, thinking something really awful had happened, wondering if I had done something to cause it; wondering if God was punishing me.

I was terrified, and I told no one for eight years — I believed I had done something to cause the experience, so it was a source of shame as well as fear. I often wonder, now, how many of us there are who have profound experiences, either terrifying or ecstatic, who have no one with whom to share their fear or joy. It was a lonely and isolating time for me after that vision. I sometimes think about those who never find a spiritual companion or community and die with secrets locked away in their hearts.

Seeing visions and hearing voices are experiences that are not generally talked about, and so we feel frightened when we are invited into a place beyond the norm, or when we break through a wall into a realm other than one that is familiar to us. Now, in retrospect, I know this is truly a time to seek guidance. But like myself, with such an unfamiliar and frightening experience, most people do not know where to turn. Today, unlike 1972, we are more aware of the teachings of quantum science, which tell us what mystics have known through the ages — that we are part of a universe that is beyond space and time, that all barriers and boundaries are of our own creation, and that we are at one with everything in creation.

Many people have visions or hear voices, and if those having these experiences are not grounded psychologically and spiritually, they can be swept into a whirlwind of overwhelming emotions and/or inappropriate, even dangerous activities. It is only after reflection, prayer, and guidance that we can know for sure that the vision, voice, or spiritual movement of any kind is authentic, and that we, who are receiving these experiences, are truly grounded. In the Gospel of Matthew, Jesus teaches, "A good tree can not bear bad fruit, nor can a bad tree bear good fruit. Every tree that does not bear good fruit is cut down and thrown into the fire. Thus, you will know them by their fruits." We shall know them by their fruits...that is, the experience discerned as authentic is leading us to a more fulfilling life, and if it is not discerned as authentic, it is because it is leading us down a path of destruction. I had a spiritual directee (a freelance journalist and a youth minister) call me one night because a voice told him to end his life. He refused to tell me where he was for fear I would call for help. But he did say that he did not know how he would end his life if he decided to follow the dictates of the voice. Clearly, this was not an authentic voice, but one that would lead to a path of destruction. Fear arose in me. I did the only thing I know how to do...I prayed silently and asked for God's help while I kept him on the phone. By grace, after much conversation and a promise to call again if the voice returned, he realized he truly wanted to live. Today, after much therapy, he is alive and prospering.

As I reflect upon it, I wonder what I would have experienced had I not been so frightened that day that I felt the darkness overwhelm me. If with knowledge and deepened faith and wisdom I could have sustained that level of absence and emptiness and darkness and remained present to it, would it have brought me through itself to Divine Love? I think it would have; but instead, it became a great teacher and over *time* it has led me to Divine Love.

I will refer to this experience, which I came to call my *Dark Experience of Nothingness*, often throughout my story because it is pivotal to my spiritual awakening, the deepening of my faith, the gateway to my emergence of wisdom and, most essentially, my awareness of Spirit present within me.

12

The *Dark Experience of Nothingness* has actually supported me in times of tragedy. No matter what was happening, I knew it was not ever as terrifying as this experience. I had been to the darkest part of the night, when the moon is dark and the clouds hide the stars. For a moment I felt what appeared to be Hell — an experience of total separation from love, even the memory of love — and I didn't die or disappear into its emptiness. Nor did I have the courage or faith to remain present to the experience long enough to find God in its midst.

The teaching that God is present at all times, in all places, took years for me to understand and to trust. Psalm 139 expresses this truth and resonates deeply within me. Perhaps this knowing of God's presence became a part of me as a result of an experience I had three years after the *Dark Experience of Nothingness* which I will share with you later on, as the story unfolds. I call this experience the *Ecstasy of God's Love*, when I knew in every cell of my being the promise of Psalm 139:

Where could I go to escape your spirit?

Where could I flee from your presence?

If I climb the heavens you are there,

There too if I lie in Sheol (darkness).

Where could I flee? No matter where I might go I was about to learn that God was there with me, loving me, with no conditions.

I treasure these experiences and others that will follow as my story unfolds. Their powerful threads weave and hold the story of my life into one very colorful, pulsating, and passionate tapestry. It is colored with significant and unexpected suffering, and has become more beautiful because of this.

Another memorable upsurge that shaped my life came six years after the volcanic explosion of Sean's death, only months after my divorce, in a fiery and terrifying experience of anger. The anger, as fierce and bright as the volcano, was clearing the way for another passage into the abyss, a passage that lasted for eight long years.

It was in a jumble of furniture, pots and pans, contractors, the planting of gardens at my new home, and my beginning of life after a divorce from my husband of twenty-three years, that at night I began reading *Laughter of Aphrodite,* by Carol P. Christ, a feminist theologian. About halfway through the book, I felt an intense sense of the author's message. My body stiffened with anger, and something groaned from deep within — something I had long felt but had repressed.

There was no sacred feminine image of God in my life to reflect to me my own sacredness as a woman. Her image existed in pre-history, but her stories were dismissed as pagan — as though pagan was evil. I realized that the full expression of myself as a woman had been denied and dismissed as well. And in this moment, as I read in bed, desire awakened in my heart to find and resurrect both the Mother God and my potential as a woman.

The book had awakened rage that caused my whole being to tremble as, in an instant of clarity, I saw and felt the devastation this lack of sacred feminine images had caused to the Image of God, the people of God, and the rest of Creation. As long as the Feminine Image of God is hidden in darkness, all of us, including God the Father, are incomplete, and we will long for truth and fulfillment. As Carol Christ wrote in her book, "God, like humans, has been in bondage to patriarchal History." (Christ, p. 22).

Up until this moment, I had spent my entire life in a position of subservience, not by conscious choice, but out of unconscious fear. From the moment of my birth through my childhood and marriage, I experienced concrete proof that being a powerful woman was dangerous to others and a threat to my own well-being. I continued to find ways to stand behind powerful men and male hierarchies that made my own emergence impossible. I felt safe, as long as I was hidden. I didn't realize that I had not yet been birthed, until the moment I was catapulted into a new way of seeing though Carol Christ's words. My awakening to the image of the sacred feminine reflected my own sacredness as a woman. I could no longer deny my potential, nor could I hide.

As the anger subsided, I wept far into the night. There was a full moon that night, and I can still see the light and what appeared to be a cross, superimposed over the moon. I felt the presence of Christ bathing me in light.

I had left my marriage because it had no room for me, for my essence, my gifts, and now, less than two weeks after moving into my new home and life, I was acknowledging that my church, which had been my rock, my place of refuge and ministry, was guilty of doing the same thing. Would I have to leave the church as well?

I was changing. The veils that kept me from experiencing deeper truths were being removed. My image of God was changing as well, and sometimes the turmoil and fear caused such darkness that there was no image of God for me to rest in. Only my faith held me — faith that God was present and loving me in the depths of the struggle and darkness. My faith in God was strong in spite of my religious crisis. Because I had already learned that church and God were not synonymous, I knew that I would be loved by God, no matter what I chose. This awareness made it possible for me to struggle faithfully and honestly. It was precisely my faith in God that not only sustained but also encouraged me as I struggled with the challenges of being a woman raised in the Catholic Church — a woman who was being awakened in the midst of darkness.

Three stories in this chapter are significant in my journey: *the Volcano, the Dark Experience of Nothingness*, and Carol Christ's powerful book, *The Laughter of Aphrodite*. Although they are somewhat mysterious, they are pivotal in my transformation from being asleep to awakening. Each has pointed the way and opened a door to a path that I would have otherwise missed. Over the years, I have learned to understand them at deeper and deeper levels and as the book progresses, you will see the how they have impacted my life choices.

My hope is that as you read, you will naturally move beyond my experiences, my suffering, and my joy, into your own — that this book takes you by the hand and lovingly leads you to knowing that the Divine dwells within you and guides you along your path even in the midst of darkness. With this awareness, you are free.

Recently I met a woman who was standing outside the entrance to our local prison, the Sierra Conservation Center. She was dressed in a rainbow colored hat, rainbow knee socks, sandals, and a brightly colored dress. Intrigued not only by her colors but also by her peacefulness and her joy, I addressed her. "You sure are brightly colored today." "Yes," she said and added with an enormous smile, as she opened her coat, "And I even have a rainbow ribbon around my neck for my whistle." She was a tiny, dark-skinned woman. She had one roving eye, which ordinarily would have been a distraction, but her eyes glistened with light. She had been leading a three-day seminar in the prison on alternatives to violence. We exchanged a few comments, enough for me to realize that I was standing in the presence of a very gentle, loving, and powerful woman.

Reluctantly I passed through the steel doors of the prison with my husband Dave. We headed to our class on spirituality, which we teach to men who are in prison for long terms or life. I so wanted to remain with my rainbow friend. She exuded freedom — a freedom to be herself in the way she dressed and in the way she playfully presented herself. She was a delight to behold. As our class began, I asked if any of the men had taken the course on alternatives to violence. Three of them lit up and spoke excitedly, "We met the lady with the rainbow hat, and we are different — we can change." I am quite sure that what the rainbow lady *said* was quite significant, but who she *is*, her presence, is what really teaches and empowers.

A few days later, I read a story about her in the local newspaper and realized that she had made it through her own suffering, and with the wisdom gained, was now resolved to help others. My prayer for you, as you read, is that what I have been inspired to write empowers you to open your hearts and have faith that whatever you need to be free, is being offered. May we all be people of the rainbow, for the rainbow is God's promise to bring us to freedom!

My faith in a benevolent and compassionate God is the most sacred thing I have. When I am old and can do little but reflect, it will keep me alive even as I pass to the other world. Faith has been my life support. It is the sacred container that held me together when everything else was falling apart. Like the oxygen tank that gives breath when the lungs fail, faith has breathed life into me. Along with the gift of faith, the gift of love that I received as a child from my family is most precious. These are the gifts that made it possible for my heart to remain open, even in the darkest of struggles.

Throughout my life, the Catholic church held me lovingly as well, and provided a powerful structure in which I felt safe, subsequently providing the necessary grist as I struggled to be born into my true self. I believe this is what Jesus calls being twice born.

Through the events of my life, my faith and love have evolved from knowing a God that dwells only in church and in the saints, to recognizing God as one who dwells in all creation — in the beauty and chaos of nature, in every person, including me, without condition; in every breath, cell, and moment in time. The God I know is both male and female and simultaneously neither male nor female, a benign and beneficent Spirit that breathes grace and blessings, purification and expansion, asking only that we open our hearts to receive and give fully in response. This story is part of my response.

As a child I was governed by the external laws of church and society: fear of Hell, shame of my own curious impulses, and always, guilt. It was faith that allowed me to move from this fearful place to one of love, trust, and freedom. It is a place where I am no longer bound but am guided by the Spirit dwelling within me. As I step further away from the confines of my past — its entrapments and enculturation, its "shoulds," sufferings, and misbeliefs — I live more fully in the present and in peace.

I remain grateful for all of my teachers, for the wisdom they shared, and for the structures that my family and the church provided, structures that ultimately set me free. But, *I am free*...free to search my inner world, down into the depths of the abyss, knowing that there I will find God. ✳

Reflection Questions

Many people have visionary experiences but often they do not take them seriously. An authentic visionary experience, like a dream, always has a message and is always a gift, but must be discerned for authenticity, in order to find the 'good' fruits.

Have you had visionary experiences? How did you know they were authentic?

Were you able to understand the messages behind them? If yes, did someone help you or did you try to understand the messages by yourself?

What have your visions taught you?

God communicates to each of us personally in ways that we can hear and in ways that make it possible for us to know that God is guiding us. Some people hear God in their hearts in formal prayer, at home or in church, others sense God in the beauty of nature. God communicates with some through art, color, poetry, or music. Sometimes people feel God's presence and guidance while working in the garden or cooking dinner. Dreams and visions are another way for God to communicate.

What are the ways that God communicates with you?

Are you comfortable with your relationship with God? If yes, can you explain why that is so?

If you are not comfortable, what can you do or what might you ask God do to make your relationship a better one?

If you have never had a vision, are you comfortable knowing that visions are   simply not the way God talks to you?

Meeting someone like the 'Rainbow Lady' is a moment of realization that life can and ought to be full of color and joy.

Who have you met that has inspired you?

Did you make changes in your life because of this person?

2

Acknowledging the Roots and the Rocks

I remember often hearing the story of my birth. I liked hearing how much I was loved as a baby and how happy my family was when they first saw me. These were my roots, and as a child, they held me securely. But as an adult, I began to question the ways my parents loved me, and I seriously doubted that their love was sufficient. I found myself in the midst of a cycle, spiraling down into the places where I felt I was unloved, not knowing where I would end up. These are the places where I discovered the rocks. It was frightening since much of what I believed to be true was coming up for examination. This is a cycle that I find to be common among the people I work with on retreat or in spiritual direction. It is a precursor for one who is moving from conventional thinking (following the group mind and fitting in) to post-conventional thinking (being free to think for oneself and individuating). I was an adult when I questioned the belief that my childhood was 'perfect,' and as I reflected on this in prayer, I was brought to my knees as I realized that I too was just as 'imperfect' a parent as my mother and father. The grace of this cycle was to return to my childhood belief that I was indeed loved as a child, to let go of all resentment for what I believed was not 'perfect,' and to give thanks for my childhood as it was. I realized that all experiences go into the pot that makes me who I am today. I returned to the delight of childhood memories of winter picnics on the beach, of ice skating in Central Park in New York City, and of daring adventures in the woods as we searched for fairies. The rocks are simply a part of the roots and, as I know now, a small but important part of my life.

My roots are deeper and stronger today because as I acknowledged the rocks, and felt them in my body, where I had, for years, secretly carried them, the love and compassion that arose within me transformed the pain, and the rocks became protectors of the roots. There is a magnificent old growth oak tree on a path in the forest near our home that I am reminded of. The tree is huge and grows majestically out of an enormous granite rock. The rock has split in several places to allow the tree to grow, but it also protects the tree from toppling over. They have grown together and are as one— like an aging married couple. I often go to this special tree to pray because it speaks volumes to me about the wonder of nature and reminds me always to seek the gift in life's difficulties —the rocks. The very things that I perceive as impositions or intrusions are quickly transformed into my teachers.

I was born with a full head of black hair, and my dad always said, "I did not believe you were mine because you were so big compared to the other babies, and with all that black hair, you looked like an Italian baby." Then my Godmother would laugh and add, "You looked just like Bozo. It was the funniest thing." Bozo was our cocker spaniel. But the part that was the strangest was the story of my arrival. My parents said, "You came out so fast and so powerfully that you almost killed your mother, and the doctor died of a stroke shortly after." The implication was that my birth was the cause. Dad would quickly add, "I had to go in search of blood in the middle of the night." It was true. The doctor did die and my mother almost died. I recall re-imagining my birth while on retreat many years later, and I had a felt sense of being left alone on a cold, steel grey table while the world around me was busy with the disaster that they told me I had caused. Without awareness, I translated the experience of my birth as: 'if I am powerful, I cause harm, and I will be abandoned.' This became my unconscious mantra which the cycle was uncovering as I spiraled into the dark places within me. Jesus has a saying in the New Testament, urging us not to put our light under a bushel basket, and here I was discovering that much of my self was hidden... even from me. My rocks were sharp and painful but the thought of not having them was terrifying for they had been my protection from the fear of abandonment or worse yet, annihilation. Now I know that it took great courage and God's grace to emerge from the box of conventional thinking, and bring the dark things which I had carefully hidden away, into the light. But it was ever more terrifying not to do so. Somewhere inside of me, I sensed that continuing to pretend was going to be a slow death.

In spite of my fear, I was being awakened, and sensing that as long as I connected my birth with the stories that followed the chaos of that day, and believed that I was at fault, I would continue to be imprisoned by fear and shame. I grew up feeling I was responsible not just for my mother's pain, but also for the doctor's death. I grew up believing that I did not fit into my family. I did not fit the image—too powerful, too big, too dark and sort of like a dog!   I didn't like these stories and wondered why I heard them so often, but, as a child, I never said anything. I just felt ashamed. Why my father did not like Italian people was never made clear to us, but we knew that he didn't. Perhaps it was the era, because it seemed that people were openly prejudiced. Or perhaps it was the entitlement that 'waspy' people sometimes arrogantly assume, and my father, sadly, was no exception. I wondered what he really felt when he saw me and exclaimed that I was big and looked Italian? When I was a young adult, I asked my Godmother not to say I looked like Bozo, the dog, but she liked the story too much to give it up. I never did ask my parents about the other stories. These are some of the rocks that shook my roots, and as you read, you will find more.

As a child I took my roots for granted, but as an adult I soon realized that they were enough to give me the security that I needed to fly free of the past. Deeply rooted and held in faith, in love, and in nature, the gifts of my family and my Catholic upbringing, I had the confidence to step out of the enculturated belief system in which I was raised. I recall a moment when, exploring other faiths and traditions, I became aware that my connection to Christ was so deep that I could go anywhere, explore any tradition, experience any belief system, and still be held securely by the tradition in which I had my roots... roots that would grow even stronger because I explored many ways in which people of different traditions worship and praise God. As for the rocks and grit, the painful and hard things in my life, which wove themselves into my roots... well, they were the very things that God and I carefully used to wake me up. Blessed be the rocks!!!

Faith and Love

My Catholic roots come from my paternal grandmother who came to Huntington, then a small town, on Long Island in New York. Dad loved to tell the story:

"Your grandmother came on a boat from Ireland at the age of seventeen and was hired as my father's cook," he would say, and then with a wink and a smile, "Your grandfather was a confirmed bachelor and a gentleman farmer. At the age of forty-one he was still avidly pursued by the town's spinsters. The women were horrified and angry when your grandfather fell in love with Maggie, his cook, of all things."

Up until that time the Prime family had been Presbyterian. But my spirited Irish Grandma insisted her children be raised Catholic, and so they were.

My grandmother never taught me about being Catholic. She taught me about love. I spent many weekends with her. She taught me how to cook and sew, grow vegetables and flowers. She raised chickens and ducks, and whenever I was there I helped her feed them and gather the eggs. The best time was when the newly hatched chicks were placed in the sunny kitchen window so they could be warmed and fed often. But when I would see her outside with her apron tied securely around her waist, her bluish white hair tucked up under a net, and a big axe in her hand held ready to whack off a duck's head, I'd hide my eyes. However, I never minded eating the duck after she cooked it, or her pies and cookies and ice cream. Grandma was almost always at home. I loved being with her most especially because she loved me without reserve. She was Grandma—the genuine article—the likes of which I hope to be for my grandchildren.

Our family heritage was tremendously important in my youth. Growing up, I was often reminded by my dad that I was part of the town's founding family. I have very happy memories of celebrating the tri-centennial anniversary of the founding of Huntington, New York, where I also grew up. My mother made me a costume—a dress from the 1650s—that I wore proudly as a Prime in the big parade. I felt surrounded by my ancestors every time I passed Prime Avenue, the series of antique homes with Prime placards on the front, the hospital and the library which they founded, and the museum that was on the property where the family home had formerly been. The old First Presbyterian Church, where several great-great-grandfathers were ministers, stood tall and pristine in the midst of the town.

My mother's side of the family was also Catholic, but there were Native American roots as well. My maternal grandfather was half Blackfoot Indian. It wasn't until I was in my early thirties that my Aunt Deemy told me the story:

"Your great-grandparents went west after they were married and lived on the White Swan Indian reservation in South Dakota. Your great-grandfather was the Indian agent for the tribe. Sometimes he traveled to do business and he would be gone for several days. Once, while he was gone, a tribesman entered the house through an open window. That's when your grandfather was conceived. I never heard if this was a rape or if it was something my great-grandmother invited. The family moved immediately from South Dakota to Madison, Wisconsin, where your grandfather was born."

The story was a family secret. Back then, being Native American, and especially scandalously so, was a source of shame. And to this day, some members of the family don't even believe it's true. But my grandfather, Daddy Bob, looked undeniably Blackfoot Indian. He was quiet, dignified, and warm, and I loved him totally.

He and my grandmother met in Colorado Springs. That is where my grandfather's family finally settled. My mother's mother went "out west," as she would say, to race her motorcycle on Pike's Peak. That would have been about 1920. I wish I had asked her how she managed to buy a motorcycle and get herself to Colorado, especially since she was the 16th child born into a very poor family, with only a second- grade education.

She was quite a lady. She and my grandfather returned to Huntington together after her motorcycle escapades.

My mother's Native American roots were undeniable; she wore her hair in braids and walked barefoot through the woods. She told me about all the wildflowers and the fairies that we passed. Early in my life, with my mother's teaching, I found God in nature, in the spirits of the flowers and the trees, and in the little people that lived among the moss covered rocks and streams.

Hints of Danger

I was nine or ten, coming home from the corner store a few blocks from the house with Ben, our Labrador retriever at my side, when a man stopped his car and asked for directions. When I went to his car window I saw that he was exposed and fondling himself. Terrified, I ran home as fast I could through neighbors' yards and over fences, but I never told what I had seen. I felt ashamed.

I rode my bike to the yacht club for sailing lessons that summer, and as I pulled into the parking lot the cook would often be standing naked at the window of his cottage, drapes open, pressing his pelvis against the glass. I hated the cook for doing this. I felt shame at having seen him naked. I began passing the entrance and coming to the club through the exit so I could avoid the cook, and I was angry about this because I no longer felt safe there. I did tell my parents about this, but I don't recall there being much of a response. I wonder if they even heard me. Perhaps my shame was too great to tell the story so that it could be heard. Perhaps my parents were not able to hear the story. I felt alone, unseen, and very sad. In the midst of the pain, though, I also felt hope. As a child, I had found a special place to be and when I felt sad or frightened, that is where I went... to the church in which I had been baptized and where I went on Sundays with my family. I made frequent visits to the church. Sometimes my Dad drove me and sometimes I walked about a mile to get there by myself. Those were the days when church doors were left unlocked. I don't remember praying or thinking about God, but I do recall feeling at home there. I was content just being in the silence, feeling the warmth in my heart and feeling loved, as I gazed at the statues of the saints, Mary and the crucifix, and of course the tabernacle, where the Eucharist, the Body of Christ, was kept.

I was in grammar school when I began kneeling on bobby pins while I prayed early in the morning in the privacy of my bedroom. I'm not sure I could have named the sins that I thought warranted this, but the shame I felt was insistent and I was clearly doing penance. Sometimes my knees would bleed, and always there would be the indentation of the bobby pins to let me know that I had been successful, though the pain ought to have been enough. Somehow I understood that I could do penance for the sins of others as well as my own, and hoped that my sacrifice was easing God's pain.

In the house where I grew up, there was an attic space that I could access through a small doorway in my closet. This became a special place for me to be alone at home, and it became my personal church. I spent lots of time alone, sitting on the rafters and gazing out the tiny window in the eaves. At other times I was joined by my brother and sister, and perhaps a friend or two, and I offered Holy Communion. Only I could touch the wafer. I used Necco wafers in those days and chocolate was the favorite flavor.

There was also a basement in this house. The washer and dryer were down there, and so was the devil. He hid under the stairs in the darkness. I would have to go downstairs to get the clean clothes, and I hated that chore. I still remember running back up as fast as I could to escape the devil's claws. I never told this to anyone because it was too scary. There are times even today that I find myself hurrying up the stairs... a left-over, very ingrained thought form from childhood. I learned about the devil in St. Patrick's school, which I attended through 5th grade. After that, my parents moved me to public school because my brother who was going into 4th grade couldn't read.

My first day in 6th grade at the Village Green School was bad. The teacher had all the students sing aloud individually before the class so she would know where we belonged in the choir. From the time I could recall, my family would ask me to sing *The Star-Spangled Banner* for them. Then they would all laugh because I loved to sing, but I couldn't carry a tune. It was a family joke and, at the time I thought it was funny too. The teacher turned to me, "Pamela, since you are new and I have never heard you sing, will you kindly stand in front of the class and sing *The Star-Spangled Banner for me?"* I didn't think this was a good thing. As a matter of fact I was really scared, but I did it. All the kids laughed, and the teacher got mad. I felt very embarrassed and was angry with the teacher making me sing first, and in front of everyone. The teacher's name was Miss Tietgen, and I can still see her white fluffy hair and short round body. I can't recall any of my other grammar school teachers. I never thought about my family's part in this or how teasing can harm a child. I never again sang that song alone.

In the spring of that school year our class performed a play and I had quite a big part. There was no singing! I was so excited about being in the play, and I loved my costume. I was a bright spring flower. When it was my turn to go onstage I went out calmly and faced the audience. I was so captivated by all the people who were watching me that I was speechless. I couldn't get over that they were all there waiting to hear me speak. It seemed funny to me and I began to laugh. Then the people laughed, and I laughed more. Within minutes the entire audience was laughing hysterically along with me. Miss Tietgen, horrified, closed the curtain. My dad said it was the best play he ever saw. I got a D-minus in deportment.

In ninth grade, I attended a Catholic girls' high school in a nearby town. I loved the school and the friends I made, and I also loved the sisters. We had our share of the older, strict sisters, but there were also the young, playful ones, such as Sister Mary Margaret who played softball with us. It was funny for us to see her run between bases holding up her black and white habit so she didn't trip, and watching her rosary beads fly in the wind.

The all-girls school became a haven for me and gave me a particular freedom to be outrageous in high school. My friends, Salley, Dawn and I were class leaders and class clowns throughout high school. There were no boys to attract or impress! At the same time I was aware of a strong need to follow the rules. I didn't smoke cigarettes in the woods like some of the girls. I always wore my uniform, and I went to confession regularly. Those were my goody two shoes days, and being seen as good was important to me.

The bus to high school left each morning from church, and Dad would drop me off early in time to go to Mass. This church was familiar to me because it was next to my grammar school, and I would often take some of my recess to sit in the church. I remember feeling magnetized, as though I could not move if I'd wanted to. I never said prayers. I just sat there all alone, held in the love which now I know was the magnet. On those mornings when I attended Mass before school, I also sat by myself, amid the older ladies and men in the church, but I always felt at home. I loved being there! I think this was the opening to God and to the spiritual communication that later guided me along the many turns on the path to life. God and I became good friends in that church. After Mass, I'd walk to town, a block from church, and have breakfast. I'd sit at the counter in the local luncheonette with a fresh Kaiser roll, butter and jam, and a glass of milk. I felt so grown up.

It was in high school that I learned about mortal sin and sex. One day I asked my parents if they had ever had sex without the intention of having a baby. They just stared at me in disbelief—astonished that I would dare intrude in this way. I was fifteen. I didn't need an answer. "Well, if you do, you are committing a mortal sin and will go to hell," I said with clarity and left the table. I can still see the look of shock on their faces.

It would be a few more years before I could understand that "being good" and following the rules didn't necessarily get me to heaven or secure my relationship with God. Sometimes it actually did the opposite.

Voices and Visions

Hearing voices, seeing visions, and recalling my dreams comprised an important aspect of my spiritual journey, one that often guided me. As a young child I didn't think it was strange, but I rarely had words to talk about it, so I kept it to myself. This gift came naturally to me because of my parents. Mom was very gifted psychically. She read palms as a young woman and one day had an experience, the details of which she would never share with us. She said that it frightened her so much that she never looked at another palm again, but her gift of knowing was always there.

My mother had a devotion to the Holy Spirit and was attuned to souls who wandered after death looking for help to move on. She told me never to be afraid of them but to ask them what they needed and help them as much as I could. There were two men, Rush and Burt, who lived in an apartment above us when I was about four. They became Mom's close friends. When Rush died, he would visit Mom in spirit. She and Burt would sit on the porch and tell stories about Rush's visits. It was as real to her to visit with Rush in spirit as it was to visit with Burt in real life. Although I couldn't articulate it then, I was learning that each of us has a personal spirit that lives on into eternity.

Dad didn't experience life quite the same way, and though he respected my mother's ways, he had his own way of experiencing the spiritual reality. Sometimes it was with animals. I recall one night so vividly that to this day it seems more like a dream. But it was real. Dad woke me up in the middle of the night. He took me by the hand, and we walked barefoot in our pajamas out to the front lawn. Dad told me to be very quiet and wait. He held me on his lap. The moon was full. I felt safe and warm in his arms as we sat on the grass and watched. One by one, the rabbits gathered in a circle and began to dance under the moonbeams. It was a night whose meaning delights me as much now as it did when I was three.

Dad also used to tell me about Pop, his father. I knew Pop, and I loved to sit with him while Grandma was busy in the kitchen. He was kind, and always seemed to be smiling. Pop was tall and thin and had lots of fluffy white hair. He was confined to bed the last year or so of his life with rheumatoid arthritis, and Dad helped care for him. Toward the end of his life, Pop would go in and out of sleep states and would tell my father upon waking, "You should see where I go when I close my eyes. It is so beautiful I can't even describe it." Then he would close his eyes and with a smile return to his other world.

Dad went to church with us but never felt that church attendance was necessary to earn God's love. Somehow he knew that God's love was there no matter what. So he didn't feel there was ever anything he had to do to make himself worthy of love. He had an extraordinary capacity to love, and everyone knew it, especially the children who flocked to him.

As a child, I often just knew things about people. I didn't have the ability to reflect on these experiences until I was in my forties. I was young when I realized that it wasn't safe to speak what I knew. When I was about eight years old, I was walking up the path from Saint Patrick's school, my hand in my mother's. The parish priest and one of the sisters who taught at the school passed by. As they did, I turned to my mother and said very cheerfully, "Wow, those two are in love, and they are going to get married." Mom hushed me, telling me sternly never to say that about father and sister. "After all," she said, "they are devoted to God." Well I'm sure she was right that they were devoted to God, but a few months later they left the parish and the school, and they got married, or so it was whispered throughout the church.

It didn't occur to me then that in telling the truth about what I saw and somehow knew, I had risked losing the most important relationships of my life. I had made my mother very angry, probably even embarrassed her, and had said something about a father and sister that insulted God. It was a moment of great confusion for me as my cheery little self began to learn that there were some things better left unseen and certainly unspoken. Consequently, when I began to hear voices and receive visions, I no longer said a word to anyone, not just because I didn't have words, but because it wasn't safe to speak.

The earliest time I can recall receiving personal guidance from God was when I was a senior in high school in 1959. I sat for hours in the library looking through books on religious life, trying to figure out what community of sisters I'd enter, because I knew I was going to be a sister. When finally I found the one for me, I was elated. I chose the Maryknoll sisters. I liked their white habits, and it seemed like a good idea to work in the missions. I left the library that day with an awareness that filled me with delight. I knew what I would be when I grew up. As I made my way to the chapel, I heard a voice: *You'll never be a sister; you will be married and raise a family.* It was the strangest thing. It wasn't the voice or the guidance that surprised me, but my response. I simply thought, "Yes," and from that day on I knew I'd be married and have children.

I heard the voice often during the summer of 1962, when I studied Spanish at a Jesuit University in Bilbao, Spain. That summer I turned twenty-one, and I was in love with everyone and everything. I lived in the convent next to the university with a community of cloistered nuns, but most of the time I was out with my new friends. I learned to drink wine out of a "boda" bottle (a leather flask Europeans use to drink wine), danced away many nights, received two marriage proposals, became adept in Spanish, and wrote oodles of love poetry to God. I was often drawn to sit for long periods of time in the small, dimly lit chapel. It was here I'd be reminded, But this isn't all you are going to do. At first I thought it was curious, this voice, but it frightened me as time went on. I was quite aware that listening to the voice would mean change, big, big change, and so I tried to block it out. I didn't want to know what else I would be doing. I was afraid. ✳

Reflection Questions

All children love to hear their birth stories, even if the stories have some difficult parts. My grandchildren wait excitedly every year for their birth stories on their birthdays. They never seem to hear them enough, or perhaps it is the excitement they feel as mom and dad tell the story one more time.

What stories do you recall from your birth?

How have the stories impacted you?

Most of us have something in our histories that we can point to and say, that is the experience which has caused me to be deeply wounded and fearful. It is that very experience that seems so violent or hurtful that has within it the potential to awaken us to a wisdom and truth which is hidden. We search for the healing of these wounds, never knowing the blessing they hold until we are free to accept them as a part of our path... most certainly a part we never consciously asked for!

What experiences in your past have caused you to fear and led you to believe you are not safe?

Do you still feel unsafe?

Sometimes we are so frightened that we hold the memory of painful experiences close to us as a shield. We falsely believe that nothing more can penetrate and cause more hurt if we barricade ourselves with the pain, anger, and fear. But when we do this, we also close down our ability to give and receive love, which is the greatest pain of all. When we remain present to God in the midst of the pain, and when we are able to fully feel the pain, we are taken to a depth within ourselves in which we find the grace to transform the suffering into love. This is a mysterious moment of awakening to the truth which we are about to learn.

Are you willing to gently let yourself be healed and free from the oppressiveness of past suffering?

Being willing, saying "yes", is the key to transformation. It opens the door. This takes courage because we are choosing to trust that we will be safe without the memories, beliefs, and pain of the past. This is a time for constant prayerfulness and sometimes, fasting. Fasting does not always mean refraining from eating certain foods but can also be fasting from certain thought forms like fear, resentment, or guilt. This kind of fasting makes room for God to fill our hearts with love, which engenders healing.

What would support your opening to love and healing?

How have the experiences on your path led you to wisdom and truth?

What happens to you when you focus on your blessings? What emotions emerge?

3

Losing Innocence

I lost my innocence in many different ways and at many different times. Loss of innocence happens when we realize suddenly that we are not protected from pain or fear. Loss of innocence leaves us feeling wounded and exposed. And it challenges whatever faith we have. We don't know it at the time, but losing innocence gives us an opportunity to relearn faith and make it our own.

Traumatic Birth

I was thirty-two, living in Walnut Creek, California, a suburb of San Francisco, happily married and the mother of four children: Sean age 7, Mark age 6, and Katie age 5. I was seven months pregnant with our fourth child when the difficulties began. My husband and I decided to go shopping for a portable crib. Sean and Mark were off playing with friends for the afternoon. Katie was at home, so she came along, delighted to have us all to herself. She thought this was going to be her baby and took charge of deciding which crib was the best. The smaller the crib, the better she liked it because it was easier for her to access. Shopping complete, we drove home, and as we pulled into the driveway I felt as though something broke open inside of me. My water had burst! But no, it was blood. I sat frozen in its warmth.

My husband ran to grab towels and, calling over the fence to a neighbor to watch Katie, he speedily backed us out of the driveway. Petite, five-year-old Katie stood silently at first, watching with eyes tear-swollen and face ashen. Then she cried out, waving her arms in protest, "Mommy, Mommy, Mommy!" We sped past her and headed for the nearby emergency room. I'll never forget the terror on her face. It must have mirrored my own, but I was too numb to feel.

They admitted me, kept me overnight, and waited for the bleeding to stop. Observation, probing and poking complete, the doctor sent me home with instructions not to worry and have complete bed rest. Except for trips to the bathroom, I stayed in bed for the next six weeks. I hired the children's babysitter to come during the day that summer to help with household tasks, and the neighbors were wonderfully helpful with the children. The doctor prescribed a relaxant to keep me from worry. "Drink three or four vodka and orange juice drinks a day," he said. This was 1972, well before our awareness that alcohol was not good for babies. Fortunately, I resisted his prescription and remained quiet without it, but it was a long and lonely six weeks with much too much time to wonder and worry. On the night of August 15, the Feast of Mary's Assumption into Heaven, my water finally did break. My husband rushed me to the hospital. My heart filled with fear. Labor was hours long. I refused medication so I could be alert. The pain was intense, and for the first time my husband was with me during labor. It made all the difference in the world to have him present and supportive. He encouraged me to trust being a "guinea pig" and asked me to give permission to the doctors to strap a newly arrived heart monitor around my belly to monitor the baby's heartbeat. I agreed. That mechanism was probably what saved my life, as well as Maggie's.

She began to struggle. Something was blocking her birth. The doctor gave me a shot to induce the labor and asked my husband to leave for a moment as they did this procedure. As soon as the doctor administered the shot, the heart monitor strapped to my belly dropped to zero. At the same moment, I hemorrhaged. Someone quickly placed an oxygen mask on my face, turned on the red emergency-code lights, and I heard the doctor say, "We've got about twelve minutes to get this baby out or we're gonna loose 'em both."

Somehow I knew that if I entered into the drama I would become frantic, and the doctor would sedate me. I wanted to be alert, to have some control and to keep my baby calm, but I needed help. I embraced Mary, the Holy Mother. She knew what it meant to be a mother and to be this frightened. I asked her to accompany me and my baby to bring us so close to her that we felt engulfed in her loving presence, to calm and quiet us, and to protect us both. I remember feeling her presence, her warmth and support. I was quieted.

Soon, droves of white-clad, serious-faced nurses, doctors, and attendants descended upon me. They ran down the hall, pushing me as fast as they could into surgery for an emergency C-section. I remember the big lights and the incredible bustle. They gave me a spinal tap, and it seemed to be only a few seconds before I watched with awe as the doctor pulled a lively, black-headed baby girl from my belly. The pediatrician announced that the baby was healthy. The placenta had slipped in front of the birth canal and caused the blockage, but Maggie was safely birthed and she was alive, and so was I. Her father stood, numbed, in the hallway. Sometimes I think about this moment and wonder what it was like for him. I really can't imagine it.

Before the doctor stitched me up, he suggested a tubal ligation. "After an experience like this one, you will never want another child, that's for sure," he said, matter-of-factly. I was exhausted and doing my best to stay calm, holding back a torrent of tears—tears of relief and gratitude. My whole being was shaking from the trauma. But I snapped back quickly. Open wound and all, I raised my head and responded, "Don't you dare touch my tubes." He said he was only joking. That was even worse! I closed my eyes to reconnect with Mary and settle into that quiet place within me. The doctor stitched me up, tubes and all.

I went into a depression after Maggie's birth. They said it was post-traumatic stress. It lasted about a month. I experienced deep emotional pain, most especially fear. My parents never called or wrote. Mom had already begun what was later diagnosed as Alzheimer's, and Dad had a difficult time with life-and-death trauma. They acted as though what had happened wasn't really serious. I was devastated. I couldn't understand why they had not called. I needed their love so much. I ached for them to be there for me, but I didn't have the physical and emotional strength to be the one to call. I just waited, and cried. Years later, it occurred to me that my parents were riveted in the fear of re-living the trauma of my birth. To protect themselves, they distanced themselves from me, and so from the emotions that their bodies had held for them all these years.

It was awhile before Maggie and I came home from the hospital. The other children were beside themselves with delight, especially Katie. She didn't say too much—she just took over. Maggie was, after all, her baby!

Death of a Child

My husband had a business meeting in New York City in early December, and he invited me to join him. It had been four months since Maggie's birth, and I was feeling both emotionally and physically healthy by this time. I looked forward to all of the perks that this sort of meeting would offer—a beautiful hotel on 5th Avenue, wonderful parties, shopping, fancy restaurants, the theater, and, best of all, seeing people who had become good friends over the years. We decided to take Maggie. Her grandmothers and aunties in Huntington would take care of her while we were in the city, and we would have a chance to introduce the newest member of the family to all the relatives. The older three children stayed at home with a sitter, and although they understood that we wanted to introduce Maggie to the family, I think they wondered how we could take her away from them for so long—a whole week!

When my mother first met Maggie, her eyes filled with tears, and she exclaimed, "Oh, she is so beautiful. She's like an angel." My mother was very intuitive, more so than even she would acknowledge, but it never occurred to me at the time that she was aware on some level of Maggie's fate.

Maggie was a sweet baby, and everyone wanted to hold her. She stayed with my mother-in-law, but my two youngest sisters who lived only a mile away and who were still living at home, spent lots of time with her. They loved Maggie just as Sean, Mark, and Katie did. It was easy to leave Maggie with my family without worrying, because there was so much love, and I so looked forward to our three days in the city.

I returned from the city to my mother-in-law's home on December 7, feeling pampered and looking forward to seeing Maggie and listening to the tales of the grandmothers. I have a vague recollection of that night, of feeding Maggie and going to bed exhausted from all the luxury and freedom of being in New York City.

I woke early on the morning of December 8. I had planned to go to my parents' home, about a mile away, to wrap the family Christmas presents, which we would leave for them when we left for California. It was a very special day because it was another of Mary's feast days, celebrating her Immaculate Conception. I loved Mary and felt very thankful for her presence in my life. As I kissed my sleepy husband and baby goodbye and went off to my parents, I went with a heart full of gratitude for my life as a wife and mother, and in a special way for Mary the Mother of God on her feast day.

I had been at my parents' for awhile, chatting with them and my sisters, when the phone rang. It was my husband asking me to come right away. "The baby is sick," he said. I think that's when I went numb. Heidi, my cousin's wife and good friend, had just come by to say hello, so I hopped in the car with her.

When I walked into my mother-in-law's living room I saw and felt my husband's dread. His face was ashen and his eyes downcast. "We have to go to the hospital," he said, holding Maggie close to his chest. Heidi drove us to the emergency room.

He sat in the front, and I sat behind, staring at the back of his head and the pink flannel blanket that draped over his shoulder. We checked in, and almost immediately two people clad in white came out of swinging steel doors and took the limp little body from his arms. I can still see those double doors swing open a second time and the doctor standing there saying, "I'm sorry to tell you your daughter is dead. We don't know the cause; we'll have to do an autopsy." I stood motionless while screaming silently: "NO, NO, NO, NO, NO . . ." The nurse handed us her clothes—her cold empty clothes—as if I wanted them. But I did want them. It was all I had left of her. I never held her or saw her again. We answered questions and filled out papers. I felt as lifeless and dead as my baby.

Heidi drove us back to my parents' home. She never looked at us, and the only thing she could say was, "I'm so sorry." What else could she say—what else could anyone say?

Mom knew. I never knew how she knew things, but her face was stricken with pain as we walked in the side door, our arms empty, our tear-washed faces aching for comforting words or arms or anything. In between the tears and the deadening silence we told the story. "The doctors said the body would be autopsied so we'd know the cause. Maybe it was crib death." My husband said over and over, "There must be a reason, and they are not telling us. She must have cried out for help, and I didn't hear her. I should have checked her crib when she didn't stir. It was my fault." The fact that he blamed himself for Maggie's death was terribly painful for both of us. I knew we would have to wait for the autopsy before he could stop blaming himself.

How do I describe the next minutes and hours? I was numb at first, and that was perhaps the worst. I couldn't feel, I couldn't imagine, I couldn't fathom what had happened. It was too quick, too much, too awful.

Our family and friends began to gather at my parents' home. There was one family I anxiously awaited, my Aunt Pamela and Uncle John, whose five-year-old daughter, Delyce, had died some years earlier from a brain tumor. I wanted to know how they had survived the death of their child. I wanted to know if I'd ever be happy again; if I would ever sleep or eat or laugh or play. I wanted to know if I'd ever be able to trust life or God or anyone with the security of my other children. I wondered and wondered if this empty hole in my chest and belly would ever fill up, or if I would just die in some way with my baby.

It was my Aunt Pamela to whom I went with all my fear and pain. This must have brought back all of her memories, and I think she truly hated knowing I would have to walk with this same suffering. She took me in her arms and we cried together. We just cried and cried and cried. Somehow, in that embrace, in those tears, I knew she had made it through, and I could make the journey as well.

We sat with family and friends that Friday, and our family made the arrangements for a "Mass of the Angels" the following morning. We changed our airline tickets to leave at noon, just after the funeral Mass.

That night my Aunt Deemy took my husband and me back to his mother's home, and although we were totally exhausted, there was no way we could sleep. We asked my aunt, a physician and thoracic surgeon, for some sleeping pills, and she replied with a quick and emphatic, "No!" and then said, "Someday you'll have to learn to sleep with this pain, and you might as well begin tonight." She gently added some wisdom that I'll never forget. "No medication will ever take away your pain. It will just cover it over. The sooner you face it, the sooner you'll move through it."

She left us alone. We crawled into the same single bed and held each other through the night. We never spoke, but we could hear and feel one another's tears. I never knew pain could go so deep. We had Maggie only for four months, but she had endeared herself to us in such a way that her absence was almost unbearable. Sometimes I would have flashes of her cold little body in the morgue. I often regretted that I had never seen her face or held her the day she died. I just watched her in her father's arms all covered in a tiny pink blanket. I would doze off at night and after just minutes, be suddenly awakened to the nightmare. Then I would remember—it wasn't a nightmare. It was real. I'd never hold her again. My arms ached.

On the day of the funeral, we arrived at the church. This church that had been home for me in baptism, first Holy Communion, confirmation, and my wedding, was now the place from which I would bury my child. I felt like a stranger in this church which I had not been in since we moved to California. I no longer knew the priests, and since our families made the arrangements, they did not know me. My husband and I sat in a pew on the left side, near the front. Our family and friends gathered around us. The priest came out to the altar, dressed all in white. He celebrated the Mass of the Angels—and he never even knew who the parents were. He never addressed us or spoke to us or introduced himself, or even seemed to care. I didn't really much care either. I just wanted to go home.

41

Maybe the death of a baby was too frightening for him, and it was all he could do to celebrate the Mass. I found myself wanting to make excuses for him. After all, he was a priest. But the truth was I was angry, and I buried the anger. It was too much to feel.

At the time, I remember being shocked when the priest never acknowledged us, even during his eulogy. I wondered was it ignorance, cowardice, or was he just too busy to take the time? I am quite sure that if this priest were married and had children of his own, he would never have been so cold, fearful, or too busy to extend his care.

Immediately after the funeral Mass we left for the airport. We couldn't stay any longer. It was too painful, and I needed to go home and see my children. My family, my husband's mother, and the priest, went to the cemetery to bury Maggie's little body. We never went to the gravesite. We went home. My husband and I cried away the long hours on the TWA flight back to California. I didn't care what the flight attendants or the other passengers thought. I am quite certain that although her body went to the grave, her spirit remained with us that day.

We did not tell Maggie's brothers and sister that she had died until we returned home. We called ahead, and our friends and neighbors took over to prepare for our arrival. They sent the sitter home, and our next door neighbors took the children to their home. My women friends went to the house and removed the crib, carriage, all the clothes, and anything that had to do with Maggie.

The house was stark when we walked in—it was as truly empty as our hearts.

When the children came home, we brought them into the living room and sat them down to talk. In order to save them the pain we were feeling (as though that were healthy or even possible), I told them a story, "We are blessed, because now we have a special angel in heaven that we can pray to, and she will always be with us in spirit."

The children, seven-year-old Sean, six-year-old Mark, and five-year-old Katie, said, keeping back tears, that that was fine. And Mark got so excited, he ran to tell his friends, exclaiming, "We have an angel! We have an angel!" as he went rushing down the steps. But he soon returned, and this time he was angry. "I don't want an angel, Mom. I want my sister, Maggie."

One afternoon, the phone rang and I picked it up in the bedroom. As I sat on the edge of the bed, looking at the empty space where Maggie's crib had been, a woman from a bereavement group insisted on giving me her best advice. My grief was still too new and too great for me to hear what I "should" do. And I especially closed down as she revealed to me the imposing danger of divorce if I didn't get marriage counseling right away. I didn't want to hear about the very high percentage of couples who divorce after the death of a child. It was too much even to begin to think that my marriage and my family would suffer even more loss than Maggie's death. So I refused her advice, as well as her invitation to come to a meeting for parents whose children had died.

I felt intruded upon and angry as I hung up the phone. I remember this incident, because I also felt embarrassed, but I didn't know why. It took years for me to discover the self-blame that I buried in my heart. Deep within me I believed that I was responsible for my baby's death. It wasn't simply that "if I had been there she wouldn't have died," but something even deeper. I harbored a belief that no matter what harm comes to my children, I am responsible. It is a core belief that I recognize as common among mothers, a belief that needs to be brought to consciousness and released. Because of this experience, I am more compassionate with others who grieve, and I understand that sometimes it's just too terrifying to open our hearts to discover the truth or falsehood that we hold inside or to receive help when it is offered.

A few days after Maggie's death, when the shock began to wear off and reality to set in, I recalled the *Dark Experience of Nothingness*. I remembered that this experience had been far more devastating than Maggie's death. However, the pain of losing Maggie didn't disappear. My grief for her was enormous. I had arms that ached for my child, and a family who grieved mostly in secret, but nothing could be worse than the total loss of everything I'd felt the year before when I had had the vision of the *Dark Experience of Nothingness*. With Maggie's death I could still feel love from my family, friends, and God, and I knew my heart would heal, and so would the hearts of my family. But in the depths of the *Dark Experience of Nothingness*, there was no hope, no love, no faith, no God. Although this awareness was very clear in my mind, I still could not fully articulate it to myself, and I certainly would not dare attempt to speak of it aloud. I didn't have the words or understanding, and the fear and shame caused by thinking I had displeased God remained.

Maggie had gone almost everywhere with me, so when I went to the store or the post office or met an acquaintance and I didn't have her in the baby carrier on my chest, they would immediately ask, "Where is your baby today?" Their words, spoken so cheerfully, were always sharp and painful for me. The story I told, no matter how brief, or stoically I told it, transferred the pain to each of them. I could see myself in the contorted facial expressions that expressed their grief for me and brought to the fore the grief that each carried in his or her own heart. I used to wish that everyone knew about her death so I would never have to tell the story again.

Perhaps the most painful experience in this regard was the trip to a house in Martinez, a town twenty minutes or so from our Walnut Creek home, to buy a boy's bicycle, "used but in great condition," according to the ad. Mark had left his new bike at the back wheel of our car, and we had accidentally driven over it.

When I got to the house, I rang the doorbell and a woman took me into the garage where she had "lots of good used stuff for sale." I only wanted the bike. She began to point out the bargains and hit on the baby furniture. There was a crib, a high chair, bassinet, playpen, and almost every type of toy and furniture a baby might need. I could feel the tears welling up as she tried to convince me to "take the stuff, because I don't want to have another damned pregnancy, and I sure don't want another little brat to raise." I didn't know whether to cry or scream or run or look at her and tell her of my grief. But I stayed, holding back the tears. I bought the bike and drove home. I didn't cry until I got home, and then I sobbed uncontrollably until there were no more tears. I sat in silence, staring blankly at the wall until the children came home from school.

I didn't grieve Maggie's death as well as I would have liked. Trying to protect the children from their pain by not showing my own was bad enough, but I kept my pain from everyone. I kept my deepest, most heart-wrenching pain to myself, and when I was alone, I wept. All my life I was affirmed because of my strength. Showing my tears did not fit with my misbegotten idea of strength. I feel a deep sadness for myself, because I cried so often then, but always alone. My husband went back to work, and the children went to school. I kept myself busy with household chores, friends, and the garden. We didn't really talk about Maggie, but there were times when the children came to me and asked to see her pictures. I would take them out of the drawer, and we'd sit on the bed together and look at them.

The children needed to see their sister again, and pictures were the only way. Those times were painfully sad. We sat quietly, and though our eyes might have teared, we never cried out loud. This never happened when their Dad was around. None of us talked about Maggie in his presence.

Healing Moments

The Sunday after we returned from New York and Maggie's funeral, we went to our local church. We arrived early so that I could speak to Father Harry before Mass. I wanted to tell him about Maggie. Fr. Harry Heiter was a Jesuit priest studying at the Graduate Theological Union in Berkeley, as part of his sabbatical. He lived at Saint Mary's Church in Walnut Creek and assisted the pastor. He had baptized Maggie just a few weeks before. Because of his openness and prayerfulness, I liked him very much. When I knocked on the office door, the secretary opened it, but she wouldn't let me see him. She said he was too busy. Her "no", didn't stop me. I went to the church and right into the sacristy where he was vesting for Mass. I told him about Maggie and our need for prayer and support. I cried. He just held me. He never said a word. He didn't have to, the hug said it all, and so did his presence as he celebrated the Sunday liturgy, his eyes teary the entire time.

The next week he came to the house for dinner. The children lavished him with attention, and he let them. They were fascinated by his white, priest collar and black dickie under his black jacket. By the time they finished exploring and dismantling his "costume," he sat at the dinner table in a white cotton undershirt beneath his jacket.

As my husband and I cleared the table for dessert, Katie took Father Harry's hand and disappeared down the hall. Her brothers followed. I was busy preparing dessert, but I wondered where they had gone. They returned, and the children sat down, looking very pleased.

Father sat down with tears again welling up in his eyes. The children had found a trunk with Maggie's clothes that the neighbors had left behind. Katie showed Father all of Maggie's things, and all three children told him their stories about their sister. It was in the midst of Father Harry's tears that I found the compassion and care that I needed. I sometimes remember the priest at Maggie's Mass of the Angels. He was as absent as Father Harry was present. I pray for them both.

Maggie was a gift. All children are gifts, and each comes to bless and be blessed, but Maggie's blessing was especially significant. Because of her traumatic entry and her brief life, she stirred something deep within the hearts of all who knew and loved her. I believe deep in my heart that Maggie lived those four months to give me time to recover from the trauma of her birth so that I would have the strength to survive her death. I treasure those four months.

I didn't know then how much of an instrument of transformation Maggie would be. From her loss, I have learned that we cannot be transformed until we have been utterly wounded. It is in the wounding that we are rudely shaken out of an unconscious relationship with God and into the journey of awakening to the experience of who we truly are. Although I was unable at the time to name much of what happened in me because of the loss of my child, my spirit began to wake up in small ways, even then. My grief and loss of innocence would then stir the awakening. ✳

Reflection Questions

Parents grieve the death of their children for their entire lives. Over time, the grief becomes less intense, but it never leaves the heart. Tears come spontaneously, in their own timing, and are eventually seen as a gift... the cost of love! Our whole society believes that the child is destined to out-live the parents, and when this does not happen, the response of the parents, family and community is one of utter disbelief and outrage.

"How could this be?" we ask, as though we know how it should be... as though we are in control, as though the child does not have his or her own path.

Who or what have you had to let go of because of illness, injury, separation or death?

If you have not yet let go, are you willing to do so?

What kind of support would help you? Spiritual direction and psychotherapy are possibilities and gifts you could give yourself. What else would help?

Some of us hold on to pain for fear something else will come that we will not be able to overcome. We think that the pain will eventually numb us and prevent us from further pain. Our essential and ultimate fear is that of annihilation, that we will cease to exist. Severe mental illness is a form of annihilation. I believe that we fear that further pain would drive us out of our minds. That is a possibility of course, but only if we do not hold sacred the feelings that are a natural part of loss. If we stuff the feelings and refuse to fully feel them, they will rule our lives, and, eventually, they will take over. This will be terrifying because we will be completely out of control. I have seen with myself, and many others, that the difficulty comes not from letting go but from holding on.

It is easy to let go, even though our culture teaches otherwise. The real intensity and pain comes from holding on. I let go of two of my children and of the dream of outliving them, because it was far too difficult to do otherwise. To do otherwise would be to deny reality. I was able to let go because I learned what the experience came to teach me. I learned because I had the grace, the support, and the courage to fully feel the pain to stay with all my feelings until they were transformed into love. I learned to keep my heart and hands open, to receive what is offered and to give what is asked. Learning and letting go freed all of us; it freed the children who died, myself, and those in my family who were ready to let go.

If you have let go of some very painful loss, has this changed your life?

What have you learned as a result of this letting go? Has gratitude filled the empty spaces where once you felt loss? Can you describe the feeling of gratitude?

Stirrings

4

Learning to Pray

About two months after Maggie's death, my husband's company offered him a position that would mean moving back east. It was a gesture of kindness on their part. It meant we would be close to family again at a time when I needed their companionship.

Our house sold quickly, and we moved to Duxbury, a little town south of Boston, so near the water that we could hear the foghorns and watch the sea gulls as they flew overhead.

It was a paradise for the children and me. All the sports I grew up with were now available to us. The children had sailing and swimming lessons, played tennis, and bicycled back and forth to the Duxbury Yacht Club that offered so much for all of us, winter and summer.

The children and I built a huge play structure in the yard, complete with a macramÈ ladder, wooden swings, and bars with spliced ropes, and a fort. It became a favorite spot for all the neighborhood children.

Charlie, our neighbor, raced a small sailboat like the kind I had raced as a teenager. He asked me to crew for him. I was thrilled! The days I sailed and raced were times of exhilaration and freedom. I'd come home covered with salt, wind-blown, wet, and feeling so happy.

We started to heal.

There was a Catholic church on the other side of our field, in back of the house, and we soon had a new faith community. I began teaching catechism in our home. I was preparing to teach a lesson on the love of God when I had the most extraordinary experience:

> *I am sitting at the kitchen table, looking out the window, pondering the possible ways that I can demonstrate God's love to these grammar school children, three of whom are mine. As I do so, my eyes begin to take in the spring blooms in the yard and in the field. I am suddenly overcome by their beauty, seeing them as I have never seen before... how the daffodils, crocuses, and wildflowers radiantly reflect the colors of the rainbow and the love of God. Oh, how perfect. I realize that all I have to do is take the children for a walk. They will naturally experience God's love through the beauty of creation, and that beauty will reflect for them their own beauty as well. This is all in a flash, but then the gift explodes and envelopes me in an experience of God's love that remains in my heart forever.*

I'd never felt such love. It filled me, flooded me, and took me to itself. This was the antithesis of the *Dark Experience of Nothingness* of three years before, when there was no love and no such thing as love. This was a brilliant and total expression of love. This was nothing but love. I ran to get the Bible, hoping that I could meet and know this God who had taken me entirely and enveloped me in love. God was still God the Father at this time of my life, but I must say that the love and the lover that I experienced that day had no gender. It was just Love. I call this the *Ecstasy of God's Love.*

I sought to understand this experience of Love by myself. I read the Bible whenever I had a few moments alone. I was searching. Who was this God whose love was so far beyond my scope of understanding, whose love was without limitation or condition, beginning or end? I wanted to know this God who took me so completely into " his" heart and loved me so intensely. I avoided thinking about the *Dark Experience of Nothingness*. It did remain close to my awareness, but I was still afraid to meet it more deeply.

These two experiences—of the darkness and the light, the most terrifying and the most euphoric—have become fundamental building blocks for my spirituality. I have come to live each day with the awareness of both, in a state of gratitude. That is not to say that I do not experience emotions such as fear and anger, hope and doubt, laughter, sadness, and every other feeling possible... put simply that gratitude is primary and prevalent, the others come and go, as I walk along my path

The Next Pregnancy

I became pregnant with our fifth child in the summer of 1973. It was an absolutely thrilling and yet terrifying pregnancy. By now I knew that all babies were not destined to live to old age or be born without a hitch, or to be born healthy and whole. To make matters worse, while sitting in the pediatrician's office, waiting for the children's appointment, I read an article just by chance that revealed a new study about Sudden Infant Death Syndrome. Studies had revealed that it was likely to occur more than once in a family. I didn't talk about the article I read , but it terrified me and made me cry when I was alone. One day, it became too heavy and painful to carry by myself. I blurted it out to my husband, and he looked at me startled and sad-eyed. He had read the same article, the same week, and had held it to himself as well.

My baby in utero taught me a new way to pray. I prayed constantly, knowing I wanted a healthy baby, fearing the worst. I prayed that I would have the grace and courage to accept and love my baby, no matter how long the baby lived or how healthy or unhealthy, how perfect or imperfect she was. The prayer I was learning during my pregnancy has been with me ever since: pray for what I want, embrace and give thanks for what I receive.

Every day after the children went to school, I walked through the back field to the Catholic church for morning Mass. My heart held the love I knew as a child and the love that had recently revealed itself, as I simultaneously felt the fear. There were just a few people, mostly older women, grandmothers, who gathered every day. They seemed to delight in my presence and in my growing belly. They never knew why I came, what I prayed for, or how much pain and fear I held on those mornings.

I had become friends with the priest at church. Father Joe would walk across the field to the house to have a cup of coffee with me during the day. When he saw that I was reupholstering some furniture, he brought over his great-grandfather's chair. I showed him how I did it, and we spent many days chatting as we stretched and nailed fabric across our heirlooms.

Annie's birth date was pre-arranged, as the delivery was to be a C-section. On the Friday before her birth, I went to see Father Joe. I told him that I would be going to the hospital on Monday to deliver the baby. He acknowledged my sharing but continued up the aisle of the church toward the sacristy. "I am frightened," I said, hoping he'd stop and spend a moment with me, encouraging me to trust, reminding me to pray and recall God's abiding love, or perhaps let me talk about my fear. But he did none of these things. Instead he kept walking, his black suit disappearing into the sacristy as he answered briefly, "Oh, there is nothing to worry about. Babies are born every second." And he was gone.

I could feel my heart close down. My hope for his spiritual companionship ended abruptly. A shiver went down my spine, and I forced back the tears. As I have reflected on this incident, I realize that most priests are not trained to be spiritual directors nor do they necessarily have a gift for spiritual direction, but being pastoral and compassionate seem to me to be primary components for a priest. It appeared my priest friend had neither in this moment.

This experience, like other disappointments, drove me to prayer, as I searched for solace and companionship with God. At that time, I had no one with whom to share my inner journey. Nor did I have the concept of this as a possibility. Actually, I couldn't even have articulated that I was on a journey, but there was always an awareness that the spirit—the spirit of God, of Jesus, of Mary, the angels and saints—was ever present.

I have had a deep awareness of God's presence as far back as I can remember. Even though I couldn't name this or wasn't fully conscious of what it meant, there was always a place within me where I felt truly safe and loved by God, with the exception of that one moment of the *Dark Experience of Nothingness*. Even so, I often felt lonely. It was a loneliness that came from having no one with whom I could sit and talk about what was happening deep within my heart. Without knowing what it meant or that such a thing existed or having the words to articulate my longing, I ached for spiritual companionship. It never occurred to me to try to talk to my husband about these things. We could talk about religion because I had words and concepts for religion, but I had no words to express what was happening to me at this time in my life.

I had never told Father Joe about myself or about Maggie, even though we had become friends just a few months after her death; perhaps if he'd known more of my history, he wouldn't have been so cool that day. Then again, I may have been opening a place in his heart, too painful for him to go. The call to priesthood meant a life of celibacy for a Catholic priest. He would never have children. He was a wonderful priest in so many ways, a kind and loving man, but I sensed that he carried wounds of his own. I'm not trying to make excuses for him, but I desire to deepen my compassion for priests, who, like so many other people in leadership roles, find it nearly impossible to maintain the pedestal pose that we create for them.

I was taught in school that a priest is a representative of God and that we must never say anything bad about any priest, or it would be like saying something bad about God. What an impossible position for a priest to be in! This notion came mostly from the sisters at school, but also from my mother.

It was still dark when I awakened on the second morning of April 1974. This time I didn't have to wait for labor to begin. I could feel the fluttering in my heart and my belly as I dressed. My husband drove me to the hospital. I remember so clearly the ride on the gurney down the hall to the operating room. I was so frightened that I cried the whole way. Would my faith hold me up if my baby were born dead or impaired? My husband encouraged me along the way to "just relax and trust." I didn't watch the operation this time.

When I saw my beautiful baby girl, I wept and wept with joy. Her screams and cries sounded like the best symphony I had ever heard. Though she was dark-haired and red-skinned, she wasn't Maggie. She was Annie, and she was exquisite. And, she was healthy.

Days, weeks, months went by. We were a happy family. I didn't sail or race much that summer but spent hours on the beach with the children, making sand castles, swimming, and just wandering, as we collected stones and shells. The freedom that the children felt when we were at the beach was evident. When the tide was high, they swam like fish for hours, and, when it was low, they wandered along the shoreline in search of treasures. One day Mark and Sean went off for a long walk and came back dragging an abandoned broken lobster trap. We brought it home. They proudly repaired it, and we used it as a coffee table.

I loved living in Duxbury, Massachusetts. I had lots of friends and all sorts of outdoor activities I found exciting. The children were happy; our home was wonderful. It was just one of those places that felt comfortable energetically, and in every other way. The possibility of leaving was unthinkable. While California was where I experienced the annihilation and darkness of the *Dark Experience of Nothingness,* it was in Duxbury that I felt the brilliance and warm embrace in the *Ecstasy of God's Love.*

Other Losses, Other Prayers

I never wanted to leave, certainly not to go to California. But even though that was true, the threat of my husband's being transferred loomed larger and larger. I pleaded with him to find other work, another company, something that would make it possible for us to stay. He looked at a couple of possibilities, but neither was right for him. It was fine with him to stay with this company, and go where they sent him. I didn't understand his choice to leave the Boston area at the time.

A cheerful phone call one evening put an end to my hope that we would stay in Duxbury, and began a new phase in my life. "Hi," my husband said, voice animated. "Guess what? I have the best news. I've been given a terrific opportunity, a big promotion, and a raise in salary, and we're going to move to Tennessee! Isn't that fantastic? Aren't you thrilled?"

I answered in a flat, cold voice. "How could you think that I would ever be excited about your promotion when it will mean we will have to leave a place where we have found so much happiness? How could you pretend that your transfer to Tennessee is good for our family?" Then I hung up the phone and wept.

I didn't realize it at the time, but it was the end of a dream. My husband used to tell me that I was too naive, that I trusted people too easily, and that someday my bubble would burst. He was right. My bubble had just burst.

As I have reflected on this, I understand that he couldn't step out of the business culture in which he was raised. That was who he was. And now he was on his way to the top, which was, in his mind, the way to best care for his family. I didn't understand and was devastated. I believed in a deep, yet private place within me, that his first love was not directly for me, the children, and our relationship, but rather for his career. In some ways, it was a very maturing moment because it was the beginning of my awareness that my happiness was my responsibility. I saw that he was committed elsewhere. I knew that I was important to him, but I believed it was for my role as his wife. I was bright, energetic, and pretty—a good companion at business gatherings. I was a great supporter, encouraging, and interested. I was a good mother for his children, and I loved him deeply. And yes, he loved me. That was true, but he was raised and en- culturated in such a way that he believed that I was his, and my purpose was to be there for him so that he could accomplish his career goals more easily. And I had agreed to this out of my own enculturation. All of this had begun to be clear, but it was only the beginning. It would take years for me to become fully conscious of it. Today, I watch my daughter and son and their spouses with each other and their children and am in awe of the way in which both fathers and mothers participate fully in family life and in decision-making. They have been raised in a different culture.

I learned to pray in Duxbury, because I understood more and more how alone I truly was. There was no one else who could hold my fear with me as I awaited Annie's arrival. The help I hoped for in my priest was not there. My husband was so busy with his career that even in our marriage I felt that I was on my own, at least as far as my interior life, my emotions—and especially my fears—were concerned. I was raised in a family that did not express emotions, particularly painful ones, and I did not know how to break that pattern. Only God and I could hold that pain...in prayer. Perhaps those sunny days in Duxbury were a time of kind cultivation from God. I was given that perfectly beautiful environment in which to build my own strength. I would need it for the days ahead. ✳

Reflection Questions

Prayer takes many forms and is learned over a lifetime. We can pray out of a prayer book or at a church service. Reflecting on and writing about our life can be a prayer form and we can pray with art, music, dance, and poetry. When we are filled with gratitude we are in communication with God without even mentioning God's name. Crying out to God for help is also prayer. You might not use the word prayer or God but you may meditate and give thanks to the Divine Presence or Mother Earth, or you may ask for help in a different way.

How do you pray or meditate today?

Who taught you to pray? Or meditate?

*How has your prayer or meditation
changed over the years?*

Experiences of God are both ordinary and extraordinary... ordinary, because God is always present and always desirous of communication with us, and extraordinary, because our lives are often too cluttered to hear God's voice. When we take our experiences of God seriously and reflect on them, they have enormous power to transform our lives. It is difficult to express in words our communications with God, and when we can, it is a gift. We most often see those expressions in prose, poetry, or art.

Recall your experiences of contact with God.

This can be an ecstatic moment in nature, holding a newborn infant, a heartfelt touch in prayer, a sudden and unexplained moment of elation, an invitation to ministry, even a realization that a change in behavior is called for, etc. God can even communicate through an unusual act of kindness, generosity, or compassion that comes to you through a friend, family member, or stranger, or through you to someone else. The feeling of gratitude upon receiving a gift or of joy on giving a gift can be God communicating Love. For those of you who feel disconnected from God, you may be surprised as you reflect on this question, at the many ways God is communicating with you.

Choose one such experience and describe it.

Will you use poetry, or art? Or, are prose words sufficient?

When you recall and describe an experience of God, what do you feel?

Is it difficult to find words or colors to describe your experience?

Is it joyful, peaceful, playful, etc.?

5

Emerging as Myself

Tennessee was tough from the beginning. We flew in a small plane from Memphis to an airport near Jackson and when we flew over our soon-to-be home, I looked down and saw nothing but brown...forever! I cried. We lived in the middle of the state, between Memphis and Nashville. We were surrounded by miles of flat farmland with no natural streams or lakes anywhere nearby. There were two classes of people: those with money, and those on very limited incomes. We were the former, and I felt so uncomfortable living in a community where there was such a wide economic gap.

Our neighborhood was new and very elaborate. It was different from any neighborhood or house I had ever lived in, but it was nearest the public school that we were told was the best, so that's where we settled.

Our house was unfinished when we bought it, so I chose the carpet and wallpaper, appliances, and bathroom fixtures. It was huge—over 4000 square feet, and no matter how many children or adults were visiting, it always seemed empty. The neighborhood seemed empty as well. I think it reflected what I was feeling. I missed my Duxbury life terribly. I missed the salt water and the sound of the foghorns. I missed my friends. I remember even realizing how important my relationships were with people in the market and the post office. I missed so much that my heart ached, especially at night when it was time to sleep.

Everything was new and different. With the exception of a couple of families, the people in my new neighborhood had been born and raised in Jackson, Tennessee. There were Bible classes, women's luncheons, lots of time spent on hair and nail appointments, gardeners, cleaning ladies, and fancy clothes. I mowed the grass, planted my own flowers, sewed my clothes and clothes for the girls, and rode a bicycle for miles with Annie in a child's seat on the back. I was different too!

I didn't fit in at all, but one day when it snowed, I found that I at least had a place. I was at home watching the snow fall when the phone rang. "Would you mind," one of the ladies asked coyly, "driving a few of us for our beauty appointments? We know you can drive in the snow, and we can't." Suddenly my unladylike strengths were needed, and I had a role to play in this fancy neighborhood.

I joined a Christian women's Bible group that met once a week at the house across the street. I thought this might be a way to make friends. It didn't work. I think they spent hours researching the Bible to pull together all the passages about sin and the devil so that they could scare one another into behaving. I didn't last long there. The Bible didn't scare me, but they did.

Hidden in the Dark

I experienced a different kind of darkness than the *Dark Experience of Nothingness* when we moved to Tennessee, but it was similar to the depression

I felt after Maggie's birth. It wasn't the kind of depression that kept me bedridden or inactive, but rather the kind that indicated something was wrong. I didn't smile, or laugh, or have much energy. I was lonely. I had no friends. Though my home was beautiful and new, it never felt like home. I was grieving the loss of a place and lifestyle I loved. It must have been difficult for my husband to go to his new job and worry about me at the same time. Over time and with deepened compassion, it occurred to me that he might have been torn about the choice he had made and perhaps even felt a tinge of guilt about moving me and the children away from such an idyllic lifestyle. He was angry with me for being in such a state, and I wonder if perhaps his anger was really toward himself because he felt, as men were taught to feel then, responsible for his wife's happiness. If indeed he did feel responsible, he would have experienced failure. The saddest thing of all was that we did not share our feelings with each other. We did not have the tools to do so in a healthy way. Blame was a major inhibitor: "It is your fault that I am unhappy," was how I felt inside. Rather than, "I feel sad and lonely," or even, "I feel angry that we have to live here." What I most needed was his love, a hug, and some encouraging words, but in his anger, and my silent depression (my form of anger), he told me, "You are crazy, and you need to find a psychiatrist." I fell deeper into depression.

My children were in a public school that was overpopulated, understaffed, and frightening. As they left the classroom each day for lunch, they were given a wad of toilet paper so they could go to the bathroom. The teacher said the school couldn't leave the toilet paper rolls in the bathrooms because the kids would destroy them or steal them. I offered to volunteer many times but was never allowed to go into the classrooms. They still used corporal punishment, and my children came home with stories that terrified them and made me cry. After many information-gathering trips to Jackson, I had been assured it was the best public school in the area. I felt sad about the school, sad that my children were having this experience, but even sadder for the children that would continue to have it.

I didn't want to put the children in a private school because I valued integration. This was perhaps a typical community in the South, and there was a heavy black population, most of whom were poor. I remember seeing a long row of small, broken-down shacks lining one of the streets on the way to school, the very first day. I didn't want to see this. I wanted to pretend that we all had plenty. It was painful, and I didn't know how to make the picture in my mind go away, nor did I know what to do to change the picture. It all felt so overwhelming. Some of my children's friends lived in those shacks. One day, one of the boys in Sean's class told him "You better be careful. There are some rich white folks who live up the street a ways. They are mean. They beat kids like you and me." Sean was horrified and embarrassed because he knew he was one of those white folks. I felt embarrassed too.

The children were in the public school for the month of May and part of June. But it was clear that in the fall they would go to private school. It was not to separate them from others, but so they could be educated and feel safe. The children's classmates did not worry me, but their teachers did!

It wasn't just the loneliness, the big empty house, or feeling as though I didn't fit into the neighborhood that caused my depression. The children's school experience was also a very significant factor. But something even more disturbing burned deep within that I wouldn't discover for a few years. It had to do with a growing awareness that my marriage wasn't what I had dreamed it would be or pretended it was.

My depression didn't last very long—maybe a month—but it seemed like forever. It was unusual for me to remain unhappy for very long, and I was so uncomfortable that I was forced to reach out for help. I turned to God.

Feeling lost and helpless, I flopped down in the green overstuffed chair in our living room and started to cry. I was alone in the house, so without thought I cried out loud to God, "Please help me. I'm so depressed and I am frightened and lonely. Help me God, please help me!" I had hardly finished my plea when I heard back, *"I've been waiting for you."*

That moment was the end of the depression, and a deepening of my relationship with God. With stunning clarity, I knew then that the *Love* I had experienced three years before while planning a catechism class for the children was a permanent state. I knew then that I could enter into that love any time I chose, because God was always waiting and hoping for me to surrender to *Love*. As I opened to what I needed, I could feel warmth in my chest. As my heart filled and stretched, there was also an ache, a tender, sweet pain.

We bought a VW camper while in Jackson, and the whole family had fun exploring the countryside on weekends. Twice, we all drove back to Duxbury in the summer. It took us about twenty hours, and my husband and I took turns driving through the night. I recall once when it was my turn. It was about 5:30 a.m. Sean, Mark, Katie, and Annie were squeezed into the front with me, and we watched the sun rise. It was absolutely exhilarating. I still remember the fullness and gratitude I experienced when I saw this, an everyday event that this morning seemed so extraordinary. And what made it even more special was that I knew my children saw and felt it with me.

We had immediately joined the local Catholic Church in Jackson, which seemed to be a lively community, and got to know the pastor. We invited him to dinner. He was a happy-hearted man. It was at the dinner table that night that we all were made to face questions concerning the biggest mystery of Maggie's death: Where was she now? Somehow the story of Maggie had come into our dinner conversation, and one of the children proudly announced that she was an angel. Father spoke up forcefully, explaining the theology of angels and stating quite clearly, "Maggie is not an angel," and that was that!

I can still see the faces of the children, and I can still feel the big lump that formed in my throat. Father didn't say what she was, just what she wasn't. Nor did he say where she was.

I didn't have much theology at that time, just what I had received in high school and college. I knew that Maggie wasn't in limbo (a strange place that priests used to say unbaptized babies went) because she had been baptized, and it couldn't be purgatory, because that was for people who had to do penance for their sins. She must be in heaven, but I didn't know what it meant for Maggie to be in heaven. At least the idea of being an angel was something I could imagine. I didn't like what the priest said, nor did I like the way he said it. It was as though he had slammed the door in or faces. Suddenly I felt I had no authority to determine the whereabouts of my baby. I was what is called a conventional Catholic—boxed in by the law and by authority figures—so I never said a word to my pastor. I did know God's love, and, although I may not have known where Maggie was, I did know that she was with God in a place of Love... that seemed to me to be the place of the angels.

Being a part of the church was important to me, and I wanted to find a place within the church in Jackson, even though I found the priest to be less than compassionate. I wanted to be part of the Church community and wanted to participate in the liturgy.

I decided to teach catechism again in Jackson, but this time for the high school students. It was a delight to be with the teens. It was also a challenge! All I wanted to do was share with them how much God loved them, but all they were interested in talking about was sex and sin. We had a question box so that they could anonymously ask the things they would never have dared ask in front of the class, questions like, "Is French kissing a mortal sin or a venial sin?" I got the question-box idea from my own tenth-grade catechism class. We asked the same questions that were showing up in the box twenty years later!

Graced with an Opening

As difficult as Tennessee was for me, there were many special experiences. But there is one in particular that is very dear to my heart.

Father David Knight came to the parish to give a talk. I was taken by his sincerity, so I bought his book, *On the Way*. I read it with a pen in hand, carefully noting and taking in the ideas and words as though they were long lost friends.

The book was a treasure. It was where I first read about the importance of lay people, like me, as ministers in the church. I was both excited and curious as I read. The seeds within me were being nurtured, gently, in the dark.

It was not only the book that was a treasure but also the community he ministered to and prayed with in Memphis. It was a contemplative community, one that experienced the presence of the Spirit of Jesus in their hearts and in their midst. Looking back on that time, it is clear now that this contemplative aspect was what drew me. I couldn't name it but I could feel it, and it flooded me with joy.

My husband traveled quite a bit. He would take a limousine to the Memphis airport early in the mornings when he left, and I would pick him up when he returned. This travel time was a special time for us, because we would have dinner together and time alone to catch up, but it was an even more special time for me. I would leave early in the day so I'd have time at this quiet community Father Knight had created. If someone had whispered in my ear then that years later I'd be founding something similar, I'd never have believed them. There were videos, and tapes, and a library, and quiet places in which to sit and think and simply be. There were people living there who were in transition, people needing a place to stay, but most importantly for me, there was prayer. Every evening at five o'clock, people gathered in a small, simple room and sat on the floor around a makeshift altar—set on cement blocks and covered with colorful cloths. Together we celebrated the love of God, boldly and contemplatively, with music and singing, in the breaking of the bread, in the sharing of the word of God, and in revealing our needs and blessings.

If Father's book was food for me, this was a feast. It was an experience of what he had written, and it was meeting my deep, often unacknowledged hunger to be in a circle of prayerful people who celebrated as one body. I was growing and bursting on the inside, but still had no one near me with whom to share and no one who could reflect back to me what was happening. It never occurred to me to talk with Father Knight. I didn't know I could have. I had not yet fully become aware of the notion of a spiritual journey or of the possibility of spiritual companionship with another person.

Closer to the Truth

By the spring of 1977, far sooner than expected, the work my husband had come to Tennessee to do was completed. He was a capable and respected businessman, and his career was well on its way.

We were transferred back to California, and though it was a relief to be leaving Tennessee, I was still secretly terrified of returning. *That Dark*

Experience of Nothingness was still a source of shame and fear, never far from my awareness, and we were moving back to where it had happened. The children, now in an Episcopal Day School in which they were prospering and felt really loved, were reluctant to move this time. They had lots of friends and were happy. Nonetheless, off we went. Perhaps they were experiencing what I had felt when we left Duxbury. There was no choice, or so it appeared.

We bought a large home in Lafayette, an affluent town about a half hour from Oakland, where my husband worked. We chose Lafayette because the public schools were highly rated. This time it was true. Both the house and the property needed lots of refurbishing, but there was great potential! This was the fourth house we had owned, and three of the four had been in very bad shape when we purchased them. It was becoming clear that refurbishing a house was one of my gifts, and something that gave me a sense of accomplishment—not that raising children wasn't enough!

Right after we moved that June, my husband left for the summer to take a crash course in being an executive. That was good for him, but hard for us. The children and I worked clearing the property. It certainly wasn't their favorite summer, but there was something special about the way we worked together. The property was overgrown with berry bushes, and entangled in their thorns were lots of dead or dying trees. It was a snarly mess at best. I learned to use a chain saw to cut up the trees, and the children learned to work right along with me. We wore long pants, long sleeved shirts and bandannas on our heads, and we pulled those berry bushes out one by one. Then we planted flowers, and ground cover, and a few fruit trees. I loved being with them that summer, and all that the five of us accomplished. They were so generous with their help, and we were a team. But I missed their father and so did they.

My sense of being less important than my husband's career was growing, and I was starting to name the feelings. Anger, disappointment, and sadness were finding homes in my heart. I was approaching the realization that my experience of importance, my happiness, and my well-being are ultimately my responsibility—a birthing that is painful because it requires letting go of blame and self-pity.

Moving is always stressful, but the timing of this particular move made it more difficult for the three older children. As new kids on the block, Sean's entrance into the public junior high school, and Mark and Katie's entrance into sixth grade was hard on them. After the small, friendly private school in which they were successful students and athletes, and where they were very popular, this was an enormous shock. I knew the move was painful, but I didn't know what to do about it. I am ashamed to say, I ignored it. Everyone thought Mark and Katie were twins because they were in the same class, but Mark had repeated kindergarten. He had spent the first year of kindergarten looking out the window. He was a dreamer then, and he is still a dreamer. Now he is able to create beauty out of his dreams, but then, neither he, nor I, nor his teachers understood the artistic gift that was Mark's.

Annie went to nursery school. The local college offered an outreach course at the same church where the nursery school was located. The church also offered a Bible study class. I attended both, but the two classes were polarized. The college course was about freedom and self-conscious choosing. The teacher would say things like, "Being yourself is fun, safe, and easy!" This was news to me. I didn't even know what it meant, but somehow it resonated with me.

The Bible study class reminded me of the ladies' group in Jackson. I'd leave the class feeling as though I had to watch myself carefully lest I sin against God, who kept tabs on everything I did, whose rules were mostly a mystery, and who held the threat of Hell over my head if I failed to comply. I didn't stay at the Bible study for long. Even though I longed to know more about God and scripture, this class didn't fit with my personal experiences of God, and I surely didn't want to be scared and even more boxed into "being good." Without much awareness, I was beginning to step out of the boxes and challenge what "being good" meant.

I liked the college course. It was just a beginning, something like what New Englanders say in September as the leaves begin to change—they say fall is peeping out. Well, the idea that I had an "I" was beginning to peep out. Up until then, I was daughter, wife, mother, never simply me. It was both exciting and terrifying to discover more of "me."

It was this college outreach class that began to open my heart and awareness. I could feel a shift within me. It was very exciting and a little frightening... like rafting down a river not knowing what was ahead. Something was rapidly changing within me, and it had a direct link to my experiences of the dark and the light, of fear and love. Once again the influences of my spiritual life were definitely felt. But they were just peeping out, too. I was being led. I didn't have a paddle, and I was being whisked down the river.

I knew that God loved me. I knew that that relationship was alive because God spoke to me. But I didn't really understand it. I just felt it in my heart. What I did not know was that I was resistant to letting God love me, all of me, completely. As I got in touch with my own life, my deeper gifts, and my inner calling, I was able to experience true intimacy with God more fully. I was being urged to recognize and use more of the gifts I had been given. I was being moved tiny centimeters at a time toward being more of me, the one created by God, on purpose. I was on the way. And, I still am... on the way.

My true self, and therefore many of my choices, was still hidden and directed by my early experiences: my birth, my marriage, my culture, parental guidance, and the church hierarchy. The challenge of allowing the deeper me to rise to consciousness was to be my life-long journey.

I had a vision of myself emerge in prayer one day that both shocked and resonated with me at the same time.

I was encased in a huge cube of ice, and the ice was melting under the warmth of the sun.

That vision, a moment of grace, revealed both God and myself to me. I saw myself being freed from the ice, the cold, harsh wrappings of enculturation, and I felt the warmth of God's love melting the ice. This is a deepening of the *Ecstasy of God's Love* which I first experienced as I prepared for the children's class on God's love. There are many times in which I felt God's love and care. There are also many times in which I have felt God healing me. God, and God's helpers, work continuously to heal and awaken those of us who pray to love as God loves... with our whole hearts. Some say this prayer to love as God loves is a very courageous prayer because when God hears our prayer, God takes us seriously and we are led along a path of intense purification. We are being taken into love, and sometimes the way is dark and frightening, which is why a spiritual guide is so important. I could have gotten lost in fear many times without it.

I was happy in Lafayette as a mother, and even the corporate wife job was easy and rewarding for me. I did a great job of fixing up the house and had lots of friends. It was a rare day that I didn't receive a compliment about my strength, creativity, or energy. I was living my life well, but there was something deeper that was trying to emerge, and somewhere inside I knew it. The ice was melting.

In September of 1978, I heard the voice again very clearly, and with very specific guidance. I was sitting on a picnic bench in my backyard, admiring the flowers, being soothed by the cool, green grass, sipping iced tea and taking a break from some refinishing work I was doing in the kitchen. It felt good to sit in the sunshine. It was fall and the children were in school, my husband at work. I was alone. My life was different now—there had been some difficulties and suffering. The pain had been instrumental in helping to make me as sensitive as I had been in my childhood. I was seeing more of the truth and feeling more of my own emotions. But the revelations, though true, weren't easy to acknowledge or to integrate. At times like this moment when I was alone and quiet in the back yard, I could reflect on my life. It was then that I heard the voice again. Though these were not the exact words, they describe as best as I can recall, what I heard:

Go back to school. Study theology so you can understand more about the movement of God in your life. Study some psychology to understand more about your mind and emotions, and study something about the body and physical well-being. Then put them together.

It was that voice, the one directly intervening in my life once again, telling me to go to graduate school. I had never thought about going to graduate school. I felt content at home, or so I thought. Somewhere inside, however, I recognized that I was growing restless. It was the "more" emerging: "This is not all you will be doing." The invitation which led me to study not only filled a need but awakened a joy within me that I wouldn't otherwise have discovered.

I was stunned and at the same time felt embraced. I didn't question the voice. I knew deep in my heart that what I heard was real, and that it was the truth. I also felt fear run through me. If I followed this guidance, my life would change dramatically, most especially my marriage. But there was no choice. It was time, and I knew it. The particulars of my studies would naturally fall into place; all I had to do was say "yes." And yes it was. I never intended to go to graduate school. I was happy to have finished college. The experience in my backyard changed my life forever. I instantaneously accepted the invitation, as though my deepest self, which I did not yet know, said, "Yes." And before I knew it, I was on my way to awakening. ✳

Reflection Questions

Moving, along with the death of a loved one, divorce and job change, is one of the top causes of stress. These stresses can cause depression as well as other symptoms, such as grief, anger, fear, etc. We often forget to be gentle, compassionate and respectful with ourselves and our loved ones at these times. We have high expectations and need ourselves and others to be "fine" all of the time. When we fail to let ourselves feel the real emotions, we end up exaggerating them. We either explode or go numb, completely repressing the feelings, creating the most painful state—the state of non-being.

> *Recall a time when you moved, changed jobs or had some other very significant experience.*
>
> *Was it a difficult adjustment for you?*
>
> *Did you experience depression, loneliness, anger, fear, or other difficult emotions?*

Books have been one of my primary teachers, but there have also been some extraordinary people in my life who have been my teachers, and some heart-wrenching experiences as well. Teachers that have a significant impact on us, because they awaken us in some way, are always cherished.

What has influenced and taught you the most?

*How have your teachers changed, supported, or
enlightened you?*

*How have you been a teacher for others? What impact has
this had on you?*

We are all impacted by the culture in which we are raised. Some of the
things we learn are healthy and some are not. Once we become aware
that we are programmed, we can make choices to release those messages
and teachings that are not helpful or true for us. I grew up in a family that
celebrated Christmas Eve with lots of champagne and a tree-trimming
party. The party went on into the wee hours and my parents were always
weary-eyed in the morning. I can recall many times when the presents
were unwrapped and sometimes lost. As an adult, I carried on this tradition. Then one day I realized that I was not really having the Christmas
experience that I wanted and at that point choose to leave behind my
family tradition. We can also affirm the beliefs that are healthy and even
enhance them. We are free to make choices, when we begin to think for
ourselves. This is a maturing process that may take years.

*What is the culture in which you were raised? What family
or community beliefs or traditions have you continued?*

What traditions or beliefs have you decided to discontinue?

*How has the culture in which you were raised impacted your
life as a married, partnered, single, or divorced person?*

*Are you at peace with or are you resentful toward the tradi-
tions and beliefs in which you were raised?*

I have come to believe that we have asked to learn "to love with our whole
hearts," and that our experiences are our most significant teachers. I am
therefore learning to treasure all of my experiences as gateways to love
and to God.

Do you agree with this thinking?

6

Following the Spirit

There must have been some powerful planetary alignments that fall of 1978, along with God's angels being especially vigilant, because not only did I receive guidance to go to graduate school, I was guided to the school where I would study.

At Mass one Sunday, it was announced that Mike Marnell, a Jesuit priest and student of theology at Berkeley, would be coming to our parish to teach a course on New Testament scriptures. I experienced twinges of excitement as I listened to the announcement and decided to sign up. I had tried to study scripture once with the ladies in Jackson and later on when we moved to California, but had not succeeded. I wondered what made me so uncomfortable with these teachings. I can see clearly now that they were too far from my felt sense of the *Ecstasy of God's Love*, that I had been given that day as I prepared to teach catechism. They were more about sin and fear than about love. But Mike was young and enthusiastic and his teachings made the scriptures come to life. I met the radical, spirit-filled Jesus, who passionately followed his Spirit regardless of the law or the consequences, and I was hooked. I wanted more.

At the end of the course Mike took me aside and asked, "Have you ever considered studying theology?" I was speechless. It felt as if I was the target of a conspiracy, or at least miraculous synchronicity. It had been only a short while since my experience of hearing the call to go to graduate school, and now the answer was before me. It was the beginning of my awareness that not only was I guided, but the way would be made clear. Did "the voice" speak to him as well? "Here is the phone number of the Jesuit School of Theology and the name of the woman who will answer your questions," he said as though it was decided that I would call. At that point I had only one question but did not voice it: "Was it possible for a wife and a mother to study theology at the Jesuit school in Berkeley? Didn't I need to be a member of a religious community?" He smiled and said, "Good luck," then turned and left the church hall.

A Mother at School

I made the phone call without hesitation, almost robotically. It was as if I had no choice but to take the next step, even though I didn't know where it would lead.

Lorna, the woman Mike had led me to, had a kind voice and a warm laugh. After she assured me that I would be welcome at the school, I agreed to make an appointment to visit with her the following week.

After that call, everything was in motion. Lorna explained all the possible ways of being a student: full-time, part-time, or auditor. I was told I could even sit in the back of the class without participating. "Here's the syllabus for next semester's classes," she said. "Read through it to see if any class interests you."

I didn't even wait until I got home to read the syllabus, but sat in the car and scoured the pages. A sudden rush of energy caused me to laugh and cry at the same time. I wanted to study practically everything they offered. I had never found much beyond the social life at college very energizing, so my sudden interest in graduate school felt completely foreign to me. But I knew the desire was authentic. It grabbed my heart as nothing had before.

I zoomed home and filled out all of the papers. I sent a letter off to Boston College to get a copy of my college transcript. When the children came home from school, I was dancing around the kitchen, preparing dinner. I couldn't wait for my husband to come home so I could tell him. Annie would be in kindergarten, and the others would be at school all day. I could take one class a semester to begin with, and that wouldn't interfere with my life at home.

When I told my husband, he wasn't excited. In fact, he was visibly upset. "You can do whatever you want, but just remember," he said sharply, "your chores come first."

My chores? The words stuck in my throat. What were my chores? Was he referring to the care of the children, or the house, or his own needs?

As he went off to read the mail, I became aware that his response to my excitement might have been similar to my response to his news of the move to Tennessee. Now we were both following our paths, and it was the beginning of a great divide, a divide that would grow rather than diminish over time. Though he never denied me the money to pay for my studies, he would never share in my excitement. I felt a great sadness in my heart, but the call within me was far greater. I often wonder still if my husband felt sad too.

The Graduate School of Theology is comprised of nine theological schools and although I was a student of the Jesuit School, I took classes from many professors in the various schools. On my first day of graduate school, I remember so well sitting on a bench in a garden outside the classroom, eagerly waiting for my first class to begin. It was on the letters of Saint Paul. It was of interest to me because I always wondered why women should wear veils in church and be obedient to their husbands, or why St. Paul said that it was better to get married than to sin, and, if you couldn't avoid sin, get married. So much of his writing about women and marriage seemed strange to me, and I wanted to know why he wrote such things.

77

It was the class suggested by my adviser because as he said "it is a lower level class and you probably can do the work."

Father Harry, a short, white-haired Jesuit priest who had been president of the school several years before, had serious hesitations about accepting me as a student. Years later, he and I laughed about that, but at the time, he was concerned. "Well, looking at your philosophy grades at Boston college, I see you didn't do very well," he said sternly, peering over glasses that rode halfway down his nose. "I don't think you'll do very well here either. These graduate courses are very difficult."

I heard him, but it didn't make much sense to me. "I don't think you have to worry about me, Father. God has sent me here, and if God wants me here, I'll have what I need, even if the courses are difficult."

Father Harry was wearing a white Irish knit sweater that day, and when I responded this way, his face turned as white as the sweater. He never said another word.

I did, however, sign up as a "person at the back of the room who never spoke but just listened." Despite what I said to Father Harry, I was terribly afraid that I couldn't study anymore. After all, I was thirty-eight years old, and for the last sixteen years I had done nothing but cook, clean, entertain, care for the children, and run car pools. How could I imagine myself reading theology books, taking tests, and writing papers?

I felt excited and proud for having the courage to do something so different and seemingly unattainable. I was also frightened. It was so new, and it was nothing I had ever thought I would be doing. My stomach was filled with butterflies as at last it was time for class, and I got up from the bench and walked into the room. I sat in the last row, as prescribed, hoping I would not be noticed. There were close to eighty students. I watched as the professor stood before the class. His name was Neal Flanagan, O.S.M. He was a Roman Catholic priest in the community of the Servites of Mary, about sixty-ish, a small man with gray hair and a beard. He called out each person's name, and, when he got to mine, he paused and then asked me if I'd see him at the break.

I waited until the students that flocked around him at the break drifted away before approaching him. He asked, "Why haven't you taken the class for credit?"

"I am a wife and mother, not a student"

He stared straight at me and said, "I'll bet that within two weeks you sign up to take this class for credit."

After the break he resumed the class and spent about fifteen minutes talking about Mother as the metaphor for the true meaning of the word "servant"—selfless service in the reign of God. I walked out of that class in a heightened state.

When I got home that afternoon, I took particular care to do everything I would normally do. I realized I needed my husband's encouragement in the midst of my fear, as much as I needed to share my excitement. He was my best friend.

The first text I had to read as an assignment for the class was thick and dense. I sat in my study reading, and realized at page 100, that I hadn't remembered a word I had just read. Instead I had mentally organized the car pool, the week's meals, and a shopping list. This made me pray. My worst fear was that my concentration and focus for anything other than running the household was shot. I begged God for help, and my prayers were answered. Never again after that did I deal with such unconscious distraction. I'll never know if grace interceded and supercharged my brain or if I simply realized the importance of willing myself to concentrate as I read and studied. It didn't matter. That I could study effectively at this stage in my life was a true gift. And whichever it was, I was thankful to God. Neal Flanagan won the bet. I signed up for credit before the second week, and I continued to admire how he knew just how to challenge me.

I thought perhaps my husband would come around once he saw how happy it made me, but he never did. He never asked me about my studies, and, if I attempted to speak about them, he cut me off. "It doesn't interest me," he'd say. He was born and raised a Roman Catholic, but was not drawn to the mystical side of the church. "That's for people in religious life," he said. He was more interested in having me study something that would be appropriate conversation material at business socials. I created two worlds, one that I could share at home and one that I couldn't. I appeared to be a normal wife and mother. My life with my children was joyful because of who they were—exuberant, playful, and curious—and because of the overwhelming love I had for each of them. Their presence filled the empty spaces as my husband and I became less and less available for each other, but the sadness of the separation lay heavy in my heart. The other life was at school, where I was developing a community of friends with whom I shared my spiritual life. This was an enormous grace that brought me much joy.

As a wife and mother, I was very much a minority at the Jesuit school in 1979. Most of the students were in religious life, but this didn't matter to me. From the time I was a child, I'd heard my father speak about the importance of feeling comfortable with all people. "It doesn't matter how rich or poor people are, how powerful or simple, whether they are red or black or yellow-skinned, or what they believe; we are all the same." He never said we are all God's children, but I think that's what he was getting at.

I was fascinated by the classes, the conversation, and most of all by the growing awareness that my experiences of God were worthy of reflection and celebration. I was feeling nurtured.

I'd get the children off to school and leave for my class. As I approached the freeway, my exhilaration would grow, and the sign "FREE WAY" came alive with bright, flashing, neon lights, validating my excitement.

My final paper, "Who is Paul For Me, and Who is Christ For Paul?" was long and tedious, but exciting. I didn't know if it was good or bad. I just wrote it. A few days after submitting it, I found a note written by Sean, stuck to the refrigerator. "Your professor called. He said your paper was outstanding, and he wanted to say thank you." I cried.

My paper was returned to me by mail. I anxiously opened the yellow manila envelope and when I saw the "A", a wave of delight ran through me. I felt so proud. I paged through the paper, reading the red ink notes that Neal had written. This was the beginning of my realization that I had been thinking and living in a box that was much too small. Throughout the paper, Neal had circled the word 'He,' whenever I had used it to signify God. Neal wrote in the margins each time, "Is God only 'He?'" I understood immediately, on some level, but it was a long time before I realized that the "He" had been deeply, almost permanently, imprinted in my psyche. I felt embarrassed to have been so closed to God as a "She"—especially as a woman—and equally thankful to have been awakened.

Neal and I became friends. We took long walks and shared much of our life's journey with one another. One day as we were walking along Shattuck Avenue in Berkeley, he turned to me and stopped. "Although I am an ordained priest, my life is not lived as a priest but as a teacher, and that makes me sad." He continued after a pause and a sigh, "Even though you are not an ordained priest, your life is so full of pastoral ministries, you are much more a priest than I." At the time I didn't really understand what he meant. It actually frightened me.

People at the school often asked me why I was studying theology when Roman Catholic women could not be ordained as priests. I always responded the same way: "I don't know, except I was guided by Spirit to do so, and I love being here."

I never allowed myself to want to be a priest. After all, it was impossible. And I had to wonder if it wasn't verging on sin for me to be recognized as a priest. I wonder now if there was someplace within me that feared being discovered and excommunicated or, even worse, burned at the stake.

This wasn't the only time I felt fear around my ministry. Years later, at the Wednesday morning gatherings at La Casa, a spirituality center I founded about the time of Sean's death, there were frequent "agape," or love celebrations. Women and men sat in a circle, and we prayed from our hearts, blessing the home-baked bread and one another as we remembered the love of Jesus. As the bread was passed, the people began to say, "The body of Christ," and the one receiving would say, "Amen." This part of the prayer had never been discussed; it just happened.

I was so concerned that what was spontaneously happening was treading dangerously on church tradition that I spoke to Father Joe Powers, a Jesuit and professor of Sacramental Theology. When I explained my concern and fear, he asked one question: "Are you dressing in vestments and saying Mass?" "No," I said, a little bit horrified at the thought, "It's just an agape, a recalling of Jesus' love, and a prayer that we learn to love one another. I don't ever lead the celebration. I am a participant in the circle." Then he looked at me, eyes teary with warmth, and said, "Don't change a thing; and do not be afraid. When love is present you can't keep the Spirit out." Christ was present within us and we unconsciously acknowledged that holy presence by saying aloud, "the Body of Christ," as the bread was passed. We did not think "Christ is present," we felt the presence in our hearts and exclaimed the good news. I wonder if this is exactly what happened in those small home churches after Jesus died. For us, it seemed so simple, so natural, so organic.

But I still held fear, and now, only much later, after prayer and grace, have I realized that priesthood is a call and a gift from God, the essence of which is love. And it comes to us regardless of gender. Ordination in the Roman Catholic Church is a formal and a powerful public affirmation of God's call, and a gift—an affirmation I will never experience, because I am a woman.

Fellow Mystic Discovered

The second class I chose to take was also pivotal. In it, I began to wake up even more to the way in which God was not only present, but guiding me. This class would underlie my work in spiritual direction for the rest of my life. It was about St. John of the Cross, a sixteenth-century mystic and saint. Father Harry told me I couldn't take the class because it would be far too difficult for me, and he emphasized *far*. It was an upper-level class, one of the most difficult, and taught by one of the most intellectually demanding professors at the school. Father Harry said no. I said "yes." I don't know why I wanted to take the class. I had never even heard of St. John of the Cross, but, when I read the syllabus, that course stood out to me more than anything else.

Finally, in desperation, Father Harry told me that the only way he would let me sign up for the class was if I talked to the professor personally and got permission. I said okay. I called the number he gave me and left a message. It was late summer, and I was in the midst of planting a fall garden when Annie, phone held in her hand, close to her mouth, yelled to me from the front door, "Mom, come quick. Some weird guy is on the phone, says his name is Feather Buckley. He wants to talk to you."

I ran to the phone, sure my chances of getting into his class now were doomed, hoping he had heard Father, not Feather. I explained a little nervously that I wanted to take his class on St. John of the Cross and that I had to have his permission.

"Who are you?" he asked.

"A mother," I sputtered. He laughed and said, "I'd be honored to have you in my class."

This was now the second professor who had lifted up my role as mother way beyond the cultural norm. I felt so much joy in the acknowledgment. What I was also beginning to experience was that because my life was different from that of someone in religious life, my insights and opinions were often of value to other students. I saw life from a different perspective.

Father Harry had said it would be a difficult class, and he was right. For the first few weeks of class I wrote down phrases and words that I had never heard. Then I'd go to the library and look them up. I never felt overwhelmed or discouraged, but it was challenging. The second week of class, one of the women students arrived with a big bag of lemons that she shared with the rest of us. Her name was Pat Benson and she was a Dominican sister who was studying for her PhD in Spirituality. We became friends immediately. Not only did she help me understand the theological rhetoric, but we would spend hours talking about God and love, prayer and the dark night. She was my first spiritual companion.

One day, as we were sitting on a bench outside the classroom at break time, Pat explained to me that the charism of the Dominicans was *Truth,* and then she added, "You know that the more we are truthful with God, the more fully we are in relationship with God." I knew she was right. And I understood in that moment, that God was using my life experiences to bring me to the deepest truth and so, into God's very heart. I only had to stay awake, to pray and reflect on my daily life, to be aware of what I was being taught, and where I was being led.

I would read St. John of the Cross's poetry and prose, and, even though much of its meaning was hidden from me, there was much that I understood intuitively and felt deeply. I'd sit for hours sometimes, without a thought, just silent and empty, but absolutely captivated. What I was reading was so fulfilling and nourishing that time passed unnoticed. Sometimes, the energy of love coursing through me was so intense that

I'd have to get up and walk around, take a few deep breaths and shake myself. I was experiencing God revealing God's very self to me, and I was in the Ecstasy of God's Love once again.

> *Oh living flame of love*
> *that tenderly wounds my soul*
> *in its deepest center! Since*
> *Now you are not oppressive*
> *Now consummate! If it be your will!*
> *Tear through the veil of this sweet encounter!*

This first verse of John's poem, "The Living Flame of Love," became a mantra for me. I didn't understand it intellectually, but I felt it deeply as each word flowed through my heart.

And then the last stanza:

> *How gently and lovingly*
> *You wake in my heart,*
> *Where in secret You dwell alone;*
> *And in Your sweet breathing,*
> *Filled with good and glory,*
> *How tenderly You swell my heart with love.*

was a further affirmation of what I was experiencing. I would read the words and immediately find myself in another reality. It was as though I'd been transported to the world of spirit, not by my own endeavors, but by God's—taken by God, to God. All I was doing was reading words, but those words were like a chariot with wings—silently, lightly, swiftly moving me into spirit.

St. John wrote about the experience of "Nada," which is translated in English as "nothing." I didn't understand what he meant, but I knew that someday it would be revealed to me. All I knew was that I had to be empty of everything to be filled with God. The thought delighted me. I just didn't know how to empty myself.

I was moved by every bit of St. John's poetry, and his prose as well. Neither were easy to understand, especially then, but both felt familiar and they continuously opened my heart. Sometimes my heart would ache from being stretched, and sometimes it would ache to be stretched beyond its limitations.

It wasn't just during class or when I was reading the assignments that I felt myself transported. The words and feelings became my companions and would wake me at other times. I didn't mind this "dream state" in the middle of the night, but daytime dream states sometimes proved challenging. I once visited the Smithsonian Air and Space Museum with my husband on a business trip. I floated through the museum. I've never really liked museums, and an airplane museum was especially boring to me, so I let myself be taken. A couple of times my husband asked, "Are you OK?" wondering if I was sick, because he'd see me staring blankly at a wall or staircase. He never had any awareness that, although I was physically present, my heart and spirit were fully engaged elsewhere.

After a while I learned how to allow this deep meditation to happen without it being apparent to others. I had to remain even more aware than usual of what I was experiencing. I was feeling the sensation of love in the presence of God while going about my life. It became normal after awhile, but I was surprised by a further awareness. When I wasn't feeling the sensation of love, I felt lost, and I knew something else was happening to me. It didn't take long to figure out that the times I felt lost were when I was engaged in thought, emotions, or activities that were contrary to the truth—not in harmony with God.

As I studied the mystics, I began to understand something of the purification that is a necessary part of the spiritual journey. Purification was taking place in my life. I was being refined. I was learning to discern spirits, realizing that there were different energies or voices within me and around me. These energies, or spirits, were often in contradiction to the Holy Spirit, encouraging me to distrust and doubt my own spirit, my deepest knowings and longings.

I was learning also about those feelings and desires, thoughts and activities that hindered my experience of oneness with God. I was learning about the will, and about bringing my will into harmony with God's will, until there was only one will. "Contraries cannot co-exist," became a mantra for me. The voices, energies, spirits, feelings, thoughts, and actions in me were being purified. And the contraries were being transformed, bit by bit.

85

The blessing of purification and the grace that followed it mesmerized me. Moving between light and darkness, and experiencing the beauty of each, I began to wonder if my *Dark Experience of Nothingness* had been something other than a shameful nightmare that I had caused. But I didn't yet perceive it as a profound grace from God. After years of reflection, I now wonder if the *Dark Experience of Nothingness* isn't the "Nada" that is the basis of St. John's theology—the moment that there is absolutely nothing for me to have or think or be, when I am completely empty, surrendered and free, when I can "tear through the veil of this sweet encounter," and am at one with God and all creation. Was this 'black experience' one in which for a moment my slate was wiped clean of enculturated beliefs and fears so that I could discover the one I was created to be, the one imprinted on my soul?

Graduate school continued to be a joy for me, and I was learning on many different levels. One day I had an intuitive flash, a knowing, that transformed the way I approached theology from then on:

> *As I am walking to class I suddenly know deep in my being*
> *that although the books I am reading, the doctrine, the*
> *church councils and teachings I am learning are important,*
> *the information is useless to me unless, through prayer and*
> *reflection, it deepens my personal understanding of God and*
> *my life experience.*

This intuitive knowing also influenced my role as wife and mother. I naturally applied it to my life at home. I could see now that there were many traditions and beliefs which were taught to me by my family, the community, and the church in which I was raised that I was questioning in my prayer. I recall one day knowing that if I gave myself permission to do as I chose, I would encourage the children to do the same, providing the choice was not harmful. One day when Annie was in high school, she told me she wanted a tattoo. It seemed very inappropriate, until I began, by some strange occurrence, to allow myself to imagine myself with a tattoo! "Annie, I think it might be fun to have a tattoo also, maybe a butterfly on my ankle." Annie was horrified. "No, mom. If you get a tattoo you will eventually have tattoos all over your body. It's like an addiction." I laughed! The inappropriateness of having a tattoo was gone, and all that was left was the freedom to let Annie explore being Annie. Annie got her tattoo, only one, which she later wanted to remove but I never did get one. In a comical sort of way, I was being taught to discern the ways of God, the ways of freedom, and to discover what brought about healthy families and relationships. I was finding my true self and making room for others to dare to do the same. I was stepping away from the ways of the world and into the ways of God... a very risky step unless one is willing to make "mistakes" and possibly be ostracized for breaking "the rules".

It was during graduate studies, especially as I studied the mystics, that I received some understanding of being guided by the Holy Spirit. I was also given a context for my inner reality, which made it possible for me to reflect on my experience and appreciate God's work in my life. Reading and studying psychology helped as well; I recall learning that people who hear voices and have visions are often said to have lost touch with reality, are diagnosed as crazy, and sent to treatment centers for intense therapy. I found this thought-provoking and wondered what made one experience a gift and another a moment of insanity. I realized again that the decision I had made as a child to keep my visions, voices and inner knowings, to myself was indeed wise. I probably would have frightened people, and they, in turn, would have frightened me.

In the winter of my second year of graduate school I wrote the following as part of an assignment. As I read it now, I realize that the impact of my immersion in theology and psychology was enormous. It brought long-awaited light into the darkness.

"For many years there existed deep within me a fallacy which read like this: It is my responsibility as a 'good' daughter, friend, wife, mother, to be sure that my family is happy.

I had assumed the role of super-giver—caring for and nurturing all those who surrounded me. It was a caring that had a "should" attached to it, and therefore was not freely given. It was a role that was often a heavy burden, at times very lonesome; a role chosen unconsciously for it appeared to be a safe place from which to attempt, without awareness, to control the happiness of another.

The super-giver role worked quite well, however, as long as I remained within the confines of my private garden and denied the existence and possible truths of other realities... like my own hidden longings. It worked as long as I maintained my role of dependence on, and subservience to, my parents and husband, and for as long as they continued to meet my physical needs and my needs for a protector. And it worked also as long as I needed few praises other than those pats on the back I got for being such a 'good person' as I cared for them.

But then things began to change, and it didn't begin with a "boom" for me, but rather with gentle and constant prodding. And it didn't begin from just outside with the women's movement, with books that I had been reading, and with classes that I had begun to take, "just by chance." But the change was also from within, as a movement of the Spirit. I was blossoming and the sun and the rain and the fertilizer that were at work came in the form of the people and courses in graduate school and my reflections in prayer. I was awakening to the ways I had held close reins on my happiness and the happiness of my family, on "my role and your role," on always putting reality into compartments. It became clear that I was doing the same thing with God. I was in control! Or so I thought.

It was a lonesome place because I was not really myself, nor did I know what I felt, really felt, or what I needed, or even that I had a right to my feelings or needs. I mistakenly believed I could create safety in my relationships by organizing and controlling myself to fit the situation. Although most all of my growth had been stunted, there had not been a death, and I began to notice new shoots peeking through. My private garden was suddenly getting too small. The rusty hinges on the garden gate were being oiled and began to open again. The trees were being pruned and the sunlight was finally beginning to make its debut. All of these changes seemed strange; the garden began to look almost naked, almost beyond recognition. And I felt a sense of loss and sadness. It was winter. In retrospect I realize that the change created new life, new growth, and a freer and more spacious garden in which to live more fully. Had this not occurred, I would have continued to exist for a while longer, perhaps forever, scrunched down, in isolation rather than in freedom; caught in the confines and limits of time, in compartments and cramped quarters, rather than in the beauty and the expansiveness of each moment as a gift—gift to be celebrated." ✳

Reflection Questions

If we follow the promptings of the heart, we find God. We find ourselves, and we find true joy! We unearth our gifts and talents along with the courage to use them. Since we are one of a kind, our gifts are always a blessing to the community.

What longings within your heart have you become aware of? Which of those have you fulfilled?

Do you recall a specific time when you felt your heart expanded by God's love?

Do you recall moments of exhilaration when you dared to break out of your fear and try something new?

7

Discovering Spiritual Companionship

Since childhood, my life had been filled with spiritual experiences. My intuition told me that these were valid and that I must pay attention to them, but never had any other person listened to my stories of spiritual experience or reflected any of that wisdom back to me. I didn't realize what a loss this was until a new opportunity presented itself during graduate school.

Someone to Walk Alongside Me

One day I was talking with four or five of my classmates, sisters, and priests, in the lounge of the Jesuit School of Theology. We had been discussing our scripture class and sharing stories about the saints as we ate our brown bag lunches. I began to share one of my experiences of God. My revelation poured out as comfortably as if it was an everyday experience. When I looked up I saw strange discomfort on their faces, and I stopped talking. Our conversation eventually continued, but without reference to my story. Their response was familiar to me from my childhood. It indicated that I had entered an area that made people feel uncomfortable. Now I was learning that it was acceptable to speak about experiences of God, when it was about the saints and scripture, but not experiences in the present, and certainly not my personal experiences of God.

A few days later one of the professors approached me and asked if I had a spiritual director. I said no, and then told her I didn't know what a spiritual director was. She explained that a spiritual director was someone with whom I could share my spiritual journey so that I could receive guidance and support along the way. She thought it was important for me to have one, especially since I was married, as a way to integrate my spirituality into my life as a wife and mother. I left with the name of the person in charge of spiritual direction for the school. I called and was given the name and phone number of someone whose name I recognized as a guest lecturer in a class I was taking. Another of those synchronistic moments was occurring. When I'd first seen him in the class, I had been struck by a sense that he would be a very important person in my life.

And so, every other Tuesday, I made my way up the steps to the big front door of the Jesuit house and rang the bell. Those Tuesdays became sacred, because for the first time in my life there was someone who was listening to me in a very special way, someone who wanted to hear my story, my experiences, my feelings as a wife, a mother, a student— someone who helped me find God in the stories I told. That first day he led me up the expansive walnut stairs to the second floor. He was dark-haired, tall and thin, and about my age. His room was small and simple. A beautiful crucifix hung on the wall, and the sunlight streamed through the windows as we sat on straight-backed chairs. I was feeling apprehensive, but his warm welcome calmed me immediately. He prayed from his heart that the Spirit would be with us, guiding our time together, and then he asked me to tell him why I had come. He was the first person who ever really, fully listened to me, and it was all I could do to keep from crying. I had waited so long.

He was generous with his time and with his story, whenever it applied, but most of all he spoke about God's love with such an eloquence and with such faith that I began to share less and less so I could have more time listening to him. It wasn't long before he figured out what I was doing and cautioned me. "This is your time to be heard," he explained gently, "and you must use the time for that reason and no other."

One day I stood at the front door of the Jesuit residence with so much fear that I was almost frozen. Every time I thought about ringing the bell, something came over me, and it was all I could do to keep from running. The week before he had suggested that I begin a retreat called The Exercises of Saint Ignatius of Loyola. "This will be a nine- to twelve-month commitment," he said, "And we'll meet once a week at my office to share what is happening in your prayer. Your life at home will be as usual, except for your daily prayer. Through your prayer, God will call you naturally to reflect on the way you are living your life relative to the scripture passage you are praying. You will have to agree to a minimum of one hour of prayer a day, meditating on a specific piece of scripture. During your retreat you will be immersing yourself in the life of Jesus, in the midst of your daily activities at home. Are you interested in this?"

I knew a little bit about Saint Ignatius of Loyola, the founder of the Jesuits, from my class on St. John of the Cross. I knew that through his life and religious experiences, St. Ignatius had "found God in all things." As a result, he never experienced more than fifteen minutes without peace, no matter how grave the occurrence or how significant the loss. That made an enormous impression on me and I wondered how it could be possible to live that way myself. At the time, I could not even conceptualize what it meant.

The fear that I felt as I stood at my spiritual director's front door was familiar and showed up every time I approached something that would threaten to change my life. Sometimes it was so severe that it felt as though an evil spirit had grasped my heart, but other times it felt more like my old familiar fear of change, a fear that took me years to shake. Perhaps it was both.

I was fairly comfortable with who I was at this time, but I didn't know what changes would occur, or who I would become after the retreat. The answer awaited me on the other side of the front door, if only I could ring the bell. Before I could make my decision, the door opened, and my director stood before me. I stepped over the threshold and began my retreat.

There are many graces available through the Ignatian Retreat. Finding God in all things is perhaps the most significant, but all of the graces or gifts of the retreat flow together and rest on each other. There is the gift of freedom—freedom to love with one's whole heart; the gift of intimacy with Jesus; the gift of feeling God's delight in the wonder of creation and in me as well. There are also the gifts of the awakening of the Holy Spirit within and the experience of darkness, evil, and even a descent into Hell... to find and offer the light to those who hide in darkness. The gift of joy emerges out of experiencing God's love, as does trust and the deep desire to share generously with others the gifts received. The Retreat was a profound gift, and, even though I didn't realize it at the time, it was life-changing. I didn't receive every grace or even most of the graces that were possible during the retreat, but I received abundantly. Each of the graces were awakened in me, but the fullness of those graces came, and will continue to come, over time. The abundance still flows today. I am finding God in all things and am discovering how to be peaceful in fifteen minutes no matter what happens, because I understand what that means now. The first moments of this awakening occurred as a grace of the retreat, as well as the assurance that God and I would continue to journey together until all of the graces were fully awakened in me... even if we had to finish up in the afterworld.

During the year-long retreat, I had the opportunity to deepen my friendship with Jesus, as I meandered meditatively through the New Testament, reflecting on his life, entering the scenes as though I were there, feeling as much as I could what he and others might be feeling, and taking that experience and those values deeply into my heart. I began to read scripture in a way that invited me to feel and taste and touch Jesus as he went about his life. I received glimpses of who he was, and I saw and shared glimpses of who I was—truly was! As I read and prayed on the New Testament scripture, I came to know Jesus as a friend who both listened to my story and told me his. I met a man who could see through every made-up belief, all self-deception, shame, resentment, fear, and whatever else I might clothe myself in. Jesus could see beyond all barriers to the beloved within me. Through his eyes I began to see myself as God's beloved daughter, even when my choices, words, or thoughts didn't live up to who I truly am. I know who I am. He showed me that each of us can see what He sees, if we are willing. The love is always waiting to flow through all of us. This knowing was happening in my thoughts, in my emotions, but most of all, in my heart.

I walked along with Jesus in the meditations as he healed the sick, expelled demons, and called forth the holy within the people he met. I walked with him as he faced fear, cried, became angry, made mistakes, honored women, challenged many with his love, and as he died and rose and returned.

Jesus, my friend and my teacher, was entering my heart as beloved. Not only did I have a companion in my spiritual director, but the Spirit of Christ was there with me. I knew it. What was begun as a year long retreat was becoming a part of my life and would underlie my choices forever.

Although I believed that the voices, visions, and dreams I had received all my life were from God, it wasn't until Graduate School that I understood that these were ways the Spirit of God emerged and guided my conscious life. Following this awareness came a second profound moment of consciousness. Gradually, without a big to-do or bolts of lightening, but through an organic process in prayer, journal writing, spiritual direction, and daily reflection, over many years, I realized that the times I am in communion with the Spirit of God, or Jesus or Mary, I am also in communion with my own spirit. In those moments of communion, the will of God and my will, the Spirit of God and my spirit are in harmony. There is no separation except in my state of awareness. We are one, always have been; always will be!! This is a mysterious realization. I am not saying that I am God, but rather that God dwells within me and is having an experience as me, as I am living my life, as I am choosing darkness or light, peace or chaos, joy or sadness, generosity or fear. God is waiting for me to awaken to the awareness of who I truly am and loving me along the way. Slowly, I am surrendering to that knowing and to God—the essential reality and cause of my being.

With this awareness, I accepted responsibility for my own choices on the spiritual path. I knew I had to remain peaceful and awake so that my spirit and God's Spirit could commune. Each day it became more familiar to surrender ego's fear, letting my spirit guide my life.

The joy I feel as I am in the present, and in communion and conversation with God, is becoming an ordinary, rather than extraordinary, experience. When I have not surrendered and my spirit is not free, when fear takes hold or a moment of self-forgetfulness or hatred rises up, I can feel the belief in separation rearing its head, and the pain is enormous. It is the felt sense of pain that moves me through prayer back to the present, to oneness and to peace.

Those I Was Called to Walk Alongside

Back in 1978 just before I received the call to go to school, when Annie was about three and a half years old, I started visiting the nursing homes in town. She and I would go once a week and play bingo. Annie loved the old folks and all the attention they gave her. She played the game along with them, and I think that's where she learned how to count. I got to hear the stories of the residents, and that was fascinating to me. Many had been daily communicants at St. Perpetua's church, the same church we attended. Some had been ushers, and others had washed linens for the altar. Sadness wrenched my heart when I realized that the priest from the local Catholic church came only once a month.

The patients were wheeled into a room for Mass, and wheeled out immediately afterwards. There was no personal contact or confession time unless a patient planned ahead to schedule an appointment with the priest, something most of them never thought they could do. I was young, and morning Mass and Holy Communion were important means for me to sustain my joy and peace in the face of life's struggles. I wondered what it would be like to be at the end of my life and have little or no access to the sacraments that so nurtured me. I wondered what these women and men did with their fear, their feelings of abandonment, and their loneliness.

Without much thought, I went right to the pastor of my church. I asked to take communion to the people in the convalescent homes and pray with them. He said, "The church isn't ready for this." I responded, not hesitant or in anger, but sincerely and with clarity, "Maybe the church isn't ready, but the people are, and when you think the church is ready, let me know."

Father Brian stared at me, pounded his fist on the desk, and said, "You've been called." I didn't know what that meant or what was happening, but I did notice that he was energized and that whatever was happening was happening fast.

Father Brian was right; my request was unusual. It was 1979. Lay people, especially women, had few ministerial roles, and certainly none that involved taking Holy Communion to the sick and dying. It never occurred to me that this was impossible. All I knew was that the people needed and deserved to receive Holy Communion, and I was willing to do that for them.

Father Brian called the bishop, and that same day I not only had permission to bring communion to the nursing homes and to people confined at home, but I had the keys to the church, the sacristy and the tabernacle as well! I had been at the altar to read the scripture for Mass, but I'd never been near the tabernacle, let alone had the key.

Father never told me what to do. He just gave me the keys. I went to Pier One, an import store, and bought a small, round, brass container for the communion wafers. I went to the church and in through the sacristy door to get the tabernacle key out of a drawer. I walked cautiously to the altar and found the little gold door. I had the feeling that someone might see me and call the police, because a woman at the altar opening the sacred tabernacle where the consecrated hosts, the body of Christ, were kept was not a familiar scene.

I took about twenty consecrated communion wafers, placed them carefully in my little brass container, and put it in a side pocket of my purse. I can't even describe how I felt—scared and privileged, kind of jumpy on the inside, and singing on the outside.

It was good that I didn't know what to do, because I had to let the people teach me, and they were patient and loving teachers. They would ask me to read the scripture of the day or to tell them about the saint of the day. Some only wanted to pray an Our Father or a Hail Mary. I was in awe of their ability to remember their prayers, even when many could recall little else. It was as if those prayers, repeated since childhood, were indelibly imprinted on their hearts. When they recited the words, the memory of God's love and Faithfulness came to life.

As I witnessed this, I realized that there were some very important reasons to have rituals, prayers, music, and gestures that were repeated many times over. Some people wanted more prayer, some wanted no prayer, but every single one wanted companionship.

I was astounded at the difference the Eucharist made. What appeared on the outside to be nothing more than a thin white wafer had the power to open hearts, bring tears of gratitude, cause signs of life in some who were almost comatose, and quiet the ones who were restless.

It wasn't long before I was listening to stories of "life back then." I heard about their regrets, unfulfilled dreams, and the fears of further illness and dying—concerns that many family members couldn't bear to hear, but which I could. I recall one family in particular who often visited their ailing but very sweet great-grandmother, who was in the convalescent hospital because of the nursing care she needed. One day I walked into her birthday party. She was ninety-five that day. As they were departing, the family made plans for her ninety-sixth birthday. Once the room was quiet, the great-grandmother turned to me and said, "Somehow they can't get it through their heads that I am dying." We sat and talked for over an hour about death and God's love, something her family couldn't allow her to do.

Listening to these dear folks voice their regrets and failures made me think of the confession rite. I often wondered if the only difference between that and the conversations I was having was that I wasn't officially ordained to hear confession or to administer the sacrament of the sick.

There was Trudy, a woman in one of the convalescent homes who was almost 100 years old. She had been there for nearly six years but rarely spoke and had very few visitors. No one in the nursing home could figure out what could keep Trudy alive day after day, year after year, alone, silent, and in a darkened room. One day I came in to see my friends and bring communion. It was the same day that a new nurse began working there. In going over Trudy's chart, the nurse realized that Trudy was a Catholic and asked me if I'd visit her that day. I went to the bedside and called her name. This tiny face surrounded by straight white hair turned towards me. I said, "Trudy, I have brought Holy Communion for you." I held up the white communion wafer, which seemed to shimmer in the light from the doorway. Trudy wept gently and in between her tears she uttered softly, "It has been so long. I've waited for so long." I talked to her about God's love for her as I broke off a small piece of the host and placed it in her tiny dry mouth. I stood there silently, stroking her cheek and loving her from some mysterious place within me, someplace that melted any belief that Trudy and I were separate from one another or from God. Peace engulfed us. The following week when I returned, I learned that Trudy had died that night in her sleep. I knew what she had been waiting for, and I felt blessed beyond expression to have met her. I also felt angry that she had had to wait for so long, as though she had been forgotten. I wondered if that had been her purgatory. Maybe some day I'll know.

Meeting Betty was another blessing. She was in the final stages of multiple sclerosis. She could no longer move most of her muscles, and her speech was severely impaired. When I first met Betty she astonished me with her smile—it filled her whole face. Each week, I walked down the hall toward her room in anticipation of her joy. "I can't pray anymore," she said with tears in her eyes as she struggled with the words, her contorted mouth making strange sounds. "I can only say 'Jesus, I love you,' over and over and over. That's all." She must have felt the joy flooding my heart because she quieted down, her tears dried, and her smile became brighter than ever. The purity of Betty's prayer and the humility that I witnessed that moment will always be with me because we simultaneously felt God's love. It was palpable, because we felt it together.

The women and the men in the convalescent hospitals and those I visited in their homes taught me more than how to minister to them; they taught me to open my heart, to be present each moment, and not die regretting that I'd missed even one moment of my precious life. This was the beginning of my awareness that the moments need not be judged as good or bad but simply appreciated as gifts. I was learning about the great loss we experience when we bypass the difficult times by going numb or using some addiction. I vividly recall my friend Harriet, a very joyful, ninety-year-old lady, who, whenever I visited, told me many stories. Some of Harriet's stories were of her losses. There were the deaths of adult children, her husband's death, and hardships of all kinds, but she spoke with calmness, and I knew she was at peace with herself, with God, and with her stories. She had been there. She stayed awake, and it was a delight to be with her. I remember wanting to be like her.

There were people like Harriet, whose rooms were filled with life; a sense of peace and joy and love was present as they prepared to die.

There were also people whose rooms were cold and empty. I could feel their despair and anger. They were not ready to die, because they had missed the moments in which they had been given the opportunity to live. They were all my teachers.

Everyone I met had some regrets, but the ones who were joyful or peaceful or quiet were the ones who had happy memories to fill their hearts They had also reconciled their differences with those close to them, accepted and grown wiser from their sorrows, and had a warm, loving friendship with God. The others, the cold ones, had hearts filled with re-morse, and there seemed to be little room for love or forgiveness. I came to know most of the people in the convalescent homes, and I listened to and prayed with anyone who wanted companionship. In the Catholic Church, the official rule is that only Catholics in good standing with the church should receive Holy Communion. I offered Communion to those who expressed a desire to receive it after we had prayed together, trusting the Holy Spirit was present and guiding me.

Learning on my own was sometimes a stretch, especially since I didn't know the rules. There was the day that all of my children accom-panied me to the nursing home. We made the rounds together. Finally, there was one more person to see, and we found her in the living room. As always, I asked if she'd like to receive communion. She nodded yes. I said a prayer, and she opened her mouth as I held the host in front of her. What happened next was a first for me. She must have forgotten who I was and what I was bringing. She found the dry wafer most unpalatable. She looked at me with disgust and spit it out. I caught it with my hand. Stunned, I stared at the tiny, half-chewed mass in my palm. Knowing it was sacred, but not knowing what to do with it, I ate it. My children stared at me in horror and disgust. "How could you, Mom? How could you do that?" they whispered as we walked toward the car.

I was as stunned as they. All I could say was, "I didn't know what else to do."

It wasn't unusual for me to visit with forty or fifty people in a week, and I soon realized that it was too much for just one person. I began to invite others to join me and to teach them what I was learning.

In the winter of 1981, in one of my theology classes, the students took turns preparing and presenting an opening prayer. When it was my turn, I felt some concern because I didn't know the prayers that the other students were using or where to find them. I wrote the following meditation instead. I was nervous as I read:

"There are no steps leading into this house—this house for the aged and the infirm—only black asphalt that gently slopes from the street to the edge of the front door. If it weren't for drains, the water from a good storm would become a river running through the main hall, and somehow that's how I feel as I approach the entrance—as if I were being carried in the flow of this river—this imaginary water, which, as it moves, touches, and changes all it meets, moving gently and invisibly through the rooms and hallways. Perhaps it's the water, the 'living water' that carries me to all who live in that house, carries me to them to love them with God's love ñ to touch them with the warmth of God's embrace, and to bring into their lives of lonely isolation even one moment of peace.

Mary sits in her chair, but her head is resting on the table; the hard and cold Formica imprints leaving a mark on her forehead, a mark of pain. When I gently wake her and call her name softly, Mary begins to lift her head, and as she does, she begins her chant, "She is on the way, she is on the way," until her eyes meet mine. She recognizes me and quiets. We pray together. Though her lips move, her prayer is silent. She receives Holy Communion, and in the tenderness of the moment, Mary takes my hand and with her eyes she blesses me. A moment more and her head begins to droop as she leans toward the Formica table, she begins her chant again, only this time I hear, "God is on the way, God is on the way."

The hall is dim and the rooms small and plain—many of them almost lifeless. Mrs. Benson lies in bed, confined by cold metal bars and a weakened, crippled body. She holds her beautiful rosary beads, blessed by the Pope—her treasure. She prays silently, but when she sees me come to her bedside, her eyes alight with childlike expectation and she asks, "Have you brought Holy Communion?" When I nod yes, her eyes close; she bows her head and begins the painful act of contrition—painfully, because she is so close in her poverty, her pain, and her humility to the goodness of God that she must see reflected in God's eyes her own human frailty, and she begs for mercy. She lifts her eyes when she finishes her prayer, and, with words barely audible, she utters, "He is so good, my God, and I am so poor. . . ." She continues, "... but God loves me anyway." And then, looking at me, she says, "And God loves you, too."

Down the halls, in and out of many rooms, touching and being touched, loving and being loved—by the lonely, the poor, the sick, and the dying, I know that I have touched the depth of the wonder of the Spirit of Christ... I have met Christ not only in poverty, isolation, humility, and pain, but also in trust, faith, hope, and love. I have met the wonder that mystifies, that unifies, and that teaches what truly matters. In the hearts of these old people I have met wisdom, and wish to share its blessing."

When I finished praying it, there was absolute silence as the students' and professors' tear-filled eyes met mine.

My experiences at home with the children and my husband and with the people in the convalescent hospitals were all woven together with my meditations on the scriptures for the Ignatian Retreat.

It was challenging to see my life alongside the life and choices of Jesus. I was becoming more aware of my habits—did I drink too much alcohol? Eat too much sugar? Discipline the children from fear rather than love? What about my thoughts and emotions—the resentments, unkindness, fear or anger I held in my heart? How could I avoid what were becoming obvious obstacles to opening my heart to God's love? St. Paul's words, "No longer I, but Christ living within me," didn't mean that I was free to live as Christ lived, but rather that the light was revealing my once-hidden, un-Christ-like behaviors. The ego-driven, "I", still had a hold on my heart and I still made choices from disordered thoughts, emotions, and habits. I was beginning to know the difference between a decision made from love and one made from fear, from unhealed wounds, or a need to please or be seen as a kind person. My disordered attachments were becoming painfully obvious. I wept often as I was shown all the places where I failed to love. My director told me early in the retreat, "There will be times when you will experience great shame as God lifts the veil for you to see your failings. You will be on your knees begging God for forgiveness." And then he added, "First, you will feel the shame, and then, if the shame is truly God's work in you, it will quickly be followed by gratitude. The shame will call you to repentance and invite you to make amends and change your ways. The gratitude will open your heart, and you will experience a sweetness as you thank God for revealing the previously held secrets, giving you the needed freedom to be more Christ-like." It was during the retreat that I understood that the cook and the man in the car who sexually abused me by exposing themselves to me so long ago were two of my teachers. All these years, I had chosen to nurture the resentment and the fear which kept me emotionally attached to them in very destructive ways. Through prayer and grace, I turned my attention to God and asked for help to release my anger and be healed of the impact of their actions. I asked God to forgive me for allowing this to harm me for so many years. I understood that the actions of these men were a result of their own pain and wounding, that it was not about me, that the shame I carried was theirs. I could only hope, as I prayerfully released the anger and shame that lingered within me as an uninvited guest, that the attachment to them would finally be broken and the lightness and joy buried in childhood would re-emerge.

I learned to pray for healing, for forgiveness, for compassion and, held gratitude for all the wisdom that this and every experience holds for me. Finally, I learned to pray for my teachers... those who teach me with love, and those who teach me through fear and abuse.

I pray that all may find the healing love of Christ and am aware that, like Christ, we sometimes have to go through hell to find our compassionate hearts. With compassion we naturally extend invitations to those living in darkness.

I learned that when I made choices from love, it meant that my spirit was in harmony with the Spirit of God and my choices would then have the potential of being a blessing if those involved were open. But if I chose because of fear or hatred, or a need to be loved or to manipulate, or for any reason that was contrary to the will and the love of God, then I would be choosing from a disordered part of myself and my choices would have the potential to cause harm. This disordered part did not require harsh judgment, but only to be noticed, and, through prayer and perhaps some guidance, loved into healing.

It was difficult for me to recognize disordered attachments because they were so bound up with my need to keep peace and please everyone, especially my husband. This was especially apparent with disciplining the children. I often backed down, even when I did not agree with him. Sometimes, I did not even let myself know that I felt a disciplinary action was wrong. I did the same with enforcing the laws of the church. I obeyed them to a fault and sometimes demanded my children do the same. This was to please God, so that we would get into Heaven. Only much later, as I came to fully accept the loving God I knew, did I understand that those choices were emotionally and spiritually unhealthy. It was years before I realized that my need to keep peace was manipulative and controlling. I was afraid to stand up to my husband. I feared it might bring out his anger, and rather than have a "fight," I opted to be quiet. It never occurred to me that I might bring out my own anger. This was buried too deeply. It is often the case in marriages that the couple is polarized. One holds all the anger while the other "appears" docile. And then, because one remains silent, a greater dysfunction is possible. As I kept what I erroneously thought of as peace, and remained docile, I sacrificed the truth and caused harm to all involved. I was not free enough, nor did I trust God enough, to allow chaos. I did not know about "constructive" arguing. It took me many years to learn that when each person expresses his or her opinion there is the possibility of coming to an even deeper truth. The choice to be silent and accept what I believed to be wrong rather than "rock the boat" was a direct result of my birth trauma. A very hidden and fearful part of me believed that it was not safe to express myself honestly, or to "cause" chaos, and if I did, I would surely be abandoned as I had been abandoned in the midst of the chaos of my birth. I feared my husband would leave me. And even more terrifying, if I caused chaos, God would leave me. The choices I made out of fear were disordered and kept me from living my life with integrity. I still didn't fully recognize that I had a right to a life, to my feelings, opinions and needs, or that I had a spirit to guide me. ✳

Reflection Questions

Spiritual direction is an art which originated in the Catholic Church with the Desert Mothers and Fathers, perhaps around 300 A.D. These men and women were called by God to live in the desert as hermits. Their experience of simplicity and purification drew them very close to God. People were drawn to them for healing and guidance. As time went on, spiritual direction became a ministry for monks, priests and vowed religious women and men, and most recently, the laity also have been called. The call to be a spiritual director comes from God, and is recognized as a call when people begin asking an individual to be their spiritual director. Although it is an honor to be invited to be someone's spiritual director, it is a most humbling ministry. The holiness of the directee is humbling in itself, but the constant call in prayer of the director for the help of God, who is the real director, is even more humbling. Spiritual direction is a great blessing and a significant challenge. To be so intimately involved in the faith life of another is most definitely a blessing, and it consistently challenges the director to be more faithful.

> *What are the ways that you have been guided to deepen*
> *your relationship with God?*

Our images of God are just that—images. God somehow is always more than we can imagine but we try our best. When my awareness of God is being expanded, I lose my image and have to wait for a new image to emerge out of the darkness. God moved me from an image of the all-mighty, all-powerful God who had rules that I did not know and which I feared would put me in Hell, to an image of God who loves without condition, at all times, no matter what I do or fail to do. When that happened, my whole worldview changed. My view of myself, my family, and the whole universe, has never been the same. I began spinning with new awareness. But in the midst of that shift, I thought I was losing my faith and my mind. I was terrified.

> *How do you envision God? As Father God, or Mother God,*
> *as Jesus, or as a Hindu God, such as Shiva or Shakti, etc.?*

Or do you experience God in some abstract way... as ineffable grace; as divine principles of love permeating the universe, etc.? Maybe you do not even use the term "God."

How important is your image of God? Has your image of God changed over the years? What has that been like for you?

I think about Gandhi and his love for Jesus and many others who are not Christian who love and respect the teachings of this Master. So, I ask the following question to both Christians and non-Christians:

Who is Jesus for you? Is Jesus a teacher, a friend, a wisdom figure, a savior, a healer, the Light of the World, God ? Do you feel His presence guiding you?

Would you like to feel His presence and guidance?

If it seems true that every experience has the potential to be a teacher, what in your life has taught you something important?

Shatterings

8

Entering a Purifying Process

Purification became a familiar word in my reading and in my spiritual direction meetings. "It is a grace to be purified," my spiritual director repeated over and over. Purification was an experience of divine light, revealing the self-sabotaging and destructive tendencies and habits that created the illusion of separation from God, self, and others. These habits and tendencies were the things that prevented me from truly being myself. The purification of these habits may have been a grace, but it was hard. It was difficult to see the things I had hidden from myself: my childhood wounds, unhealthy family dynamics, issues in my marriage, struggles with my children, and of course, the underlying fears and withheld anger.

Destructive Fears

One of the most deeply held fears I had to face was the fear of Hell. Hell for me was an image of enormous flames lighting a freezing cold, dismal hole filled with people screaming in agony; but even worse was God's wrath and the unimaginable and terrifying separation from God. Although I discovered that I unconsciously feared abandonment on all levels, the most deeply buried and most significant fear was of being abandoned by God. *The Dark Experience of Nothingness* was this fear made real in an instant. Unconscious for the most part, this fear controlled me more than I suspected. In truth, it totally countered my trust in an unconditionally loving God. I could not consciously hold both, so I buried Hell. This deep, unconscious fear held enormous power. My fear of Hell revealed itself in an unforgettable incident that involved my children. At the time I did not realize what was underneath the terror and rage that erupted within me.

The family went to church faithfully every Sunday morning. Though it was a ritual, it was becoming a challenge. Annie either teased unmercifully and laughed with her siblings throughout the Mass or, if separated from them, sat stone-faced. We bribed her with bubble gum so she would sing.

Mark and Sean reluctantly washed and dressed for church, and Katie, though appearing cooperative, found it as boring as the others did. We bribed them with breakfast at a restaurant or a stop at the candy store, so they would be more agreeable. In my mind, church attendance was imperative unless you were very sick. It was a mortal sin in those days if you did not attend Mass without a good reason, and mortal sins took you to Hell.

Sean and Mark were about thirteen and twelve the day they decided to go to church on their own. They were attempting to become more independent. It was the same summer they went backpacking in the Sierras by themselves. Their adventures were exhilarating, and at times terrifying. But this Sunday's adventure was different. When they came back from church, I asked them something about the Mass, something like, "Who celebrated the Mass?" or "What was the Gospel?" I had no suspicion that they hadn't gone, I was just chatting. I knew instantly that something was strange. I questioned them more, this time peering at them with suspicion. "Did you two really go to church? Tell me the truth!" Sheepishly, they confessed that they had been at the donut shop, not church.

I wish I had responded differently. I wish I had laughed! But fear overwhelmed me. They had missed Mass, and they had lied. With anger, I yelled, "How dare you lie to me? How dare you pretend to want to go to church by yourselves, knowing you were going to the donut shop?" The words MORTAL SIN flashed wildly in my head. I was failing in my job to teach my children to be obedient and honest. I created Hell for myself and my children that day, with the internalized fear and rage that shamed, terrified, and punished them. "You two are horribly disobedient. I cannot believe you really did this, and I am not sure how to punish you, but you will be punished." There was no room for God's love, for compassion or kindness. My fear was too great; so too the responsibility that I had falsely assumed as mine.

"Get the bucket, cleaning fluid and brushes from under the sink and scrub the Mexican deck tiles until they are perfectly clean," I said in a harsh voice. They silently obeyed me and with heads down they moved to pick up the buckets. It was summer, and it was hot. I can still see them scrubbing those tiles under the heat of the sun as the rest of us swam in the pool. I wish I could erase that image. I now know Hell is not somewhere in an imaginary hole. It is here. It is in the fear that leads someone like me to treat her children in such an abusive manner. It is in war and rape and starvation in our own communities with people who are alive today... our brothers and sisters. And we don't go to Hell because we miss Mass or tell a lie to our parents, though I do not encourage either. We are in Hell, which is the pain of self-created separation, when we are out of alignment with the truth of who we are, with God, with our family and friends. The more out of alignment we are, the more awful the Hell and the more we can create Hell for others. With enlightened awareness my boys, and I could have had an open, loving conversation about church and God, truth and trust. Instead, because of my raging terror, it became a nightmare, an experience of punishment and fear, where I transferred to them the very worst of my theology: "If you are not good, you will go to Hell."

It was a long time before I could articulate the abusive nature of what I had done or understand that I was dealing with the internalized fear of Hell—that controlling monster embedded in me like a computer chip robotically running a program. I simply lived with the shame and fear hidden away. Toward the end of my graduate studies I understood the unfairness of what I had done and why I had done it. I talked to all of my children, and I apologized, asking for their forgiveness. I remember the looks of sadness on their faces as I spoke. I was sad too. They didn't say much. They just listened. I am sure my apology was more for me than for them because I did feel their forgiveness. Forgiving myself was another matter. That would take prayer, grace and time, as would their healing. By the time I apologized, one of my sons had already died. I spoke to him in the spirit world in prayer and asked for his forgiveness. I asked all of the children to be forgiven for my intolerance, my ignorance, and for the awful way I had punished them. I knew that the impact of the experience had profoundly affected all of the children, but especially Sean and Mark. I asked for God's forgiveness and to forgive myself before God. I knew as well that this experience negatively impacted the children's relationship to church and, more importantly, to God. I am deeply saddened when I hear preaching or see books that preach fear instead of love, the theology of sin rather than the theology of grace, and teach the threat of Hell rather than the love of God as a basis for "good" behavior.

St. John of the Cross writes about the dark night of the senses and the dark night of the spirit as times of purification. He explains that not only is the sin eradicated but the root out of which the sin emerges is destroyed. The unconscious belief that God's love is conditional is an enormous root. My very optimistic self believes it is being destroyed, bit by bit, individual by individual, until collectively we know and celebrate fully the love that is ours, no matter what—no matter what we have done or failed to do! I realize as I reflect on this experience with my children, that Hell is within my heart and torments me through fear, guilt, shame, and the belief that we can be separated from God's love. I don't have to go anywhere to be in Hell. It lives in my mind every time, even for a microsecond, I doubt God's presence and love.

Healing Graces

Fortunately, I received many graces that helped me nurture my children in healthier ways.

The most significant of these were my graduate studies, in which I had the opportunity to reflect on and understand my life, in the light of God's presence and love. Sometimes when people have a profound experience of God's love, as I had years before on that spring day when preparing to teach catechism, their lives are immediately healed and transformed. That did not happen for me, but the experience did lay the groundwork for the transformations that followed.

Two beliefs grew out of reflections that eventually opened the way, for me, for love to overcome fear. The most significant is the belief that everything that happens to me brings me to God and to consciousness, and therefore I must embrace all experience. The second, difficult as it is sometimes, is that I am called to love as I am loved. Slowly, sometimes painfully so, I realized that whatever I did could be used by God for good, even the Hell I created for my children that day. I could only pray that someday my children would grow because of the experience, rather than be burdened by it. I asked my children's forgiveness, expressing my sorrow and my shame. With their forgiveness and my self-forgiveness, each of us had the freedom to grow. Loving my children is all I am really called to do, advising or guiding only if I am invited, and interfering only when they are in danger of harming themselves or others. With this new understanding, parenting became so much simpler, and paved the way for peace and joy in our relationships.

But these understandings were not instantaneous. They developed within me, over time and with the help of my children. When Mark escaped out of his bedroom window one day and took the car because I had punished him, I realized I had to treat him differently. He was sixteen, and I was parenting him once again in an over-controlling and insensitive way. I knew that if I continued parenting him without the love and freedom he demanded, he would leave. I can only attribute this knowing to grace. Children come into our lives for many reasons, but the main one I experience over and over is that they come as teachers. I was learning, little by little.

There was a day when, in utter exasperation because his behavior had been so outrageous (or so I thought at the time), I burst forth with an even more outrageous question. "Mark," I said, almost breathless with frustration, "Who chose whom? Did I choose you to be my son or did you choose me to be your mother?" Mark looked at me as though I had completely lost my marbles and said without a moment's hesitation, "That's the most ridiculous question you've ever asked me. The answer is obvious. I chose you, because you were not awake enough to have chosen me." I gulped, but somewhere inside I knew he was right, though I couldn't really explain why. "Well then," I said calmly, "If you chose me, maybe you ought to figure out why, and maybe we can figure out how we can get along a little better." Oddly enough, we did make some significant and healthy changes after that.

My early religious training was based on fear. It caused very fundamentalist thinking and abusive behavior. It caused the Hell that I created in harshly disciplining my children. Fear outweighed love, the law outweighed the Spirit, and the rigidity of fundamentalist thinking blanketed my spirit and God's Spirit within me. It took years of prayer, courage, purification, and grace for God's love to free my heart and guide my life. Freedom is a grace I long for, one that I am blessed to receive, bit by bit.

Light and Progress

The mystics write that during periods of purification there is a constant flow of divine light. At first the experience is sweet, and one longs for more. But then the intensity of the light begins to reveal the truth. Self-revelation is humbling. Although my narrow-mindedness, impatience, resistance, and judgments were revealed to me, I couldn't change myself or fix most of what I saw. I could only acknowledge and pray for transforming grace. Some changes we can make ourselves, and there are other changes that only God can make, with our cooperation. And then, I had to learn that some things never change. These are the weeds among the wheat that we must learn to live with, in humility. All of this transforming grace is described in the poetry and prose of St. John of the Cross.

There are two parts to the spiritual journey which St. John of the Cross writes about in his poetry. He uses the metaphor of night to describe the spiritual journey. The first part of the journey, the night of the senses, is concerned with the person's departure from the imperfections and the unhealthy appetites of the senses. This might be something like continuing to have relationships that are unhealthy and unsupportive, or it might be spending too much time watching television, or spreading gossip, or any number of habits, addictions, and choices that are not conducive to deepening one's spiritual life. Because on the spiritual journey the soul is being stripped of its destructive thought-forms and habits, there is pain. Actually, the pain is caused by the damaging lifestyles or beliefs because they interfere with the person's ability to experience joy. As the light shines and we recognize the unhealthy behavior, with willpower and grace, we can change. However, until change takes place, there is either considerable shame and pain, or there is continued denial. The first obstacle that I became aware of and had to change on my spiritual journey was my belief that I didn't have enough time for prayer. I made a choice to get to bed early and to rise early so I would have the quiet time I needed before my family awoke.

Addictions to such things as food, alcohol, or work and unexamined habits are the obstacles that need to be overcome because they limit our freedom. One of the gifts of my prayer and reflection was the realization that watching television too late at night and drinking more than one glass of wine with dinner were habits that kept me from rising early enough to have time for prayer. My focus was changing. My interior life was deepening and my desire to develop spiritually was swiftly becoming a priority. This did not mean that my husband or my children were becoming less of a priority but that my spirit, the part of me that was essential for the fullness of life, was emerging and desiring to be integrated into my life as wife and mother.

The second part of the night that St. John identifies is called the night of the spirit and is concerned with bringing to consciousness the sources of our erroneous beliefs and deeply held fears. Our hidden fears, regrets, hurts, and misconceptions, control our behavior. Much of my behavior was co-dependent and was a direct result of past fears, especially fear of abandonment, which originated at my birth. I am struck by the profound impact the chaos of my birth had on me. The story, told and retold over the years, imprisoned me in the shadow of shame and in fear of disclosing the desire to be fully and powerfully alive for more than half of my life. Co-dependence revealed itself in my need to take care of others whether they asked for help or not. I felt "happy and good" as long as I was helping someone, but I never took myself into account or let myself know my own needs. I didn't think I had needs. As a child, hearing the stories of my birth, I assumed guilt and shame that were not mine. Shame and guilt were the cause of my co-dependent behaviors, forcing me to prove that I was "good." Helping others assured my being seen as worthwhile, or so I thought. All of these behaviors and more emerged in the light, as I journeyed. But, I was coming to understand how powerfully the unconscious influenced the conscious life. The unconscious fear of my power, which I believed was destructive, and the decision to remain independent from everyone, even God... to never surrender fully to love, due to the perception of being abandoned at birth, were incredibly influential in all of my decisions. Until I was able to bring them into the light, they controlled me.

When I began to emerge as a person with identifiable needs, I felt the terror of my birth. I found that the story my family repeated over and over had become mine—my image of my father as he drove through the town looking for some rare blood type was one of terror, my mother who almost died and the doctor who did die were innocent victims, and I, a new born baby girl who lay cold and alone on a steel grey table, was the cause of it all.

So with that as my entrance, why would I ever dare be myself? Why would I be forthright, exuberant, excited about life, and delighted to be fully in the light? Why would I ever trust that I deserved to be loved or that, if I let my love loose, others would not be harmed? No, as a matter of fact, I would do everything possible not to be myself, because it was dangerous, or so I believed! Was it possible that one of the reasons I was so attracted to my husband was his power? I could and would for many years hide behind him, never really speaking up with clarity about what I wanted or needed or knew, never feeling as though I deserved to be heard, or met, or fully loved, and afraid that if I did, it could be dangerous. And so it was!

As long as I made my family's story mine, I would carry guilt, shame, and fear. I would be fearful of my power, of being myself, and I would never allow myself to be truly vulnerable... open to being loved. As I looked back at this time and attempted to comfort that baby who was me, I realized that I had even decided that it was not safe to let God's love in all the way. I could not even trust God. It was as though I put my little hand up and said to God, "You were not there when I needed you, and you are not going to come into my heart now." It has taken years of reflection, therapies of all kinds, and spiritual direction to uncover the false beliefs so as to free this child to surrender and to trust.

It took years of prayer and grace to recognize the fear of abandonment and destruction, and the decision to remain aloof that arose from my birth. I had to go back to that image many, many times in prayer to re-envision myself as a baby. In the re-imaging I would see myself held and caressed in the arms of Mary, my spiritual mother, until I no longer felt abandoned.

It took even more prayer and grace to heal the ways that this fear imprisoned me, causing pain to myself and others. I could feel the exuberance of coming into the world, but then also the shame, the fear, the guilt of coming in so powerfully that I caused such chaos.

Some of the healing for this wound occurred in Hawaii in 1989 during a Christmas vacation, a year and a half after my marriage ended. The children were celebrating the holidays again with their dad and although I missed being with them terribly, I had learned how to deal with the separation in healthy ways. At first, I tried spending the holidays with friends or family, but that only increased the loneliness. Trying to be a part of other peoples' traditions increased my awareness that our family traditions were gone. I found another way to care for myself. I spent that Christmas alone in a charming oceanfront bed-and-breakfast on the coast of Kauai. It was beautiful, and I was happy for time just "to be." I was on retreat. On Christmas morning, I went down to the ocean to some shallow pools that I'd found a few days before. I felt free to take off my swimsuit because no one else was on this private beach. The sun shone brilliantly and I was toasty even in my nakedness. I could feel my heart beat as I prepared to enter the darkness of my mother's womb. I slowly immersed myself in the water. Floating, I blissfully surrendered and let myself be held in the warm, salty fluid... the birthing waters of my mother.

I closed my eyes and entered the darkness. I imagined the strong rhythmic pulsations as her body prepared to birth me. I felt like the morning sun, like Jesus. Then I heard the angels sing; it was glorious. I knew that even if the physical event of my birth was traumatic, the spiritual event was celebrated, and God was pleased. I felt God's love, as mother, embrace me and restore the innocence, and all the while the angels sang. That day, God's light revealed and healed much of the pain of my birth, as God became the doctor who joyfully birthed me anew in the Pacific Ocean. On that Christmas day, my exuberance was received and welcomed, but it took even more healing to free me from the fear of coming fully to life as a woman in a powerful exuberant way. I cooperated with God by being present and saying, "yes." Years and years of prayer, reflection, spiritual direction, and therapy came together and I was freed from the deeply held belief that I, as an eight-pound baby girl, was the cause of my mother's hemorrhage and near death and the doctor's fatal stroke.

As I continued to dig deeply into my conscious and unconscious beliefs, my eating habits changed. At first I felt I couldn't eat beef, and then I couldn't eat poultry. I could tolerate fish. Until one day, while dining at a very fancy San Francisco restaurant with my husband, I looked at the menu and my stomach heaved. Fish was no longer an option. I became a vegetarian. I think now that the need for clarity was instrumental in my choice to eat as a vegetarian. Somehow fasting was an important part of my journey, although I didn't understand my choices as fasting until many years later.

During that same time it became evident that I couldn't drink wine or any form of alcohol. That was a more conscious choice, because I knew something was happening within me that required great clarity, and I didn't want anything to get in the way.

I continued this intuitive fasting for nearly five years, then, one Thanksgiving morning after five years of fasting, as I was preparing a turkey dinner with all the trimmings for my family, it was as though the curtain was lifted and I knew my fast from meat and fish was over. From that day on I have chosen to fast in different ways. Most especially I pray for the grace to fast from foods that are not healthy for me, such as sugar. I also fast from thoughts that are not life-giving. Self-deprecating inner talk, blaming others, judging rather than noticing, and projecting negativity are all detrimental to my life and to the lives of others. I fast from emotions that limit my freedom and cloak my spirit by tending to them and not allowing them to run my life. Resentment, prolonged anger, rage, doubt, fear, and hatred are some of the emotions that are harmful if left untended. In tending to my emotions, I have learned that every emotion has a story. If I am willing to embrace an emotion with love and sit with it with compassion, it will eventually tell me its story. Once it has experienced my willingness to listen, it will soften, and with continued listening, the emotion will transform. I will have learned what it came to teach and will no longer be trapped by it or feel the need to act out.

All emotions are gifts and must be embraced with compassion to allow them to be heard, rather than ignored and acted out. When heard, emotions have the power to transform, to create, and to inform. They will guide us to a deeper realization of ourselves and others. They will also bring us to the source of our being, the God of love and compassion, which is their ultimate intention. If left unheard, our feelings will fester, causing physical, spiritual, and psychological disturbances. Feelings are like children who pull on our apron strings, longing to be heard. If pushed away too often, they will either act out aggressively or crawl into a dark corner, where the pain of not being heard is held at bay with the other unheard feelings. We sometimes experience this state as depression.

My parents didn't know how to listen to their important feelings and could not teach me to listen to mine. It wasn't until I began graduate school and experienced the gift of being heard by my first spiritual director that I experienced my first felt sense of the power of my emotions, a power I am learning about still. I am now tending to my feelings, the ones that hurt or scare me and the ones that delight me. I am the caring friend as I listen to myself. ✳

Reflection Questions

Purification is a gift, but the sense of gift does not become apparent until the work of cleansing is complete. In the midst of purification, we will feel loss, pain, shame, fear, and many other negative emotions. I learned something about this when Sean and Mark had a pet snake,. When the snake was shedding her skin, she became restless and unapproachable. She did not eat. She was in darkness, because the old skin covered her eyes. It was difficult for her to move. I think she must have been confused and angry. But had she not shed her skin, she would have stopped growing, maybe even died.

Have you had realizations that you need to purify your
heart, transform your habits,or make some changes?
What has that been like for you?

Joy, peace, love and compassion are gifts that we eventually learn to consciously choose, regardless of what is happening around us. We do this simply because they are the most expansive and delightful emotions. Certainly, there are times when we feel anger, fear, doubt, sadness, or even despondency, but those emotions are meant to be short-lived. Once they serve their purpose and we learn why they have come to us, we return naturally to the more expansive and delightful emotions. It isn't always simple to remain in these more expansive and delightful emotions, granted there is much in our lives and our world that calls us into fear or pain. But more importantly, it often feels uncomfortable or even frightening to remain in the light with gratitude, rather than returning to the old ways of nurturing complaints and aggravations.

All emotions are gifts, even the difficult ones. But those difficult ones will rule our lives and even ruin them if we allow it. All feelings are meant to be embraced with love. Some we embrace to learn from and transform, and others we embrace because it feels good. Both embraces free our creativity and our sense of self. Both inform us and can transform us. This is hard work, but we do the work faithfully, when we realize that the only other option is to numb ourselves into that dark corner of not feeling. I remember doing this, and the pain is excruciating.

> *Here is a list of some common emotions: joy, peace, fear, hatred, love, anger, guilt, shame, sadness, despair, surprise, delight, rage, pity, etc. Which emotions are you most comfortable with, and which ones do you hide from yourself and others?*

Clearly, I can say now that beliefs which are bound up with unheard emotions interfere with loving unconditionally. Beliefs can do great harm, and they can be most beneficial. Discerning healthy and unhealthy beliefs is a life-long challenge.

> *Have you ever acted upon your beliefs and harmed another person?*
>
> *Have you ever failed to stand up for what you believe? If so, what resulted in your failure to speak up?*
>
> *Are there habits or beliefs in your life that keep you from what you really want to be or do?*

As you respond to these questions, remember that you are never alone. The angels, your angels, are with you, helping you to lighten your load, to grow in wisdom, and to become free. As we see and own and release our unhealthy ways, and as we change our habits, we enter into the realm of God, and we are at home. Purification is what makes this possible. Do not waste too much time regretting what has been, rather keep your eyes on what you are receiving now. If you are seeing clearly, you will notice that love is all there really is; the rest is fiction, a made-up story whose purpose is over. It is a story which needs to return to its originator to be transformed into love.

9

Recognizing Unhealthy Patterns

In the spring of my second year of graduate school, just months before one of my darkest moments, my studies became even more enlightening. It was at that time I came across an episode in the life of Leo Tolstoy and recognized in his story of darkness, something similar to my *Dark Experience of Nothingness*. He was catapulted into a period of extreme self-doubt, and as he lost himself in the darkness, he also lost touch with reality and felt as though he might end his life. It was shortly after this episode that Tolstoy wrote *Confessions* and according to him began his last period of awakening to the truth. While St. John of the Cross was illuminating my experience of God's presence, Leo Tolstoy was helping me to understand my darkness. I felt such a kinship with both authors and a sense of relief knowing that I was not alone. I, like Tolstoy, was being awakened in and through the darkness. My beliefs were being challenged... not just my religious beliefs but my beliefs about myself as a woman. This could never have happened to me without the faithful embrace of God.

I knew and felt that being a wife and, for me especially, a mother, was a gift, but I had not realized that I had other gifts or that I had choices. I fell into marriage because it was what was expected, and now I was falling into something else, and it was a surprise. I was invited by one of the professors to present talks about my personal experiences as a laywoman in the church to the Jesuits who were preparing for ordination to the priesthood. The professor told me she hoped that my presentations would open the hearts of these soon-to-be priests. "Compassion and love must influence the ways in which priests teach the laws of the church," she said.

God or Church

One of the first talks I shared with these priests had to do with confession. I recalled the time when my husband and I had been married for three and a half years, and I was seven months pregnant with our third child. Worried about my health and our financial concerns, my husband gave me a choice, "After the birth of this child, separate bedrooms, or birth control." Although I wasn't surprised by this ultimatum, it terrified me. It was a week before Easter, and I went to confession to talk to the priest about it and to confess that I thought birth control was the only feasible answer. The priest in the confessional became irate. He told me to leave the confessional and the church and not to return until I could promise to be a good Catholic and follow all the rules.

Shame and fear overwhelmed me. The church had been my haven. What would I do? Although I didn't want to practice birth control, the rhythm method wasn't working, and I knew it was either my marriage or my God! This was a powerful moment in my faith-life. I didn't leave the church. I went to Mass, but for more than a year, I never received communion. I grieved this loss deeply. Sitting there in the pew while everyone else went to Communion, I felt isolated, ashamed, and terribly sad. I was not fully a part of the Body of Christ, the community in which I worshipped. I was not worthy to receive communion. It was a long, lonely year until, one Sunday, a Franciscan priest came to the church. I went to speak with him. He told me that if I practiced birth control, I had to promise myself and God that I would be welcoming if I conceived a child. "It is up to your husband and you whether or not you have another child. This is a matter of conscience and prayer." Then he added, "You are free to receive communion." His permission freed me. He was so different from the priest I met in the confessional. I remember them both in prayer. I pray for the first priest with compassion, and the second I pray for with gratitude because he was so compassionate.

This was the first time I experienced an unconditionally loving God. It preceded my experience of the *Ecstasy of God's Love,* but it paved the way for God to awaken me. The possibility that God and the church might be on different tracks at times was a huge aha! I knew I would have God's love and presence, even though I might not be welcomed in church as a Catholic in good standing.

As I related this story, some of the young men preparing for priesthood were open-minded, awaiting every word I said, feeling the pain with me, and freely expressing their sorrow. Others, who were more concerned with law than love, struggled as I told the story, and I could read the disapproval on their faces. In these moments, the remnants of shame would surface, shame that I carried because of the priest in the confessional, but also the remains of the shame of previous abuse, which had not been healed. I'd have to pray with all my heart to keep these demons of shame at bay.

The Franciscan priest was like the young men who now listened to me with open hearts. I felt loved. The other priest was like the young men were looking at me with disapproval. Only this time, my experience of God's love left little room for shame.

There is a prayer we say just before receiving Holy Communion: "O Lord, I am not worthy to receive you, but only say the word and I shall be healed." Feeling unworthy was familiar; it was bred into me. I prayed this prayer with sincerity, not out of humility as it is intended, but out of fear. Then one day I realized that I was tired of feeling unworthy, especially at this most sacred time, so I decided to change the prayer, and I omitted the part about not being worthy. I was praying with all my heart to experience God's love and forgiveness, rather than the unworthiness that shame encouraged. It was healing for me to realize that the origin of shame was abuse and did not belong to me but to the abuser, but every once in a while a bit more shame would surface, and I'd have to return quickly to the awareness of God's love and return the shame to its owner. It was at this time that I could pray the prayer " O, Lord I am not worthy," with the awareness that I am being made worthy in the midst of God's love... in my present state. I had come to see clearly, by grace, that I often fail to love as I am loved. I could feel my unworthiness in a healthy way, humbly acknowledging that although I would like to be free from sin, I am not. I am human and I am a sinner. I am only learning to be holy.

Change and Challenge

I was excited about my life, but the changes I was making internally were challenging my marriage. I was beginning to question the role I had assumed: I was the one who provided for everyone's well-being at home, and, if there were time or energy left, I could attend to my own needs. The greatest change was to acknowledge that I actually did have needs apart from my family, but it took a long time and much reflection to name them. With the spiritual awakening that was taking place and the questions that were rising up, it was becoming essential that I have companionship with those who were willing and able to engage me at that level. The children were too young, my husband was not interested, and my friends were not yet ready. So I began to make friends with the sisters and priests I met in class. I had very little time just for myself, but the extra time I did have was spent with my books, classes, and new friends. Sometimes there were retreats or special programs offered that I could not attend because of my family's needs, so I would ask God for the same insight and blessings I would have received had I gone. I always felt that my prayers were answered.

I was spending significant time in prayer and journaling each morning. This happened as a result of a purifying grace that revealed to me the importance of taking time for prayer, and the realization that I had no excuse for not doing so. It became routine to rise somewhere between four and five a.m. The study off our bedroom had become my special room, and I would go in each morning for an hour or two of silence and prayer. It took discipline, but I treasured this time immensely. Everyone else was asleep. The house was silent. There were no external interruptions. I was alone with God and had time to reflect on my daily life and integrate it with my spiritual life. It was so powerful to experience my two worlds merging.

There were many dynamics in our family, as there are in all families, that I needed to reflect upon. Some were healthy, and some were not. I can't pretend to understand father-son relationships, but in our family they were strained, especially as the boys went through their teens. There was a harsh anger and often an inability on the part of father and sons to listen to each other. My husband's expectations for himself and for the children were very high. Sometimes the children found those expectations unreachable, and at times incomprehensible.

The anger and disappointment I was experiencing in my relationship with my husband was growing. I could feel my discontent and anger leaking out into my relationships with the children. Although I reflected prayerfully on my impatience with the children, I didn't really understand that it was related to the disease within the marriage. But as the pain deepened, I realized I needed help.

A close friend recommended a therapist she knew who had an excellent reputation. It was a relief to make the phone call. I felt comfortable talking to her and was anxious to begin therapy. Her office was in the living room of her home, and when she opened the door a waft of incense enveloped me. I just stood there and stared at her. She was shorter and younger than I, with curly black hair, and she wore a colorful flowing dress. She wore no makeup but had a huge smile and a warmth about her that was calming. The room was as colorfully dressed as she was, and candles were lit alongside the incense.

"What can I do for you?" she asked.

My answer was somewhat hesitant. "I'm here because I'm having trouble with my marriage and I need help to make some changes so my husband and I can be happy together."

She just stared at me without responding for the longest time. Then she said in a clear, stern voice, "The first thing we have to do together is work on your depression, and then we can look at your marriage."

"Depression?"

"Yes, you are in a depression."

Nothing could have surprised me more at the time, but I was doing everything I could to make myself fit, in a relationship that had no room for me. The marriage was already over, but I hadn't yet discovered that. I was working hard at the pretense, and in the process I was repressing and suppressing everything real within me. That is bound to cause depression.

It wasn't only the spiritual truth I sought, but the truth of who I was, and soon I found there was no difference. In both therapy and spiritual direction I was asking hard questions about myself as a wife and mother. One day, I was surprised in prayer by the revelation that fear still controlled many of my choices and that I didn't really know how to love.

I had made choices out of fear or guilt for many years because I was ignorant, but that was slowly changing as I became aware. There were a multitude of challenges that my teenage children presented every day, many of which moved me to the point of terror.

The awareness that my job as mother was to love my children and be there when they asked for guidance, or when they were in real danger, was slow in coming. The more this truth became my reality, the more relaxed I became. But sometimes I didn't hear their call for help or recognize that danger was at hand. I denied the impact that their dad's anger was having on all of us. Perhaps I was too busy suppressing my own anger and fears, as well as the mounting pain, as the gap between my husband and myself deepened. We didn't talk about this. It just happened.

There is a saying, "People do the best they can with the tools they have." We didn't have many tools. I lived with fear I couldn't name—fear that the ever-widening gap I was experiencing with my husband would grow beyond the possibility of repair. If I'd had the freedom to express my fear and my anger, perhaps the outcome would have been different, but I didn't. I didn't have the words, nor did I have the sense that I had the right to feel, let alone the right to express, my feelings. Even with spiritual direction and therapy, I didn't have the words to engage my husband in a dialogue or an argument. We had polarized. He expressed his anger, and I went silent. We both held fear in our hearts, and both of us did the very thing we most feared. We separated emotionally—he to his work, and me to my studies and new friendships. And the gap continued to grow.

Every once in a while something would happen to wake me out of my pretense that everything between us was just fine. One morning I was sitting out in the back yard, meditating. There was a black hose on the lawn, left there by the gardener, intended for the sprinkling system. Suddenly, in the meditation, I saw the black hose wrapped tightly around my body and heard the words, "Your marriage is strangling you." Stunned, I sat for a long time in silence, and then drew the image in my journal.

My life with God became my salvation. It was a place of self-discovery, and it was also a place where I found peace. My image of God changed often. Sometimes it was God the father (I didn't really identify yet with God as mother). Sometimes the image was Jesus. Often I would find myself with Mary, the mother of Jesus, or Mary Magdalene, the beloved of Jesus. Sometimes I would be with one of my spirit friends, like St. John of the Cross, or Theresa of Avila, or Ignatius of Loyola.

Sometimes I would draw or write prose or poetry. Usually these would be times of quiet in which I would feel enormous love and presence. Even when I was exploring my shadow side, my shame, my unacknowledged anger or hurt, I felt God's love and Presence. I was like a moth naturally drawn to the light, and the light was burning through whatever separated me from truth.

Each morning after prayer I would crawl back in bed next to my husband. He rarely missed me, but would have, had I not been there when his alarm went off. Our time in the morning was our most special time, a time when we could remember the love we felt for each other. It was as though the night would wash away our difficulties, and we would hold one another, often surrendering to the desire for union that to my amazement remained intact until the end. These were moments of hope when most of the other moments seemed bleak.

Regardless of my marriage trials, the summers were busy. My main commitments were for car pools. I'd drive the children to swim lessons and swim meets, camp activities and hobbies and outings. Planning our summer vacation was also time-consuming. All of these activities meant that I had to remain close to home.

I found the organizing and driving that was necessary to keep the children busy in California to be difficult. I was afraid that a summer away from theology school would mean I'd revert to my old ways, lose my connections to my new friends, and to myself and to God. Of course that wasn't true at all, but it took one summer away from my new life to prove that it was okay to take a break. It was one of those summers that changed my life forever.

A Revealing Incident

Our friends from Duxbury were visiting with their four children, and we were having a delightful time sightseeing with them, showing them all the best of our new life.

We piled into two cars one day—cars stuffed with camping equipment, coolers of food, and water toys, and headed for Yosemite. I was deeply sad as we left for our trip, because Sean was not with us. He was having some difficulty with school and needed to take summer school classes. I decided that he could not go with us because he had to learn that his choice not to study had consequences.

I have deeply regretted this choice ever since. I made it out of fear. I made it out of a belief that punishment or deprivation would teach Sean a lesson. In retrospect, I realize that what he needed was to be loved and encouraged to believe in himself. I feared that he would continue to fail if I didn't step in with a punishment, and in doing so I supported the very fear that he struggled against, rather than giving him the love he needed. In those days so many of my decisions issued from fear rather than love or wisdom.

Sean must have felt terribly angry, maybe even enraged, at my decision, and shame in front of his siblings and his childhood friends that he had to stay at home because he had summer school. Or, maybe the feelings were so strong, he went numb. I never did find out.

We had a "babysitter" for him. Sean was sixteen, and it was almost a sure bet that without someone in the house, he would have summer bashes in our absence. But I made an even greater mistake with the babysitter. She was someone I had come to know through church, a very sweet, bright, young woman who was the victim of tremendous childhood abuse. She wore the pain of her childhood trauma on the outside. Her body, her facial expressions, and her clothing, all expressed her need to hide the horror she had lived with. She was glad to be at the house; the house and the pool were beautiful, and Sean would be busy with summer school and studies.

But of course Sean was not happy when I told him who was coming. How could I not have realized how painful this would be for him? What would his friends think? It was bad enough that we left him behind, but now something worse; he had a young woman mirroring his stuffed emotion, the rage and hurt, and the shame. I know he must have wondered how I could do this to him. In retrospect, I wonder too.

On the camping trip I continued to rise at four or five, making my way to the river with my journal and colors in hand. I never went anywhere without my journal. It had become my friend, and it held my conversations with God, the joys and challenges of my daily life as well as my tears. It was often difficult for me to express or clearly write my experiences in my journal, and so poetry and art became an important means for self-expression. I came to love colors, especially chalk pastels, mostly because they are so forgiving. My fingers and hands were often an art piece in themselves, as I smoothed and smeared the colors on my journal pages. So, off I went, gingerly, tiptoeing out of the tent to sit in silence by the river. I still recall the feeling of delight as I gathered my things together. It was an adventure to follow a gentle call deep in my heart to come to the quiet place to meet the beloved. The moon was full, making the early morning experience even more beautiful, as I watched the moon set and the sun rise.

On Sunday morning, as I sat in silence looking at the river bubbling and listening to the birds as they awakened, I had a vision. This vision was very clear, and even though I can not say if it was in my mind or my imagination, or if it really manifested on the river, I can say it was as real as I was real:

> *I see a woman hunched over. She is completely dressed in*
> *black, with a black shawl covering her head and shoulders.*
> *She is weeping. As she turns towards me, I see that her face*
> *is filled with grief. "My child is dead," she says. I cry with*
> *her, thinking all the while that it is a visit from Mary who*
> *is sharing the grief over the death of Jesus. I am deeply*
> *touched. I draw the picture in my journal, and I write*
> *about it.*

I returned to the camp before everyone was awake carrying the grieving mother in my heart. The image is still vivid today, and I can imagine myself there almost instantly.

Sean was fairly cheerful when we arrived home. I paid the young woman, and she left. The only thing Sean ever said about those three days was that I was never to bring that girl home again. Inside he must have been terribly upset, but those emotions were not expressed to me—and perhaps not even available to him.

There really wasn't room for emotional expression in our Lafayette home. I was far too busy trying to keep the "peace." I still did everything I could to quell my own feelings, except for the "nice" ones, and even then I monitored my expression. Today I recognize this as serious codependent behavior. Sadly, I taught my children to do the same.

Roots in Family History

I had learned this behavior from my family of origin. In my childhood home, when my parents had a disagreement, Mom fumed silently in the kitchen, and Dad rocked rhythmically back and forth in a rocking chair in the living room. He did most of the cooking in our home so whenever

I saw Mom in the kitchen, I wondered what was happening. When I saw Dad in the rocker, I knew. Eventually whatever "it" was would pass, and life would continue as "normal."

Dad's big problem was with his boundaries. Sometimes he acted in inappropriate ways. I have vivid memories of those yacht club dances where he and Mom would join their friends for dinner and dancing. We teenagers had our own parties in a separate room but often wound up with the adults.

From the time I can recall, cocktails and cocktail parties were an everyday occurrence. That was when people were not alcoholics unless they fell into the gutter, drunk, like the man next door who would get off the Long Island Railroad after work in New York City and land flat on his back in the parking lot. Maybe he had a note in his wallet to call my Dad when this happened, or maybe someone called his wife and she called Dad, but off Dad would go to the rescue. My parents were not declared alcoholics, even though they drank excessively, because they could almost always walk.

It was at those yacht club parties that Dad would have too much to drink. He danced so roughly with me that my dress would tear or my jewelry would break. What was worse was watching my mother sitting alone while he danced with other women—women who were young and pretty. Though they might have been younger than Mom, it would have been hard for them to be prettier.

Some of the women liked to dance with Dad, but I could tell that others were uncomfortable and wanted to escape. He was a big man, handsome and strong, and he was passionate. When he had too much to drink, his passion was like a loose cannon, and for most, it was a bit scary. I felt enormous confusion watching all of this, especially watching Mom, alone and sad.

At home, Dad was so attentive to Mom. He pinched and tugged at her, always wanting to snuggle and kiss, always telling her she was pretty and that he loved her. But he forgot her at parties. That seemed strange, and it must have made me very angry. That's why I felt confusion. The anger I experienced toward Dad would have been too scary to feel. I didn't know at the time that I could acknowledge his shortcomings and still love and respect him.

Sometimes I'd walk over to Mom's table to say hello, but I didn't do that too often. I didn't want her to know that I saw her pain. But even worse, when I'd say, "Hi Mom," she'd sometimes act as though I wasn't there. She was in a daze, a daze that was familiar; she was the one who wasn't there.

Her dazed state happened often, and I felt so alone at those times. Sometimes I'd come home from school and say, "Hi Mom, I'm home," and she wouldn't answer me. She would be playing the piano or aimlessly wandering around, and she would just stare, with no response. Sometimes she'd laugh at what I said or did, but the laughter was out of place, and I'd know she really didn't see or hear me—like the time I rushed in because I had blood on my underpants. I was scared because I hadn't been told about menstruation. I was twelve. Mom looked at me and laughed, then walked away. Later on she explained why I was bleeding, and took me to the store so I could run in and buy perhaps the most embarrassing item possible for a twelve-year-old girl, a Kotex pad!

I never did find out why my mother wasn't there for me, why she laughed inappropriately, or why she never helped me understand the beauty and the wonder of my bleeding. Mom used to tell me after I had children that it was important to discipline my children, but I must take care never to break their spirits. I think her mother did in fact break her spirit. Her mother, my grandmother, Rob, who we called Robbie, who married my Native American grandfather, Daddy Bob, was the youngest of sixteen children born into a very poor family. She had to go to work at age eight and continued to work her whole life. She was self-educated. And though she did love us, she had a mean streak that was unpredictable and fierce.

Maybe Mom's absences were due to the intensity of pain she suffered as a child. Maybe she learned to escape to another reality where it was more peaceful and where she felt safe. Maybe when things got difficult for her with Dad, when the pain got to be too much, she just took off in her mind for a while as a way to find peace.

Mom was very bright and so beautiful. Her hair was dark brown and thick, even when she was old. She contributed to the community in lots of ways, always welcomed children and teenagers who were struggling at home, and always delighted my friends, as well as my sisters' and brother's friends, even though there were five of us. Both Mom and Dad were deeply loved by many people, and still today I have friends who tell me how much they appreciated their generosity and love, and the fun they had at our house. Most never knew the inside story of the family. Even I didn't really let myself feel or see the truth as it happened. It felt safer to pretend that it was just fine.

So I raised my children the same way. Even though I didn't drink as my parents had, I was raised in what today would be called an alcoholic family, and I learned very early: *don't trust, don't feel, and don't tell; keep hidden the emotions, especially fear and anger, even from yourself.* I was, however, about to experience the biggest wake-up call of my life, and that familiar experience, *don't trust, don't feel and don't tell,* was to be blown wide open. ✳

Reflection Questions

Our personalities are a composite of our experiences and we respond to life according to those experiences until we become aware of them and begin the work of transformation. Laws are intended to protect us, to safeguard our lives, but sometimes they do the opposite. There are laws about gay marriages, birth control, divorce, abortion; laws about what constitutes rape, sexual abuse, marital violence, etc.

Do you feel protected by the laws of your church or your community?

Do you feel that you have been hurt by the laws of the church or temple or community in which you were raised? Does that affect you today?

Being seen as "good" is something we outgrow, and eventually we only care to be seen as true to ourselves and to God. When we make choices out of a desire to please others, disregarding ourselves, we are most always choosing out of guilt or shame.

What choices have you made or do you continue to make out of fear, shame, or guilt?

Are there instances in your past in which you have been punished or have punished another for which you still feel shame or sadness?

Our parents have an enormous influence on us. They teach us by what they say or do not say and what they do or do not do. We learn over time which teachings or examples are helpful and which are not. We try to eliminate the unhealthy influences but it is not always easy to do so. These behaviors are often very deeply embedded in us. If we struggle with the habit of repeating unhealthy behaviors, knowing they are unhealthy, then we add shame and guilt and even self-hatred to our burden. If we are able to transform our lives, we experience great joy and freedom.

How has your relationship with your parents affected your relationships with others, especially your romantic relationships? Have you been able to free yourself from unhealthy teachings?

It is always helpful to celebrate our accomplishments, even if they are minor ones. Gratitude is in partnership with love, and whatever we can do to fill ourselves with either opens the door for more of both. Self-criticism is fine because it can lead to an awareness of how to make healthier choices. However, if we do not quickly move to gratitude, we will be in the hands of an energy or spirit which desires our demise, one who invites feelings of worthlessness. That will not be our loving Father/Mother God. Even when our own parents or teachers have despaired of us, God will always call us to Him/Her self with a warm embrace, and this will ultimately lead to love of self. St. Bernard of Clairvaux, a 12th century monk, writes that self-love is the highest form of love and results directly from God's love of us. He shares that if God loves us it would be rude of us not to love ourselves. I pray never to be so rude.

10

Losing My Son

Shortly after our return from Yosemite, I received an early-morning call from Father Brian, our pastor. He told me that Mr. Hansen, a man I had been visiting, had just died. I had grown to love him and his family, and the pastor knew that. I quickly dressed and went to the 6:30 a.m. Mass. I filled my container with hosts and went to the family home. The whole family was gathered, grieving the death of their grandfather, father, and husband. I grieved along with them as we prayed together. There were more of us than there were communion wafers. We shared the already small wafers among us, and, as we did so, I felt the Spirit's presence radiating in our hearts. In the midst of this very dark moment, the light shone brightly. That was the morning of July 11, 1981, a day I won't forget.

House on Fire

I returned from the Hansen's feeling both blessed and sad. The children stayed home to swim and play while my husband and I spent the rest of the day in Napa, visiting wineries with our Duxbury friends.

When we arrived home in the early afternoon we found the yard flooded with neighbors. The house was charred, blackened by fire, and the children, huddled in a clump, were terrified. The story rolled out:

Unbeknownst to us, Sean and Mark had gone to Chinatown the week before to buy firecrackers for the Fourth of July. They had saved a few, and Sean had lit them that morning. Without them realizing it, one landed on the wood shingle roof on this very hot, dry, July day. They told us that a stranger knocked on the front door. She said, "You kids better get out of this house immediately. It's on fire. I'll call the fire department." And she did, then disappeared. No one ever saw her again.

The fire truck had come and gone before we arrived home. A neighbor told the children not to talk to anyone about the fire until we got home, so the Fire Chief had left, apparently very angry. The fire destroyed half the house, leaving the other half with severe smoke damage.

Our friends went back to Duxbury the next day, and we started looking for a house to rent. By this time I knew, at least intellectually, that the feelings that each of us held, especially Sean, needed to be expressed, and that it wasn't going to happen without help. The whole family went to a therapist. It was helpful, because we had a chance to talk about the fire, what it was like, our fears and our mistakes, and, how each of us felt. It seemed as though one session was enough.

But a few days later I discovered Sean on his bicycle laden with newspapers. He had seen an article about the fire in the local paper that morning and had ridden to town to buy as many papers as he could carry so that people wouldn't read the story. It was an account of the fire with input from the Fire Chief. The headlines read something like, "Rich

Lafayette Boy Burns House Down," and the article was about Sean. The article said many things that were not true—but many things that caused Sean to feel shame. To make matters worse, it was syndicated, and my father, whom Sean adored, called because he had read the article. Although this didn't cause Sean's trauma or depression, I suspect it was a huge contributing factor. I wish I had realized then that we needed more family therapy, but I didn't. Sean never showed any signs that he was suffering, but my awareness at that time was not very developed.

The days were filled with insurance people and insurance claims; sorting through the things in the house; cleaning and packing our clothes; making arrangements for all that was salvageable to be cleaned and stored. We had to rent furniture and outfit the kitchen in a rental house.

One day Sean and I were in a thrift store buying things for the kitchen. He disappeared and returned with a tea cozy on his head. The white liner covered his face, and the blue and white outer covering stood stiffly above his head. He looked like a masked cartoon character. I burst out laughing, and so did he.

That was just how Sean was. He loved to laugh and did all sorts of things to make others laugh as well. He was an extravert but hid his more fearful and difficult emotions within himself. I didn't understand then that there were ways to engage him in conversation that might help him express whatever was painful or frightening. I didn't know how to do this for myself, let alone for my children. He stayed with me most of the time through these days, helping me with all the chores that needed to be done. The others were often with me too, but Sean seemed to be nearby almost all of the time.

He and Mark were great pals. They had matching ten-speed bicycles and would ride for hours, exploring back roads. They challenged themselves daily with bigger hills and longer rides. Their personalities were very different. Mark was quiet and reflective. He loved to spend hours by himself, fishing at the reservoir across the street. Sean was boisterous! He loved crowds, the larger the better. He was adventurous, and he loved unusual things. He had a pet rat he named Kissy. He and Kissy had routines that entertained the other children. He also had snakes, which fascinated him, and, though Mark was fine with the snakes, I don't remember any of the rest of us liking them too much. Both Sean and Mark liked the outdoors, physical challenges, and adventure, and this is how they spent a good deal of their time together.

The fire left all of us stunned, but Katie and Annie were especially affected. It was frightening for them. Although there was significant smoke damage throughout the house, nothing in their bedrooms was destroyed. None of us overtly placed blame for the fire or pointed a finger at Sean, but we all knew that Sean painfully carried the brunt of it. Buying the firecrackers and lighting them had been his ideas.

Katie and Annie had a friendship very similar to that of the boys. They spent their time together differently but were great companions even though there was a seven-year age difference.

Suicide

We found a house for rent in the neighborhood, only a couple of blocks from our home that had burned. It was on a small, side street, set down in a hollow. There was a large, bright living room and kitchen, two bedrooms and two bathrooms on the main floor, and a bedroom, bathroom, and family room with very little light, on the lower level. The house was relatively new, not very well-built, and felt very cold. But it was a place to live, and it was convenient.

It was strange in many ways. Its layout and the way it was situated on the property were part of that, but even more peculiar was its energy. Mark wouldn't go into the house unless I was at home, even if he had a friend with him. He said the house was haunted. I felt uncomfortable around the man who owned the house, and I often wondered if something awful had happened there. There were strange noises, the hangers in the closet would rattle, and the downstairs where the boys slept had an eerie feeling. It never occurred to me that this might be a problem, but it was. And I'll never know how much.

Because I no longer had my special room, I'd wait until my husband left for work in the morning to take time for prayer, and I would pray in our bedroom. On August 4, 1981, while praying, I had a very significant vision, although at the time I didn't know just how significant it was.

> *I saw myself dangling, feet off the ground, with my hands grasping a bar. I heard the words, "Let go of everything, even the desire to let go." With that I let go of the bar and fell in a heap on the ground.*

In my prayer that morning, God was preparing me for a volcanic eruption that did indeed leave me in a heap on the ground but also gave me a way to stand again by learning to let go of everything that might keep me down. As I was concluding the journaling of my prayer, Sean came down the hall and stood outside our bedroom as he called to me, "Mom, I'm going to Mrs. Jones' this morning to mow the grass." This was one of his summer jobs. I hollered back, "Okay, see you later," and added, "don't forget to take out the garbage." That was the last time I heard his voice, and those were the last words I spoke to him. I so wished they had been, "Okay, see you later. I love you." I wish I had gone out to hug him. I wish, I wish, I wish. I left the house shortly after Sean did.

Mark and Katie went to their swimming lessons and friends' houses. Annie had gone to Lake Tahoe with her friend Erin, and I went to the convalescent hospital to meet with Ann and Mike, a couple from my parish who were in training to become Eucharistic ministers. They accompanied me that morning, and I introduced them to each of the people. We prayed together as the people in the convalescent hospital received Holy Communion.

As we stood out front on the sidewalk, finishing our conversation, fire trucks and an ambulance went by with sirens blaring. I suggested we pray a moment for the people involved, because that was what my mother taught me to do as a child. Then we said goodbye, and I headed toward our rental home. I could have gone a shorter way, but decided to go past our burned house. As I turned the corner, I saw that the ambulance and fire trucks were in the driveway of our fire charred house. There was a car there as well that I didn't recognize. I instinctively pulled into the driveway. A man approached me and asked who I was. He introduced himself as the county coroner. His face was stark. He said, "Your son is dead." I went numb. I must have. It was the only way I could hear the man's horrifying words without going crazy. Actually, as I think back to that terrifying moment, I could have gone insane. The words I was hearing were just that horrific. "A neighbor, Kim, came over and identified your son," he told me.

Shaken to my core, and afraid to ask I almost whispered, "Which son?"

"Sean," he responded.

Neither answer would have been a good one, but now I knew which son was in the ambulance. It was too much to take in as real, "I want to see Sean, I want to see my son."

"No," he responded.

His response felt cold. Crying, I pleaded with him, pulling on his jacket. "Please let me see him. How will I ever really know it is Sean if I don't see his body?"

"No," he said again.

"Please," I begged, "just let me see his left toe. Sean had a minor operation, and I will recognize the scar. Please, please let me see my son."

Again he said, "No," and he got into his car and closed the door.

I stood there alone, withholding the screams and wails of a mother in unmitigated agony as he drove away. I just stood there watching that car and the ambulance that followed, holding the body of my son.

I think it was a policeman who called my husband and told him to come home. He didn't tell him why. Somehow I managed to drive. I picked up Mark. Mark knew the minute he saw me that something was wrong. The words flew out of my mouth. "Your brother is dead, and we have to go home." He stared blankly, his body rigid, sharing the shock with me. He just nodded, "yes." The tears came moments later, but it took all of us a long time for the other emotions to catch up.

I called a neighbor to pick up Katie. Annie was still in Tahoe. I was terribly worried because she was only seven. What was it going to be like for her when she came home the next day? We were alone in the rented house. The four of us stood motionless and numb in the kitchen staring at each other and not knowing what to say or do. It was unreal. It was too much to believe.

We still didn't know what had happened. And there are parts of Sean's story that we would never know, but we needed whatever information we could get. We called the police station. Sean had been shot in the head with a rifle. They said it looked like suicide, but they couldn't find a note. I couldn't believe it was suicide. Maybe it was an accident, maybe murder. Anything but suicide. I couldn't believe Sean would kill himself. He was such a fun-loving, outgoing kid, so filled with humor and laughter, so filled with life. Sean was always surrounded by people, and they looked up to him. Even adults admired him because he was so filled with adventure and courage and curiosity. He lived on the edge, always trying something new and challenging. But he wasn't the kind of kid who was destructive. He just never really acknowledged most limitations.

School was one of the limitations he couldn't avoid. Sean was bored in school. He had so much energy that being confined in a chair in a crowded classroom, or anywhere that didn't feel free, was more than awful for Sean—it was unbearable. I knew this about him. I could feel his sadness, but even more, I could feel his joy when he was free—like the times when he flew down a steep hill on his bicycle.

And it was Sean's desire for freedom that inspired me as we planned his funeral and made the decisions that were before us after his death. I knew that symbolically a small, enclosed box buried in the earth would not be right for Sean.

Journal Entry
Friday, August 7, 1981

Today Sean has been dead for three days. He was cremated yesterday. In prayer, I envisioned his body being wheeled into the crematorium, and at the same time that I wept I heard myself singing the Easter "Alleluia." It was the Feast of the Transfiguration, the day Jesus was transformed into light on the mountaintop. This afternoon Sean's ashes will be sprinkled on San Francisco Bay, just beyond the Golden Gate Bridge. As I write, I hear music in my heart. "One Bread, One Body," and then, "And I will raise him up."

My understanding is so limited. I pray to trust that what appears to be so brutal and filled with pain is in some way a blessing to those of us who are receptive. I trust your goodness and your compassion, my God, and I trust most of all your tenderness and love.

That evening I wrote a letter to Sean in my journal:

Dear Sean,

Sometimes I made choices that hurt you, and I ask for your forgiveness. I am so sorry. And sometimes you made choices that I did not agree with, and I forgive you. Now you have chosen death and I am heartbroken. I ache everywhere. I miss you more than I could ever express. I do not understand your choice. I don't know why you had to leave or where you are.

And then as I was expressing my love and my pain to God and to Sean I had a vision:

I see Jesus, with Sean draped on his lap, as Jesus had been draped on the lap of his mother in the Pieta. Then I see myself kneeling before them. My husband comes, and then Mark, Katie, and Annie, the other members of the family, and our friends. And then the Angels and the Saints appear too. We sing, "Sing a new song unto the Lord, let the song be sung from mountains high."

Sean died on a Tuesday and we waited until Saturday to have his funeral Mass so family and friends would have time to gather. Pat Benson, my Dominican sister friend, came to our home immediately and helped me plan Sean's funeral Mass. With Pat's help, I chose the music, the readings, and the celebrants. Our pastor, Father Brian, presided, and the assistant pastor, Father Martin, was also vested along with my priest friends and professors, Neal Flanagan, Rich Byrne, and Mike Marnell.

Journal Entry
Saturday, August 8, 1981

Today was a beautiful day; one I shall always remember. I melted when I walked into church. The most beautiful, spring-like flowers were all around the altar, so many that it was difficult for the readers and celebrants to find a pathway. It was glorious. And the church was filled with people, so much so that many had to stand.

The music, sung as if by angels, filled the church with such joy that in that moment I didn't have room for much else. The loneliness, tears, and pain remain in my heart, but the peace and the joy are greater.

"Amazing Grace" was sung after communion. It was magnificent. Somehow I knew that, just as Jesus' death had brought new life into the world, Sean's death would bring new life to many, and in particular to me. I didn't know how, I just knew in my heart it would happen.

As we left the church the musicians sang, "Though the mountains may fall and the hills turn to dust, the love of the Lord will stand," and I was flooded with a love that lifted me up, and I knew the love that touched and held Sean, the joy was almost unbearable. I felt I would burst. Though I do not understand what I write, I know that in that moment of joy I was transformed.

The double doors at the rented house were wide open the day Sean died, and for weeks after. People came regularly, bearing gifts of food and flowers, sitting with us and sharing our grief. It was a very blessed, though sad, time.

Sometimes people said things that startled me like, "Why would God do this to you?" Or even more confusing, "God must love you so much to let you have this much pain to carry."

All I knew was that God was walking through this with me, as God had walked with Jesus and with Mary. The statue of the Pieta had come alive for me with the vision I had of Jesus holding Sean in his lap, as Mary had held Jesus. I saw Jesus putting Sean's body back together—my once handsome, vibrant son, being healed in every way as he lay in the lap of Jesus. It was a comforting image, because I knew Sean was all right.

The first night after Sean's death, my husband and I lay awake all night in our rental house and talked about Sean—our shock, our fears, our concerns about Mark, Katie and Annie, and most especially our feelings of guilt. We talked for hours about the things we might have done differently and the regrets we had because we hadn't realized that Sean was so depressed.

Although the police had thoroughly searched the burnt house where Sean had taken his life, looking for a suicide note, they found nothing. My husband walked down to the house to look for himself. He went into Katie's room where Sean had left his bike. He reached under the seat of the bike and in the frame of the seat found the note. It read:

> *Dear mom and dad and kids,*
> *I am sorry but I*
> *just couldn't stay here*
> *any longer.*
> *I love you all very much.*
> *Don't be too sad.*
> *I'll see you in heaven*
> *someday soon.*

My husband didn't tell me he found the note. He thought it would be even more upsetting. But Mark discovered it in his dad's dresser drawer. Perhaps because the note made it clear that Sean had taken his own life, it was a gift to me. I no longer had to wonder. And Sean had known that it was time for him to leave. Even if he was besieged by dark forces or despair, he made his choice to escape his Hell, knowing that he loved us, having concern for us, and knowing that we'd meet again in Heaven. He knew God loved him and was waiting for him and he expressed his love for us. That meant everything to me.

It was terrifying to consider the depth of despair and pain he must have felt. It occurs to me that I may have tasted it in my *Dark Experience of Nothingness,* the experience that I survived only because it was so brief. I shudder thinking that this is what my son felt. But once again I am thankful for the *Dark Experience of Nothingness.* I think it is the taste of Hell that St. Theresa is said to have experienced during her life, and which she considered her most profound religious experience. She said she lived her life from that moment on with the awareness that her choices would insure she never returned to Hell because it was so horrid. Sean didn't have the chance that St. Theresa and I did. He was overcome by the horror.

I have learned to trust Sean's choice, though I wonder how much freedom he had in making it. I respect his journey, and I am profoundly transformed because Sean is my son. Although his death was tragic and I grieve still, God has used Sean's choice to die to bless me with compassion, wisdom, and the freedom to go between the worlds. I would never have chosen some of the events in my life, and in the past I have often wished my life were different. But today, I know that I am who I am because of the experiences I have encountered, and I am thankful for my entire life.

I never saw the room where Sean died, thank goodness—none of us did. My imagination is enough. Sean had taken his father's hunting rifle from the closet in the burned house and had shot himself. I never saw Sean after his death, and I do not know for sure, but I assume they would not let me see him because he was so disfigured by the gunshot wound. As I write this, my heart pounds and my hand is shaking. I weep for my son and for the desolation he endured alone.

Diane and Gary, two of my dearest friends, came to the house and spent the day tearfully and lovingly cleaning the walls, furniture, and floor. They said they couldn't imagine letting a hired stranger take care of Sean's remains, and they knew we could never do it ourselves. How does one ever express gratitude for that kind of love? A few days after everything was cleaned in his room, I went down to the house alone. The house was still torn apart and charred from the fire. I stood at his doorway and wept. I have a small suitcase that I keep in my closet. Inside the suitcase are some of Sean's schoolbooks, his special things, like a sign with his name on it and a few pieces of his clothes. Sometimes I open it up and put his shirts to my face to remember how he looked and smelled.

Sean's death was excruciatingly painful and shocking. Even today, many years later, I can feel the cross in my heart—but the fact that it was a suicide made it far worse. I wanted it to be murder or an accident, anything but suicide. Even the police, suicide prevention people, neighbors and friends, were shocked. Ten years after Sean's death, I was teaching a class on ministry to my sabbatical students. I had invited a woman to talk about working with people who threatened suicide, and the families who survived a suicide. In the middle of the class she began speaking about a sixteen-year-old Lafayette boy who committed suicide in 1981. I held my breath and stood, fearful of what she would say, my back plastered against the wall for support. "To this day," she said, "no one understands this suicide. He was a wonderful young man, and his family is lovely. I visited them myself. Sometimes we just never know what causes someone to commit suicide, and we have to let go of cultural beliefs and help the family deal with the shame that exists around suicide."

I followed the woman out to her car after the class and told her who I was. I had moved to a different house, and I had changed enough so that she didn't recognize me. She was upset and apologized profusely for using my story as example, but I thanked her because it was helpful for me to hear that Sean was remembered in a wonderful way.

Continuing Surprise and Growth

A few days after Sean's death, a woman came to the door to invite me to a meeting for bereaved parents. This time I was more mature than I had been when Maggie died. Strange as it may sound, I had learned how to grieve, how to stay open, to feel and share my experience, and especially how to receive the help I needed. But the woman at my door was in greater need than I. She told me, as her eyes welled with tears and her lips quivered, the story of the death of her son the year before. She shared with me her pain, her loss of hope, and her depression. I knew she needed companionship, but I didn't have the energy or strength to help her that day.

Her pain frightened me because mine was so new and so deep, and I didn't know how I could handle more. The thing that kept me from despair and hopelessness was my awareness of God's love—my faith. It was a time of darkness, and my pain was excruciating. My prayer was nothing but a flood of tears for weeks and months. But in between, there were moments of light and even joy in an inner awareness that said, in some mysterious way, that it was all okay and that all was perfect.

One of those moments came at a stoplight in town. I was on my way to the grocery store and waiting for the light to turn green when I began to sing "Holy God we praise thy name." I sang with a clear and soulful voice, loud and with feeling, when suddenly I realized I was singing! How could I be singing, I asked myself, just days after my son's death? Then I began to cry! They were joyful tears because this singing wasn't my usual experience, but the spirit within me who knew, no matter what was happening, that I was okay because I was in touch with my spirit and God's Spirit. I knew it was true. I was okay. I can easily recall the joy of that moment. It was another experience of the *Ecstasy of God's Love* emerging from within me, reminding me of what is truly real and calling me into itself.

Experiences of God were familiar to me in my whole life, but I had no way of holding, naming or celebrating them. They were just a normal part of my life. When I reflected on them in graduate school, they came alive. I received them in a different way, as gifts.

Sean's death brought me to a new level of consciousness. I had experienced Maggie's death and lived. I even grew spiritually through her death. Because of Maggie, I had learned how to pray and how to grieve Sean. By the time Sean died, I had a deep and conscious connection with my spirit, which deepened immeasurably as the days went on. I became more vulnerable and receptive, especially in my relationship with God. I began to have visions often. I was sitting on my small prayer bench one morning in August when I had a vision of Mary:

> *Mary is dressed in blue and white with stars in an oval shape around her. I weep as I drink in her beauty and brilliance. The stars shimmer around her. The next day she appears again. This time one of the stars is missing. I notice but don't understand why. She stays with me for a while, and then the image slowly fades. The third day she appears again, and this time Sean's face shines brightly in the place of the missing star. I just sit there and stare at my son's face. The image is breathtaking.*

I had been praying with all my heart to know where my son was. My prayers were answered first with the image of the Pieta, with Jesus healing Sean, and then with the image of Sean as a bright star in Mary's field. I experienced the sense of gratitude and relief that all mothers must feel when a child who has been lost, is suddenly found. Mary understood this.

Most of my grieving was done in the hills across the street from our home. There is a five-mile hike around the rim of the Lafayette reservoir, which I walked daily, alone. It was the time I felt free to cry my heart out because only very rarely did I pass another person. I'd walk and cry. That was my prayer. I asked for help, for understanding, and for healing. Usually I'd have some awareness, or feel the presence of God's love, and then I'd go back home and was able to take care of the children or cook dinner or whatever else was on my schedule.

One day the end of my walk came with no relief. I felt no awareness of God's presence and no reason to stop crying. As I walked down the hill toward home, disappointed that my pain was still oppressive, I heard Sean's voice. "Mom, I need your help. Please pray for me."

I flew home. My heart sang. Sean was alive. My son, who had died, was alive. The phrase, "once a mother always a mother," came to life in my heart.

He had asked for my help, my prayers, and all along I was seeking help for myself. I felt for a second the shame that comes with discovering one's ignorance and self-centeredness, but that lasted only a second. Most of all I was ecstatic, and I never grieved quite the same way after that.

Suddenly there was no separation between this world and the next, between life and death, or between Sean and me. The saints I had prayed to and who guided me were more available than ever, and I prayed faithfully to them, and to Jesus and Mary, that Sean would have the guidance and support he needed. And I truly believed that he would. I had always prayed for people who had died, but now I understood why.

Sean was on a journey which would eventually lead him to the fullness of God and his place at the "heavenly banquet." I used to believe that when we died we were immediately with God and that was the end of the story. Now I realize that whether we are alive or dead, God is always with us, but our freedom to be with God is often limited. Our fear, self-hatred, shame and guilt, resentment, and all the negative forces within us create barriers which God does not cross unless we ask, or someone intervenes and asks for us. The power of intercessory prayer for those who have died is far beyond what we can imagine. Many people, whether alive or dead, are not able to pray for themselves, and God relies on us to pray for them because it is God's desire, and our deepest, yet often unacknowledged, longing to be in the fullness of God's love.

With this awareness, which I learned from Sean, I felt an intimate relationship to those in the Spirit world—something I had previously known only intellectually. Now I knew for sure that nothing could separate me from those I love. Even if they die or turn away from me, there is always a spiritual connection between us because we have loved one another. But I also knew that to experience that love and connection, I would have to consciously choose to be in the present moment with whatever I was experiencing, trusting the gift of the present moment, and above all else, God's love. I could no longer dwell in the past nor could I hold onto the painful memories or the negative emotions (fear, self-hatred, shame and guilt, resentment, etc.). I learned to take time to go into those memories, with God as my companion so that I would not get lost in the story. I prayed for help to heal the pain and release any negative emotions that remained. The more I healed the past, the more I could live in the present and bring into that moment the wisdom, the compassion and the gratitude that emerged as a result of healing my past. My faith in God's love, which resided in the depths of my being, assured me that whatever was happening or whatever had happened was bringing me ever more deeply into the fullness of God's love.

There was indeed no separation, only changes in form. I wanted to find the lady who was depressed because of her son's death and tell her, "Its okay. He's alive and he needs your love, your encouragement, now, as he did before." I wished she could see that if she focused on her son's needs as well as her own pain, she would be better able to handle the pain, and help her son as well. The veil that St. John of the Cross talked about was becoming less and less of a barrier.

I know that it was my faith that held me during the days and weeks after Sean's death. I also know that the Spirit of Love presented herself, not only in my prayer times at home, but in the trees and the wild flowers, water and animals, as I walked in nature.

There is something that happens to me—and I suspect it is fairly universal—when I am in nature, and that something is often ecstatic. I have a sense as well that as I walk, my breathing is enhanced. And the more deeply I breathe in the air—the Spirit—the more the attributes and the gifts of the Spirit (wisdom, joy, love, freedom, peace, and so on) are available. I have heard that depressed people don't breathe deeply. I think this is true, because even now when I am deeply upset or sad, I'll go out and take a walk. At the end of the walk, I am always thankful for the effort, because my spirit is uplifted, and the joy, and my breath have returned.

During this time of grieving for Sean, I had many visions, and some were of Sean and Maggie. One of my favorite visions happened while I was having a facial with a lovely cosmetologist I had come to know. Reena finished the facial and wanted to apply some makeup. It felt playful. She told me to close my eyes so she could put on mascara. I told her I didn't really like mascara because sometimes I cried, and then my eyes would be smeared with black. She convinced me to let her apply it anyway. As I sat there staring at the wall and squinting, she blackened my eyelashes. And then I saw Sean and Maggie:

> *Maggie and Sean stand in front of me holding hands. "We came to tell you that we love you and want you to know that we are sorry our deaths have caused you pain. We want you to know that we did not intend the pain, but that it was just time for us to leave. We are proud of you...you are doing really well...and we will stay with you until you finish."*

And then they left! Well, as you might imagine, my teary eyes were smeared with black. Reena looked at me quizzically. I could hardly speak. The impact of this was profound for her then, as I explained the vision, but became even more so a few months later, when her only son was killed in a car crash.

I didn't know what the children meant by "until you finish," but I wonder if they meant my death. I feel their presence often, but I also feel the presence of many of my spirit friends, my parents and grandparents and other family members, and the saints I have come to know. My mother's readings, and then the death of my children, helped me open the door to the world of Spirit, and, because of that, I have helped others do the same.

Sean also came in a dream a few days after his funeral Mass. My husband and I were on the Mendocino coast for the weekend. We thought that if we went away to a place we loved, we would feel happy, but the grief dominated most every moment. And then the dream came:

> *Sean appears at a campground on the Sonoma coast where the Russian River comes into the ocean. He stands in the*

parking lot with a baseball cap on his head, the river behind
him. There is a brilliant, star-like diamond over his head,
and the light from it casts shimmering light beams over his
whole body. I reach for him, and he begins to leave. He is
elusive. I reach again, and he says, "No, Mom, I have to go
now. It's time."

The dream was a treasure because I know it was Sean's way of crossing through the veil to let me know he was okay—more than okay, he was great! Clearly, he was on his journey, and he was in the light. My prayers for him continue. It is an arduous journey, requiring courage and faith, even though he is "on the other side." Like his note, the dream let me know he made a choice, that I don't have to understand, nor do I have to judge. I simply have to be aware and pray.

When we returned from Mendocino, we picked the children up at a friend's home where they had stayed that weekend. Annie came running up the stairs from the playroom calling, "Mommy, Mommy. I had a dream about Sean." She described the exact dream that I had had. She cried, "Mom it was so real. I thought it really was Sean, that he had come home."

"It was real, Annie," I said softly. "Sean did come home to see you."

I am struck by the fact that it was a seven-year-old who also received the dream. I wonder if it was because she was so innocent and open to her brother's spirit coming to her. She hadn't yet been taught to fear that world. Today, I continue to be moved by the mystery of life and death. I smile deeply within as I reflect on these instances where Spirit breaks through. Gratitude wells up as I acknowledge how much presence and love surrounds me when I am free to receive it. I am at the edge of knowing that the experience I am having in the moment, no matter what it is, has the potential to bring me to our divine Mother/Father, to truth, to the awareness of the perfection of it all, and to peace, if I am willing to surrender my fear and be taken. This is a truth that is becoming fundamental to my understanding of life.

We lived in the rental home for six months. It really was a cold, strange place, but we stayed there because it was so close to home. I would never again stay in a place like that, but in 1981 I was not very discerning. My mother told me that if there were spirits present that I was to encourage them to go to the light. She said there was nothing to fear. I believed her. But now, I believe differently. The spirits, like all of us, are trying to go to the light, but there may be something to fear. The awareness that I have today is as a result of becoming more and more spiritually attuned and developing the gift of discerning spirits. Now I know that places can be inhabited by spirits that are malevolent, and those spirits can have very serious, negative effects on the people who live in their midst. Those spirits can be embodied in people or in property. The owner of the rental house was an angry man. I could see that on his face. He seemed mean, and he frightened me. I wondered if something awful had happened in his house or if the man's anger opened a doorway to evil spirits within himself... some of which he left in the house.

We moved back into our own home in January of 1982. Our newly rebuilt home was beautiful, light and airy, and we were all happy to be back, but there was a gnawing emptiness. As we settled in, we were forced to remember that we would never be a part of one of Sean's jokes or hear his laugh again.

I met the woman who had invited me to the bereavement meeting once again. It was in the grocery store. She wore black. The circles under her eyes were huge. She was living alone, because her other children and her husband had moved away. As I listened to her, I realized that she could not hear the few words I spoke. She lived closed off in her dark lonely world. She was lost. Her grief became her life, and I wondered later if it eventually killed her. As I witnessed this woman from the bereavement group slip down into the darkness due to her grief over her son's death, I watched myself awaken. I felt a deep sadness that I could not help her. She died emotionally, and I suspect not long after, she died physically. I wondered what made the difference in her grieving and my own. The only thing I could think of was faith, the faith my parents instilled in me, the faith that was deepened in all the years of Catholic education, and the faith that was blossoming exponentially in graduate school. This is a faith that has grown mysteriously by grace throughout my life, embracing me just as those granite boulders hold the old oak tree in the forest near our home. It is this faith that assures me that I am in relationship with a Mother/Father God who loves me more than I could ever imagine...a faith that tells me that God's absolute generosity will turn every one of my experiences into wisdom and bring me into God's heart, because I have received the grace to surrender and open my heart to Truth. I live with a deep knowing that comes through faith that everything is

God's gift, nothing is owed to me or owned by me, and with that, a growing sense of gratitude, regardless of the situation at hand. There was within this woman dressed in black, along with her deep grief and pain, a belief that she was entitled to have her son for as long as she lived. She was unable to free herself from her anger because of the loss of her son, and it led her from sadness and anger to depression and then to despair. We are enculturated to believe that we are "entitled" to have the life we choose, as though we own and are in control of everything in our possession, including ourselves, our health and well-being, and that of our loved ones. But that is not the truth. The feeling of entitlement leads to a haughtiness and pride when things go our way, and anger, depression, and despair when they do not.

It wasn't the rules of the church or society, the threats of Hell or the promise of Heaven; it wasn't the idea of being good or bad or the kind, or not so kind, things that people said or did that made the difference. Though some of those things helped, while others hurt. Those things do not support or lift up or heal anyone. For me, it was the awareness that I am God's daughter, loved totally as I am, that God longs for me to know this love, surrender to it and be nurtured by it. That is what made the difference in me. It is the awareness that no matter what happens, if I am willing to feel into the depths of my being, any experience can wake me up and take me more fully into love. It is having the freedom to stretch out my arms and open my heart to the heavens for healing, and know without a doubt that my prayers will be answered...that perhaps are already answered. My friend kept her pain locked in her heart as though it was all she had left of her son, and it took her life.

The Jesus who held and loved and healed Sean after his death had died too. The blood of Jesus was sacrificed, they told us in school, so that we could live. I didn't understand all of this then; it was still a mystery. Now I understand that my own son's blood was calling me to life. And though I have some words for it now, it is still mysterious. But I know it is true.

Sean's surprises never ended, even after his death. He has managed to this day to keep me on my toes. When Katie was graduating from New York University with honors and a masters of science in nutrition; and Annie was graduating from Mills College with her B.A. in Art; and Mark was turning thirty—all the same summer—there were parties galore.

In the midst of these celebrations, Sean's spirit awoke me one night and said, "You have to have a celebration for me too, because I graduated as well. I've learned how to love." I could sense his brilliance, and knew it was true. His wild spirit, his passionate and adventurous being, was becoming free.

I celebrated Sean's freedom alone. I wish now I had invited Sean's sisters and brother to join me, but I was fearful of their ridicule. I am sorry that I didn't trust them more and at least give them an opportunity to celebrate their brother's graduation. I didn't have the necessary freedom at that time.

I created an altar with a beautiful white silk scarf, a candle, and some flowers. I placed Sean's picture carefully in the center. Once I was seated and quiet, I began to speak to Sean, telling him how proud and happy I was of his accomplishment. I felt his presence with a warmth in my heart, and, even though I was crying, I began to sing. I sang to him with words that I made up, and as I sang I could feel my heart open even more. During the celebration, which was more prayer than party except for a split of champagne, I had the sense that Sean had grown beyond believing others' negative judgments about him. He had been deeply touched by God's acceptance and unconditional love, and he was indeed, free. The song that I had made up eventually brought me to my feet, and I danced in celebration of my son's freedom to love himself ñ my son who left this world because he didn't have the maturity or tools or defenses to deal with the world's harshness. Now he was living in the midst of joy and love, and in that moment, so was I. ✳

Reflection Questions

Children are the most beautiful gifts and provide the most extraordinary challenges to us. I often say to parents who are in pain that no one can hurt us as parents like our children can. They can hurt us with words and actions, with their choices or lack of choices, and with their criticisms and impatience. And no one can bring the kind of joy that comes from one's children when they express their love and appreciation of us. Children are amazing teachers for us. I think this is because we love them so much that we will do almost anything to have loving relationships with them. The greatest thing they have to teach us is that they have their own lives, and we must learn to let go. It takes a great deal of time and maturing to remain at peace and to love our children, regardless of how they are living their lives or responding to us as their parents.

> *If you have children, how have you felt hurt by their words, actions, or choices? Have you been able to heal your pain and fully engage with your children again?*

> *If you do not have children, have you experienced hurt or pain with the children of your siblings or friends? Have you been able to heal your pain and fully engage with the children again?*

Some couples grieve the death of a child while others desperately want to conceive a child and, for whatever reason, they can't. The pain for these couples can be excruciating and continues until they realize they must live without the child that they long for. There are others who have deeply held desires as well... desires for a loving spouse, a good job, or a healthy body, and find pain in their unmet desires.

> *If you want to conceive a child or if there is something important to you that you deeply desire, how do you cope with the feelings of disappointment of unmet longings?*

Sometimes things happen in our lives that appear utterly incomprehensible and absolutely impossible to overcome. We cannot imagine being normal or happy ever again and yet as time passes, the pain eases and we begin to heal. We don't ever forget the loss or the pain, but we learn to be happy again in spite of it.

> *What in your life has caused you to feel as though you could never be happy again?*

> *Have you overcome that feeling?*

11

Birthing a Spiritual Community

The days went by. The visions continued. And my daily life returned to normal. I never knew when I'd burst into tears, but the tears were always sweet, reminding me of someone I loved whom I never, ever wanted to forget.

Less than three weeks after Sean's death, I had an appointment, which I had scheduled back in May, to take my graduate exams. I had decided to formalize my studies and become a masters student at the Graduate Theological Union, and exams were a requirement. It is a mystery to me how I passed those exams, but I did. It's even a mystery how I could sit there for four hours and concentrate on the questions. I don't think I really did concentrate, nor do I believe I was just lucky. I believe I had help from the other side!

Because of the depth of my grief, the only class I could take in the fall was a class on prayer taught by Dan O'Hanlon, a Jesuit priest who profoundly affected my life. Although he has since died, I feel him present at times, and I thank God for his life as he journeys more and more deeply into God's Divine Presence.

Each week after class I would hand in my journal with reflections on the particular prayer form we were learning. His comments were a gift, as was his class. But his presence and willingness to be authentic were the most special blessings. His expansiveness opened me to a wide range of possibilities regarding prayer and images of God.

He was involved in communication between theologians from the East and West at a time when this wasn't widely accepted. When I told Dan that my current prayer was nothing but tears, he responded that under the tears I would find peace, and it was true. He reminded me that in the depths of my grief, God's presence and God's peace would never leave me, that I would find God loving me in the depths of pain—if I had the courage to go there. Like the new moon, though it is dark, the light is always there, though obscured by a dark shadow.

It was faith that held me, and it was growing stronger. I could believe that after the darkness receded, I would again see the light. In the book, Jesus before Christianity, Albert Nolan writes, "Faith is not taught. It's caught." I was catching Dan's faith.

The grace made possible by my *Dark Experience of Nothingness* once again deepened as I realized that although the pain I was in was excruciating, it was nothing like those moments of darkness when nothing at all existed or had ever existed. I might not have Sean, but I had love, and I had the rest of my family. I had life.

Finding Peace

In September, a month after Sean's death, women began gathering on Wednesday mornings, this time at our rented house. This gathering had started the previous spring after three women in one week had asked me the very same question, "How do you find peace when life is filled with turmoil and suffering?" I invited the women to join me to talk about our spiritual journeys and pray together, never dreaming that my life would soon be in turmoil and my peacefulness shattered. Women originally met for three months, and in June we had decided to take a summer break because the car pools and summer events with our children left little free time. When we met again that September, after Sean's death, the question they had originally asked was now my question: How was *I* finding peace in the midst of *my* suffering? The group was no longer four. The room was overflowing. Each Wednesday I presented the material on prayer that I had learned the day before in Dan O'Hanlon's class on prayer. He became the godfather of our group.

I continued to teach everything I was learning, and I continued to search for peace under the tears. What I didn't know at the time was that the tears were creating a route into my depths, and that's where I eventually found my spirit.

All I knew at the time was that my heart was torn open and the sadness was almost overwhelming at times. I slept more than usual and often went to my room to be alone with Sean's spirit and with God in my sadness. Our first Christmas was almost unbearable, as were all holidays that first year. It was all I could do to buy and decorate a tree. I have no recollection of presents that year, except the gift of my sister, Nina and her husband, Mark, who came to be with us. They were a godsend for us, but I knew it was hard for them to be in the midst of so much sorrow.

But there were significant moments that Christmas, moments in which the gentle rains and the winds were cleansing my inner world and preparing me to see God more clearly than ever before. One morning I was praying, and tears filled my eyes. "How much I miss you, Sean," I said, and then heard:

> Mom, don't cry for me—this is going to be the best Christmas ever. For heaven is filled with light and love. There is peace beyond all your dreams; joy that is endless and filled with song. There is music and there is dancing—everyone is free and warm and loving. . . . Mom, don't cry for me. Rather let your heart fill with joy for I am loved fully and

163

*know the hope for which I so longed. Mom, I am light and
will shine for you and for all who watch . . . look often and
see my star; listen and I shall guide all of you to a deeper
place of love and of light. I love you all and am with you always. Be open. Have no fears and teach all who come, the
love of Jesus.*

No one really understood what was happening within me, that in the
midst of the pain I was experiencing the world of spirit and the love of
God in the most profound and ecstatic ways.

I was painfully aware that I did not care what I wore or how I
looked. I was just glad that I got dressed each day. I understood why older
women, often widows of European descent, wore black. It reflected the
colorlessness of a grieving heart. As the months passed I began to heal.

Dreams

While voices and visions guide me, dreams are significant for me as well. I
record my dreams every morning and use them as a way to become more
aware of ways in which Spirit is guiding me. The dream that follows was especially meaningful because it is a dream in which I experienced Jesus coming to me at a time in my life that I really needed His help. The morning I
awoke from this dream I was so moved that I wept with joy. I felt so touched
and so blessed. I didn't really understand what the dream meant, but I did-
n't need to—the experience of Jesus coming to me was enough of a gift:

*I am in church. I am seated on the left side, in the middle of
the church, in the middle of the pew. Jesus is on the altar. He
is brilliant and dressed in white. He holds the cup elevated
above his head, and although I have a sense that in the silence he is in communion with the Holy Spirit, his eyes are
locked with mine. I am entranced.*

*Then Jesus comes down the aisle toward me, his eyes still
fixed on me. He stops at my pew. Silently he passes the cup*

down the aisle, indicating with his hand that it is for me. I
take a sip and pass it back. He looks into the cup and passes
it back with one word, "Drink." I do so and pass it back. A
third time he sends the cup back to me, and this time he
says, "Drink it all. It is all for you." I drink every bit and
send it back to him.

Throughout the years I have held this dream close to my heart. The symbolism has many layers, some of which I will understand only as time goes on, but the one symbol and interpretation I most often focus on now is the cup and its significance.

The cup represents many things, but here it is symbolic of the feminine, both in its womblike shape and its contents—the blood which Jesus sheds that we might have new life. Women also shed blood, and our blood along with its cup, the womb, has the capacity to bring forth new life. Jesus is honoring my feminine power at a time when I am growing disheartened by the continued oppression of women in the world and in the Roman Catholic Church. Jesus insists three times that I take seriously the gift of my womanhood and live it as fully as possible. It also represents the suffering I experienced with the deaths of two children and the collapse of my marriage six years after Sean's death and the challenge I am given as I struggle with injustices toward women. In particular, it represents my own struggle with that which is forbidden within the church... the call of women to ordained priesthood, most especially the call to preach the word of God to the community at a Eucharistic liturgy. The cup also represents the pain of being told that I am not even able to speak aloud my inner calling. My heart is soothed by the words of St. Francis of Assisi, "Preach the Gospel at all times and when necessary use words." I pray often to preach and to minister to others by the way I live because that is all I have to give. If I cannot consecrate the bread and wine, then I can pray to become that which I long to consecrate and in that way feed the people who are hungering. I pray continuously that all people in the Church, including the hierarchy, will fully awaken and celebrate the awareness that women are called by the Holy Spirit to ordained ministry. It was no accident that Jesus Christ chose Mary Magdalene to be the first to preach the Good News. I pray for this not only for the Catholic Church, but I pray as well knowing that the Church's oppression of women dramatically impacts the continued oppression of women throughout the world. The cup that Jesus offers is my cup, which I drink in memory of Jesus. If I truly receive the cup that is offered, I will suffer with him and with the world.

In the Gospel of Matthew, Jesus asks the sons of Zebedee, "Can you drink the chalice that I am going to drink?" I think Jesus is saying, "Can you accept the suffering that comes your way, or will you live in resentment, wishing your life were different?" Sometimes I ask Jesus in prayer, "Did you come to me in the dream to encourage me to continue to accept my life as it is? Did you come to help me see that suffering often comes unexpectedly and to be prepared because we never know the hour or the day? Did you come to me imploring me to accept the things I cannot change and do my very best to change those injustices which I can? I do know that you invite me, Jesus, to be aware of certain injustices so that I can hold them in my heart with you... a privilege and an honor." The cup is offered that I might have the courage to suffer fully, rise and be filled with the Spirit of Christ. I receive the gift of living beyond the suffering because Jesus has shown me the way.

But with this gift comes the command to love freely and to forgive those who have caused harm and perhaps continue to do so. This loving and forgiving of those whom I perceive to be my "enemies" has been tremendously challenging, and the freedom to do so, to love as I am loved, is a gift which always emerges out of prayer and God's grace. There have been times that I have had a desire or made a decision to be forgiving. I have prayed continuously for the freedom to forgive and have even thought it was done, but the gift is never complete until I feel the forgiveness flowing from my heart. I find that the deepest forgiveness I always need is to forgive myself for withholding my love from others when my conditions for deserving love are not met. At the same time that I have withheld my love, I have expected God to love me without any conditions. I feel sad for being so ignorant and proud. Sometimes I have waited a long time for the gift of forgiveness to come from my heart and I have experienced the pain as well as the humility of having to wait. The growth that has taken place in the waiting has been the key to opening my heart. The key or teaching is as much a gift as the opening of my heart. Discerning that I need to forgive myself for being weighed down with resentment or anger by someone's perceived or real offense makes me aware that I have taken the other's action as personal and used it to darken and depress me, when in fact it was part of the other person's journey. We simply met along the path, and so I have the opportunity to learn something important for my awakening. Each of us is on a journey of awakening. We cross paths and are catalysts for each other's growth but if there is growth, it is because we ask to grow.

While on my daily walk in the beauty of nature recently, I found myself reflecting on my life. As I did so, I could see how God has used all the events of my life to bring me to joy. One of my special spiritual friends, Padre Pio, a recent saint whose sanctuary I visited in Italy, said this quite well. "Those who suffer in love will lead a very privileged life."

Encountering our teachers is often very stressful, and we struggle until we remember to ask the question, "What am I to learn now?" I encountered many teachers in our prayer circle, which was fast expanding into a spirituality center that would eventually be called La Casa de la Luz. One in particular stands out to me. She was a bright and energetic woman who worked alongside me as a secretary and began using her skills to help the emerging center become more visible in the community. Everything seemed to be going along well, until one day at a meeting she exploded in a rage directed at me and after many accusations and insults, she stormed out of the meeting. I was stunned and silent, as were the other people at the meeting. I took seriously everything she said. A few days later, after reflecting on what she had said about me, with my spiritual director and in prayer, I tried to talk with her. She remained angry and refused. I realized that my job was to step aside and let her rage and accusations pass me by. I held her in love, from a distance, as she cleaned out her desk and left the center. With my history of feeling guilty when things went wrong, or in the face of another's anger directed at me, I had to struggle with the temptation to take on her projections.

When my heart is open and the grace is given to love and to forgive, I feel light and free and joyful—and I know I have risen. It is Jesus who teaches this as He hangs in agony, taking in the sins of His crucifiers but not taking them on. Their cruelty did not take away His love, but rather, His love became transforming grace. This is what I think about when I hear it said that, "Jesus takes away the sins of the world." He takes them in, holds them, and His love offers the possibility of transformation. In my willingness to take "in" but not "on" my secretary's rage, I received the cup that Jesus offers in that moment. It was a great learning for me, and I was grateful for the opportunity. I send gratitude to this woman in prayer, and hope she too has been blessed by this happening.

Almost by surprise, I found myself admiring the flowers in the garden and wearing colorful clothes again. It was a sign that the wounds from the death of my son were healing. Once again I was spontaneously singing songs of God's presence and love. I was receiving and accepting invitations to give talks at the Graduate Theological Union, where I was studying, and spiritual direction became my most significant ministry.

The Expansion of Spiritual Direction

The Christology class I took in the spring of 1981, a few months before Sean's death, was an awakening. Kenan Osborne, a bright and humorous Franciscan priest with a down-to-earth personality, explained High Christology (a Jesus who was born with the Wisdom of God) and Low Christology (a Jesus who grew in wisdom). He invited us to reflect on the ways we lived our theology: "If you can't do spiritual direction at the Greyhound bus station, you probably aren't really doing spiritual direction."

I was already doing spiritual direction, so his "out of the blue" comment struck a deep chord within me. It was an invitation to live my theology wherever I was, in whatever way seemed appropriate. Even a smile might be enough. And my faith was growing, as the awareness of the light within me (the presence of the Holy Spirit) deepened.

Clearly my mother's faith had been fundamental to my awakening to the presence of the Holy Spirit—which had been happening since I was a child. But now, as an adult studying theology, I was growing in the knowledge necessary to articulate my faith. I was finally gaining the language that enabled me to express my religious experience, and I was developing the background and affirmation I needed to validate that experience.

On August 3, the day before Sean died, I had received a letter from Rich Byrne, a Paulist priest who had been my spiritual direction professor, asking me to be a spiritual director for the School of Applied Theology, a sabbatical program for people in ministry: sisters, brothers, priests, and lay people. I was surprised and deeply touched. But with Sean's death and my grief, I seriously doubted my ability to guide others. It never occurred to me that Rich would encourage me otherwise, but he did.

My spiritual director had moved back east the week before Sean's death. I asked Rich if he would be my new spiritual director. After taking my request to prayer, he accepted, but with some trepidation; perhaps it was my grief that made him hesitate. For the next year, I shared my pain, my poetry, my art, and my questions. Rich listened with the openness and love that I so needed at that time in my life. There was a freedom about him that invited me to express myself, without needing to understand or judge the experiences I was having.

At first it was a strange experience to have a new spiritual director. I missed working with my first spiritual director, and I was happy when I could occasionally speak with him by phone—like the day I told him about Sean's death. He spoke to me with such kindness and warmth that I could feel my heart softening. He encouraged me to remember often that God was present and loving all of us. He also said he'd be praying for us. To this day, he celebrates Mass for us on the anniversary of Maggie's death and on the anniversary of Sean's death. Sometimes I forget to keep my promise to pray for people. He never has forgotten this promise he made to me.

In September, a month after Sean's death, with Rich's encouragement, I accepted the invitation to be a spiritual director for the School of Applied Theology. I had only been seeing people for spiritual direction for about a year, and now I was being invited to be a spiritual director for sabbatical students, most of whom were priests, sisters, and brothers. I stood before forty women and men, telling them who I was, while wondering why they would choose me when there were such prayerful, educated, experienced spiritual directors available who were sisters, brothers, or priests. A surprise was in store for me.

Not only did several of the sabbatical students ask me to be their spiritual director, but one of the professors, a priest, asked me to be his as well. I really don't know what attracted them, but I can't help wonder if my heart was so broken open that the Spirit shone through.

The ministry of spiritual direction was, and continues to be, an enormous grace. As I listen to the stories of the people who come to me, I am filled with love and compassion. I find myself saying the things that are most important for me to remember.

It's an enormous blessing to become aware of God's presence with an individual who is struggling through purification, shame, fear, or any of the challenging, or even joyful, moments on the spiritual journey. Both the spiritual director and the person being directed are blessed in this process. It always seemed that whatever breakthrough I had experienced in my own prayer life, or reading, or in spiritual direction, was exactly what I needed for the next person with whom I'd be doing spiritual direction.

Whatever ministry I am involved with continues to be my teacher. I receive what the Spirit is teaching me, and then I offer what I have learned to another person who, like me, is on an amazing journey. ✴

Reflection Questions

Creativity is God's gift emerging from within us and becoming manifest in the world. When our hearts are broken open through a significant loss, our creative gifts have an opportunity to burst forth. As our hearts heal, we begin to recognize a new movement coming from within us, a birthing of our creativity.

What are your losses?

As you reflect on your losses, can you name creative gifts that emerged as you healed?

Have your dreams been important to you? Is there a specific dream that you might like to revisit and reflect upon to deepen your awareness of who you are?

There are so many ways for us to become self-aware and each awareness invites greater freedom to love and be loved... and therefore, more joy. Our work is to discover the ways to this awareness which work for us. Prayer is primary for me, but sometimes I am so filled with emotion that the only way I can pray is actively... like walking or drawing, journaling or dancing. I learned to be very free with my prayer and to vary it. It is important for those of you who pray frequently and deeply, to have spiritual direction, to talk over your prayer, for support, and to discern how it is impacting your life. Be with God as beloved in whatever way best meets your needs. I liken my relationship with God to my relationship with my husband. If I find out that my husband likes to sit with me on the porch swing, I would not assume that he always or only wants to be with me in that way. It is like that with God—a real live relationship!

Being in an honest and intimate relationship with God guarantees self-awareness, and ultimately, self-awareness guarantees joy.

12

Ending My Marriage

By 1983 I had acquired enough credits to graduate, and so I started writing my thesis. I wrote the draft of my thesis in a cabin on the Sonora Pass, very near where I live and write today, almost twenty-five years later. While my children and husband skied, I wrote. It was an ecstatic experience to spend days reflecting and writing about my faith journey, in light of my course work and the books that had influenced me. Upon presenting this draft to my thesis director, he sent me to the library to look at what others had written, convinced that I could not write about my personal journey and expect to graduate. I persisted, and with the gracious help of a professor, Clare Fischer, at the Starr King School of Ministry, I finally wrote the thesis and entitled it "Through Journey to Mission."

When Clare first read the thesis, she looked at me warmly and said, "You've written a book. We have to turn it into a thesis, and then you'll have to turn it back into a book." I think the book you are now reading is what Clare was suggesting.

My thesis was accepted, and in May of 1984 I graduated with a Master's in Systematic Theology. La Casa, the spirituality center, was growing and I was more involved in teaching and in doing spiritual direction. I was feeling both blessed and challenged by my ministry. Immediately following my graduation, I was walking up the street towards the Jesuit School of Theology. Frank, one of my Jesuit professors and my spiritual director from 1982-1993, passed by and stopped.

"Congratulations," he said. "How does it feel to be a theologian?" Then he smiled and continued on his way.

I stood there dumbfounded. I had never thought of myself in this way, and wondered what it meant.

I understood that the gift of my studies was my ability to step outside of my enculturated beliefs and learn to think for myself, to reflect on my experience of God, and to speak from my own heart. I learned to trust the voice of the Spirit who guided my life so faithfully, and to discern those voices that spoke falsely. No, I was not, nor would I ever be, a theologian as normally defined, but I knew God was in my heart, and I could speak what I heard and knew from within. One day, I came across a quote from Evagrius Ponticus, a 4th century Christian monk and ascetic who wrote, "A theologian is one who prays, and one who prays is a theologian".

A Beginning and an End

I had graduated, and I was thankful and proud. The women and men in the La Casa community prepared a celebration at my home in Lafayette. The house was filled with Lafayette and La Casa friends and school friends and professors. My children and husband had come to my graduation. I felt the children's excitement. I think they were proud of me. My husband acknowledged my accomplishments with a diamond and ruby ring, which was also a birthday and anniversary present. It was beautiful, and I was delighted. We were still pretending that the marriage was fine; little was said about the disharmony between us. We had been married for twenty years.

He and I had first met during our freshman year in college and had fallen in love on New Year's Eve. We dated for five years. Even though our dating experience was fraught with struggles, I remained in the relationship and in love. At that time I lacked self-esteem and so wanted to be married to him that I refused to see what was real. Even so, I have never once believed that it was it a mistake that we were married. Without that marriage I certainly would not have my children, the most precious—and challenging—of my gifts. And without that marriage I probably would not have learned what I most needed to learn—how to find my spirit and free myself. I believe that all of the people who come into my life are teachers, and my first husband was certainly one of my most significant teachers. I will always be grateful to him for the learning, but, most of all, I will love him forever for the children we were privileged to bring into the world together. Our story is one of joy and sorrow, not unlike most stories.

On Christmas Eve, 1963, alone with him in my parents' den, I opened a small box. Inside I saw a pair of gloves with a diamond ring sparkling on one of the fingers, I heard his question, "Will you marry me?" The "yes" came easily, since I had often dreamed of this moment.

Before we left the den to tell the family, who were gathered in the living room, he took me over to the light to show me the flaw in the diamond. I didn't want to see it. I never wanted to see the flaw.

Our first argument was just after our wedding ceremony as we stood in the church vestibule waiting for the guests to pass by and toss the rice.

"I haven't packed my suitcase for the honeymoon, so you go on to the reception," he said blithely, "and I'll come along later."

I did not take this well. I had a knot in my stomach and I could feel tears welling up. The dream I held as a bride was being threatened. I kept my composure outwardly, for the folks gathered around, and through a smile I spoke softly and clearly but not kindly, "I am NOT walking into our wedding reception alone." I never cried. I kept tears at bay, with the anger.

Still smiling, but feeling terribly hurt and angry on the inside, I went through the tunnel of people, hearing their cheers, arm in arm with my new husband, feeling the rice fall on my veil and shoulders. Then we walked the block and a half to his mother's house, I in my wedding dress and veil, and he in his tux, to pack his suitcase and his "honeymoon business briefcase." With years of learning and some wisdom gained, I now realize that I could have chosen to act differently and actually laughed at the perceived inconvenience. I could even have helped him pack instead of sulking, but I was too stuck in how it "should be" to have had such an insight.

Divorce is an extremely high probability for parents whose children die. I know that the death of my children was a huge contributing factor for us. Recently I have been working as a hospice volunteer with parents who are grieving the loss of a child. As I listen to these parents and hear their grief, I am aware of the depth of their struggle in a new way. I am witnessing the marital problems that arise because of their grief, and I am aware more than ever how deeply the deaths of our children impacted our life together as a married couple. I feel deeply sad about this and would love to help others find a way through the grief with their marriages intact. A child's death creates a very painful, usually unacknowledged, unnoticed projection for the parents. If one parent has feelings such as guilt, shame, or anger about the death of the child, feelings that he or she is not aware are there, then that parent will project those feelings onto the other parent. The unconscious feelings will be seen in the other, not in the self. Even more difficult is the constant reminder of that child's life, simply because of each parent's presence. Since both are in grief, neither can truly bring solace to the other, as he or she has in the past.

But there were other reasons for our difficulties. The most significant was the very painful split I felt between my life as a wife and as a developing spiritual person. I loved and needed both parts of myself, but they didn't fit together for me. My husband remained uninterested in my studies and wouldn't celebrate with me as I discovered and explored my gifts. He once had been my best friend, and the longing I had to share my enthusiasm with him was enormous.

One afternoon a friend and I were walking in the hills. He was also a spiritual director and eventually taught with me at the Institute for Spiritual Direction, a program I created at La Casa. He had a good deal of wisdom and a developed sense of intuition. We were talking about suffering, and I was telling him about the suffering I lived with in my marriage. He asked me why I didn't say something or do something about it, and I responded quite spontaneously, "I don't want to tip the apple cart." He just stared at me in utter disbelief, and then I understood and added, "But there is no apple cart, is there?" Then I wept. These moments of grace were hard because they broke through my pretense.

My first spiritual director had returned to Berkeley briefly to finish his studies. We met at Tilden Park one day and took a walk, the first of many. Now our relationship could be more mutual because he was no longer my spiritual director. He remained a wonderful listener. We talked and listened to each other for hours. Over the years, we became best friends, soul friends. We wrote to each other, and, whenever he came to town, we walked and talked for long periods of time.

Our friendship and our love for one another grew as we shared our spiritual journeys and prayed together. A very significant part of me was being fulfilled in this relationship. I longed for my husband to be the one with whom I shared my heart and soul, but he wasn't. It felt as though I was being torn in two. My heart was divided. The split was sharp-edged and painful.

My friend and I began to co-lead retreats for the people who gathered at the spirituality center for our Wednesday morning prayer. The love I felt in his presence, and in the ministry we developed, deepened my faith that God was present even in the midst of the pain that continued to permeate my life. I have often commented to people who are struggling in their marriages that I believe this is one of the most extreme forms of suffering. I even recall feeling that the death of my marriage was more painful than the deaths of my children. I frequently cried myself to sleep at night and I begged God to guide me and to help me bear the pain.

There were many things occurring in my dream life and my prayer life that pointed toward ending my marriage. I was walking the rim trail one day when I realized I could have forty years of life remaining. At that moment I was aware that forty years were too many to live in such an unhappy relationship. I cried a lot when I was alone. I slept with my husband every night but felt a tremendous loneliness. We tried to make it okay, even to pretend, but I couldn't. It hurt too much. I begged him to go to marriage counseling with me, but he refused. I got on my knees and pleaded, but he brushed me aside with an angry response, "You made this mess. Now you fix it." He was right. I had made a mess. It was the same mess a butterfly makes when it bursts through its cocoon, but his anger was not about that. He saw that we were growing apart and there was nothing he could do to stop it.

Later on he told me, "The problem is that you have changed, and I have not." I was not the woman he married, and I wasn't playing by the unspoken rules we had set up. He was right. I was not the woman he had married. I had changed. He had not. I was more myself than I had ever been. I was growing into my true self, and I was thankful for that, even though it was creating big changes, changes that caused enormous pain for all of us. I was finally taking responsibility for my life and making choices to live the life that was my own, alongside being a wife and mother. I was learning that I wasn't born just to accommodate my husband and his career, which was the traditionally accepted role of an executive's wife at that time. This cultural value was the one with which he had been raised. His mother and father had lived by the rules I was breaking. I was rewriting the rules for myself, and it was hard for all of us.

In prayer one day I felt the call to make a private retreat so that I could reflect quietly on my marriage. I called a retreat house in Carmel and reserved a room for one week. I chose to stay in what had been the gardener's shed, which was small and simple, so simple that I could use only one plug at a time. I could have either heat or a light, but it was quiet and I was alone. Although it was winter, the weather was spectacularly beautiful, and I spent most of my time outdoors. Point Lobos, a beautiful state park was a short walk from the retreat house. In the morning I'd have breakfast and pack my lunch, along with my journal and art materials, and off I'd go. Each day I walked the paths along the ocean and into the woods, often pausing to journal or draw.

And every day whenever I'd approach a cliff, I'd hear a voice within me whisper, "Jump." At the time I was very sad and often crying as I walked, but I wasn't anywhere near being suicidal, so this whispering voice intrigued me. One day I decided to pay attention and jump the only way I knew was safe:

I sit on a log close to the cliff, close my eyes and begin to pray.
Then I imagine myself jumping off the cliff. I begin to float

through the air high above the ocean. It is ecstatic. I travel all
over the world, seeing beautiful colors of sunset and sunrise
and feeling the loving embrace of the world I visit.

Once again I had a vision that I understood only in retrospect years later. I was being shown that I would know how and when to take a leap of faith and that many blessings would follow. As you will see, I actually do travel to many places in the world and have wondrous and fulfilling adventures. I do not really understand the mysteries of visions... images that I see in my imagination such as this one, or in my mind, such as the *Dark Experience of Nothingness,* or those that are real but ethereal, such as the visions of my children or Mary, but I do know that what is revealed to me in visions, voices or dreams has kept me faithful to the path. The feeling of joy and freedom that I experienced in my body as I floated through the air has allowed me the freedom to "jump" in real life, when the time is right.

The answer I needed concerning my marriage came sixteen months later in the winter of 1987 in a spiritual direction session with Frank, who had been my spiritual director for five years. As I talked about the experience of my marriage, the pain and repression I felt, and my retreat experiences, I knew in a graced moment of clarity, that the marriage was over.

"For you to be faithful to God," Frank explained, "you must be faithful to yourself, your true self. You have to commit to becoming the woman God has created you to be. And steer away from anything that takes you away from the truth... even if it means leaving your marriage. You have worked hard to reconcile the differences with your husband and done all you could do to save the marriage. Now you must save yourself."

I left the spiritual direction room and walked to my car. I was shaking. By the time I began to drive, I was sobbing.

"What will I do," I screamed angrily at God, "if I have to leave my marriage?" The answer came immediately: *You will open a house for women in transition.* I knew it was true. It was the voice that I had heard many times before. I had no idea how it would come about, but I knew it would.

A few days later, I awakened early one morning to a voice that spoke very clearly. Again, it was the voice I knew so well: *It's time to leave. You don't know the way, but if you take the time to listen, I will guide you.*

This was in March of 1987, a Tuesday morning, the same day of the week that Sean had died, my husband's birthday, that I heard the voice, which had become like a wise and faithful companion, and I knew it was time. I went into the dressing area to tell my husband that I was leaving him, but the words stuck in my throat, and I couldn't talk. I left the room, and after I had dropped Annie off at the bus for school, I experienced a wave of depression. It was as if I had no energy, no spirit. I knew that I had failed to listen and do as I was guided. So that night, I told my husband that our marriage was over. He never said a word. I have often thought that, although it was painful, it was probably the best birthday gift I could ever have given him. It was the truth, and it set us both free. I felt a sense of peace come over me, even though I had no idea what my future life would be. I had no information about the legalities of divorce or the procedure that one follows, nor did I have any idea that I would be entitled to a share in the property we owned or the savings we had accumulated. I just knew it was time to leave.

Changing Relationships

Although the divorce papers were signed almost immediately, we decided to wait until May, when Mark and Katie would be home from college, to tell anyone of the decision to divorce. Annie was at home, and we wanted to keep things as normal as we could so that she wouldn't know about our decision. Although we continued to sleep in the same bed so as not to alert the children, we never again hugged or kissed or shared any sort of intimate word or glance. After twenty-three years of marriage, it was over, just like that. We physically separated in June of 1987 and were formally divorced in August, a year later.

When Mark and Katie came home from college, we all sat down together. We told them of our decision. They were shocked. Annie put her hands over her face, as if that would make the terrible news go away. Our difficulties were either not evident to the children or they did not let themselves know that we were so unhappy. After they had discussed the situation with each other, Mark spoke. "Mom and Dad," he said, "We can't tell you what to do. If this is what is right for you, that's your choice;

but we can tell you that you have an obligation to keep things pleasant between you for our sakes. We ask that you maintain a relationship that will make it possible for both of you to be comfortable at our birthdays, holidays, and other family celebrations. Do you agree to that?"

We said "yes." Mark continued, "We ask that you not ever talk about the other to us in a degrading way. Do you agree?"

We said "yes." I was stunned by the clarity and maturity of my son. The girls wept. Mark must have wept silently as well, but he assumed the role of protector and remained outwardly stoic.

The night we told the children about the divorce, I was finally free to sleep in another bedroom. There was no longer a secret to protect. That is when my husband really got, on a gut level, that our marriage was over. He stood at the doorway of the guest room and asked, "Why are you going to sleep here?" I felt the sadness, his and mine, but could only respond with "because our marriage is over." It was after that he agreed to go to counseling. I went with him once, but I knew it was too late. I vividly recall the psychiatrist saying to him regarding our marriage, "When you dam up a river it finds another outlet." I had found another outlet.

A week later, I flew to New York because I wanted to tell my father and my siblings in person. I walked into my dad's home. He was at the stove. Mom was already in a nursing home. Dad turned and gave me a big hug. "What's up?" he said.

"I'm leaving my husband and getting a divorce," I responded calmly, surprised that I had said it without breaking down.

He grabbed me and held me in a bear hug. My father never asked me to explain or to justify my choice. He never needed or wanted to know why. The only thing he said was, "I know you make good choices. Your decision is enough for me, and I support you one hundred percent." He wanted to know what I was planning to do about telling the rest of the family. I told him I wanted to tell them in person. He said, "Okay. I'll drive you." He was seventy-seven years old. We had to go to New Jersey and to Boston.

At one family gathering, my Aunt Deemy, a matriarch in the family and someone who loved me as though I were her daughter, began to scold me with ferocity. She told me I was making a huge mistake, that I was foolish to leave such a wonderfully successful man, and that I was ruining the family. I went numb and shrank into my chair with shame. It was then I knew why Dad had insisted on driving me to these family meetings. There were many times that I felt his protective nature and that day I really needed him. My dad stood up. He was a big man, but this day he was huge. He spoke clearly and with strength. "Don't say another word. She is my daughter. She has made a choice that is good for her, and you and no one else will dispute her choice ever again. Do you hear me?" She said "yes," and that was that. The rest of us sat in awe of the respect that Dad commanded. It was a lesson for me to hear my dad speak his truth, regardless of the outcome.

The grief over the divorce was enough, but the responses of a few family members and friends heightened the pain. I suppose what I was doing frightened people, and it was easier for some to make me wrong than to look honestly at the dissatisfaction in their own lives. This was deeply painful for me.

Some said I was crazy, others that I was committing a sin, ruining my chances for happiness, leaving the best thing that had ever happened to me, and destroying my family and my children's lives. When my brother said that I was ruining my golden years, I couldn't help but imagine myself stricken with depression, illness, emotionally or even physically dead in my golden years if I stayed in the marriage. I sat in prayer for many hours asking God to guide me and to show me the sin, if in fact leaving my husband was sinful, or crazy. As I reflect on this time in my life, I realize that I was being led by faith, and even though I was fearful, I never let the fear lead. I consider this pure grace. Not once have I felt that my choice was anything other than healthy and yet, I continue to pray to be open to seeing the truth about this choice, or any choice I make or have made.

As I have reflected upon the notion of sin I have come to see that the only sin that God cannot forgive is the sin that I deny I have committed, the sin that I keep hidden, even from myself. It is the sin that I have convinced myself didn't really happen or happened for a good reason so is not really a sin or whatever will justify my behavior. I pray daily to see my sinfulness regardless of the shame, guilt or embarrassment it may cause. I pray as well that I will have the humility to apologize and the generosity to make reparation for what I have done.

The more I released my old patterns and habits and emerged as my true self, the more I threatened those around me who weren't ready to do the same. This continues to be true. The divorce escalated the fear in those around me. Some of my friends no longer phoned or wrote. Sometimes even family members questioned my sanity, some to my face, others behind my back. But there were many more who loved and supported me through this painful time. I became more particular about who I chose to spend time with. The people I began to enjoy were those on a spiritual journey—seekers of all kinds. Their paths might be different from mine, but that didn't matter as long as we were free to tell each other the truth about the moment, what we felt or thought or hoped. I wanted to be around people who were willing to enter periods of purification and talk about those periods as gift, who questioned the status quo, who wondered daily what it meant to love, and people who encouraged me look more deeply at who I am and who God is.

My husband had the impression that I was having an affair with my priest friend. Although we were not having an affair in the way most people define the word, there was something happening between us that should have been part of my marriage but wasn't. This was threatening to my husband, rightfully so. Sadly, we never spoke of it. My friend and I never expressed our love for each other physically. There was no sex, but we shared very deeply—emotionally and spiritually. We spent a great deal of time together, walking and talking. He became my new best friend, replacing my husband who was not available for the emotional and spiritual part of life. I cried myself to sleep at night as I felt the pain of what was happening in my life. It was in part because of this friendship that I was able to find and explore being myself. It was a bittersweet gift. It eventually led to finding the courage to leave a relationship that had no room for the me. I was discovering... a me I had buried long ago, out of fear and shame.

I grieved the decision to leave my husband, but I also grieved the fact that as long as my husband believed that the "affair" caused the divorce, he would never have to look at his share of the responsibility. There could be no reconciliation, even for us to be friends. But I left, because I needed to find an accepting and loving environment in which I could be free to bloom. I didn't know how to find this with my husband. I tried, and, sadly, I failed. I felt as though I was suffocating in my own home. I knew that in order to be truly myself, and act in integrity, I would have to leave. That meant destroying a dream and breaking up the family. I grieved that as I had grieved the deaths of the children. It was excruciatingly painful to let go. It also meant that some of my family and friends would feel threatened and become angry with me. Some wouldn't understand. It meant being cut off from people whom I loved very dearly. But I had no choice if I was going to live a healthy life. There were days when I wondered if we would have survived our struggles if we did not also have to reconcile the pain of the deaths of our children. Was it just too much to handle? I have had to remind myself that the deaths of our children contributed to our pain. They did not cause it, however. Our struggles were more than ordinary marital difficulties.

One very special friendship that I struggled with was more difficult for me than any other, and that was my relationship with Mother Mary.

When I first had become engaged, I prayed daily to Mary to help me decide if my choice to be in relationship and to marry the man I loved was wise. My parents and some family members were expressing their doubts in ways that seemed cruel to me. They openly showed their disapproval through long letters, threats, and insults. This had something to do with "first daughter in the family to marry" syndrome, but I wonder now if they were also seeing the flaw that I never wanted to see.

Mary was my salvation back then. I took my pain, fear, and sadness to her in prayer. I wrote in my journal, begging to know what was true—my parents' opinions or my heart's inclination. Mary seemed to say that I must listen to my heart.

When the divorce became final, I was angry at Mary because I thought she had given me the wrong answer. It took months for me to understand that I hadn't made a mistake, and years to sort through the pain, the growth, and the awakening that took place within me because of my relationship with my husband. Mary had said "yes," and I am thankful.

Good-Bye to Home, Hello to Life

The summer of my divorce I found a house to buy, one more fixer-upper. The only flowers in the garden were plastic. It was a mess, but it had potential.

In many ways it was a reflection of how I felt. The house had a large living room for gatherings, a private backyard, and a wonderful view of the Lafayette hills. I hired a contractor and once again created a home, only this time it was for me. I tore down the rotted backyard fence, planted gardens, and cleaned the algae-ridden pool until it sparkled.

The day I moved into the "ugly" new house it had boxes and furniture piled everywhere. A couple of rooms were filled with the previous owner's belongings. My bed was set up, and I had laid out fresh linens and towels, but nothing else seemed very welcoming.

It was Maggie's birthday. My priest friend and I had just finished leading a retreat for a group of about twenty women and men. It had been a joyful week that had ended on the day of the Harmonic Convergence, August 16, 1987. That was the day for people everywhere to pray for peace throughout the world. There was an event in the sky that was exceptional, and the energy on that day was obviously heightened.

I arrived at the house after dark. Annie was staying with a friend—the other two children were away at college—so the house was empty. I was afraid to go in. This would be not only my first night in the house, but it also somehow symbolized the first night in my new life, a life without my husband and the family as I had known it. I was terrified of the loneliness I knew was coming.

I put the key in the door, and pushed it open, expecting a dark empty house. It was dark, because there were no lights on, and there were no people inside, but the house was far from empty. It is difficult to explain the moment. I was certainly not alone, and the darkness was illuminated with joy. I felt a sense of elation as I put my things down. There, in my living room, was a huge gathering of spirit beings, all singing and dancing, and welcoming me home. I had walked in to a surprise party. Although I was surprised, I never doubted the reality of what I was experiencing, nor did I think it was unusual. After all, from the time I was a child, my mother told me about the spirits. I also learned in my Catholic schooling, that holy people who had died were available to help me whenever I asked. These people are called the Communion of Saints. For me this was not an idea but a truth which I had experienced many times. The saints and the angels had become friends. But most importantly, Sean and Maggie had invited me into their world, the world of Spirit, and it had become my second home by then. So although the party was a surprise, it was no surprise to me that those who loved and guided me were there to welcome me home.

Smiling, I made my way up the spiral stairs to my bedroom, washed and dressed for my first night "alone" in my new life. As I fell asleep, I was aware only of the love bursting my heart open. The loneliness I had felt for years was gone. When I woke to sunlight filling the room, I wondered if my fullness and the welcome-home party had been a dream, but it had not. I breathed deep, full breaths. I could feel God's Presence embracing me.

The house I lived in while married sold quickly, and we divided up the furniture and all that we had accumulated. There was sadness, but the numbness was greater. Annie lived with me in the new house and visited her father on some weekends. Mark and Katie went back to college.

I don't really have words to explain what that time was like for me, but I realize now that it takes a tremendous force to break the marriage vow. It had never occurred to me that this was a possibility. Marriage was a sacrament. We were joined by God and could not be separated. In fact, it was a sin to separate. It was unthinkable. Yet, it was happening, and I was following my spirit.

My first Christmas as a divorced woman was very sad. The children went to Mexico with their father and another family. It was a trip we had planned for a long time. My dearest woman friend, Sharon, the one who helped me most after the divorce, was the wife of the couple with whom my children spent Christmas. I don't know who was the saddest, Sharon or I.

Although I had many invitations, I chose to stay at home that Christmas. On Christmas Eve I walked the streets of Berkeley, chatting with the street vendors and the people I met along the way. I bought myself a silver necklace with a cut amethyst in the center. It was my Christmas present.

On Christmas morning I set the table as though it were an altar and celebrated an Agape, a love feast. It is the way a layperson celebrates the love of God and the gift of Jesus with bread and wine. It was one of those illuminating experiences in which I was in two worlds at once. The flow of energy within me, the joy I felt, and the awareness of love was all-consuming. I became the bread, the wine, the celebrant, and there was no separation between me and the Christ whose love I celebrated.

When the children came home, they gave me a gift they had bought in Mexico. I was so excited and so were they, but when I opened the box there was nothing but broken pieces of pottery. We sat there, chins to our chests, teary eyed, and feeling a bit embarrassed. The image on the pottery was an image of a mother—now broken in pieces. When Katie went back to college that semester she made a gift for me in her pottery class. It was a large plate on which she had drawn a beautiful mother and child.

I felt as though I would have died had I not had the freedom to leave my marriage. That level of unhappiness—living daily with unmet longings—was overwhelming. Often, I was unable to focus. My prayer once again became an hour or more of feeling the pain and allowing the tears to flow, only this time I was processing not the physical death of a child but the total death of a marriage. No longer did I have my husband, my "old" best friend, but then I remembered that this "old" best friend had actually left, emotionally, a long time before I left physically. I had never felt more alone. Once again, my heart was broken open, and once again I did not die, but rather grew more into what God had created me to be, unearthing my gifts and finding ways to use them.

One of the predominant post-divorce feelings, after the initial sense of freedom and joy, was loneliness. Whenever it would emerge, I would quickly find a remedy—call a friend, go for a walk or bike ride, begin a new project, or eat (my most destructive remedy). One day, as I was getting dressed, this feeling of loneliness came over me, and it felt as dreadful as it usually did. But this time, by grace alone, I chose to stay with it. I lay down on my bed and let myself feel the loneliness. I actually embraced the loneliness as if it were a friend coming to teach me something. I felt it in my body as though it were a sharp knife piercing my heart, so painful that I might not survive its attack. I stayed with it. It hurt. I prayed for support, for guidance, for truth, and suddenly I felt an opening. It was quite a visceral sensation. In that moment I had an ecstatic experience of God's love and presence embracing me. I wept with joy. Although I thought I had learned to be faithful and present to my emotions, I realized that there were some emotions I unconsciously or semi-consciously held at bay. Loneliness was one of them. I began to pray to be vigilant and vulnerable, to not only recognize but honor my emotions, knowing now more than ever that they always brought me to God. This was a time of revelation for me and a time that I was most grateful for spiritual direction. I had just read Laughter of Aphrodite, Carol Christ's book, and in the flood of emotions that followed, I let myself feel the pain of being excluded by the church hierarchy because I am a woman. I knew God was teaching me and leading me through my emotions, especially the most intense and visceral ones. I call these moments "painful grace".

Not only did I face the loss of my marriage and the break-up of my family, but I was convinced that I would lose my adjunct faculty position at the Jesuit School of Theology, and that my ministry in spiritual direction would end. The church's stance on divorce was clear: it was not acceptable. Since I was asking for a divorce, it seemed as though I would be seen as unworthy to continue in my ministries. Instead, my ministry grew. It was made quite clear to me that if I was faithful to my spirit I would be blessed... and I was very blessed.

I received a call from Sr. Maureen Therese at the School of Applied Theology, the sabbatical program where I did spiritual direction for the students. She asked if I would be open to being a core faculty member. I accepted. My spiritual direction ministry expanded, and La Casa de la Luz came fully into being. This was "the house for women in transition" that I had been called to open. La Casa was a reminder of the voice which made and kept a promise. It had grown into a sacred place where the Spirit danced and sang her way into our hearts. The group that had originally gathered in 1981 to pray together and find peace had continued to grow and eventually become a large spirituality center. Women came from miles away to gather and share their stories. It was women awakening, and some men as well. The first eight years we had met in my home, but when crowds of people were coming every day, the neighbors complained. So we moved into a house in the business district of Lafayette. In 1988 we became a nonprofit educational organization with the help of the pro bono lawyer, Dave Kirkpatrick, who I didn't meet until 1996, but who became my husband in 2000. We called this place La Casa de la Luz (the House of the Light) because of another vision:

> *I see the house with brilliant red, yellow, and orange light*
> *coming from the earth like a fire up through the house. This*
> *fire is one of refinement, destroying only those beliefs that*
> *keep us from experiencing our oneness with God and with*
> *one another.*

> *I also see a brilliant white light coming from the heavens*
> *into the house. The light from the earth is God the Mother,*
> *and the light from the heavens is God the Father.*

I was beginning to experience the partnership of the Divine Masculine and the Divine Feminine within me, and it was emerging in my prayer. I would later look for this in a love relationship and then in marriage. Over the years La Casa grew into a community of several hundred people, offering spiritual direction and a nine-month program which trained spiritual directors which we called The Institute for Spiritual Direction. The center also offered The Institute for Sacred Healing Arts in which healers of many traditions shared their skills to encourage the gifts of, and educate the students enrolled. There were a multitude of classes on spirituality, with guest teachers, lots of social gatherings, the original Wednesday morning prayer circle, and, most essentially, companionship for those on a spiritual journey.

Shortly after my divorce, I began to travel, sometimes to give retreats and sometimes just for the experience of exploring other cultures, mostly indigenous and Third World. I also traveled to Europe as I searched for the Divine Feminine. I traveled extensively, always alone and always discovering more of myself reflected in the people I encountered. This was an ecstatic time in my life. On my return, energized and overflowing with joy, I would call the La Casa community together and share stories about my encounters and adventures.

In the 1990s I became a student of a Native American teacher, and I had the privilege of becoming part of a group that did ceremonies with him. In one of the ceremonies, I had a vision of my Blackfoot great-grand-father and my English great-grandmother which I will describe as best I can. These visions do not represent people we see in the ordinary way.

> *They stand before me. He is dressed in beautiful skins and feathers, is large, strong, and handsome, obviously a very powerful man. My great-grandmother is present in her costume, a dress like the one I wore in the parade. She is sturdy and proud, even as she asks for help. They ask me to forgive them, so they can be free from guilt and shame that resulted from their encounter on the Blackfoot Reservation the night my great-grandmother conceived my grandfather. I do not know whether this encounter was mutual or forced, but he was filled with guilt, and she with shame. I immediately understand that the guilt and shame had traveled down through the family line, and this was an opportunity to help all of us be free.*

When I told my Native American teacher what had happened, his eyes filled with tears. He said he had hoped that by bringing people of the Red race and White race together, deep reconciliation would take place. It had. And I felt tears of gratitude. ✳

Reflection Questions

Marriage is sacred. It is a gift with many aspects. Some say the most important is procreation. Others say it is companionship and love. And still others say it is a sense of belonging to a family. Yet I notice over and over with couples in spiritual direction that marriage has the distinct capacity to bring our dark, oppressive, often unacknowledged selves to the light, for the sole purpose of healing us. We only have to be willing. It is terribly hard on a marriage when one partner is willing and open to do the transformative work of marriage and the other is not. What is even more difficult and terribly sad is when both implicitly agree to go numb to the difficulties. Marriage also has the ability to bring forth our creative, imaginative selves, and to help us unearth our gifts and talents. What a joy and delight it is for one partner to experience his or her beloved coming to life.

> *What experiences do you have of marriage as*
> *transformational?*

When we decide to expand ourselves through using our creative gifts, through education or taking on a significant project, we risk the status quo of our lives because we always change and grow with expansiveness. Our lives will never be the same. They will be more.

> *What projects, creative endeavors, educational*
> *accomplishments, etc. have you courageously chosen*
> *and completed, and how have they changed your life?*

It takes courage to leave any situation that is not life-giving. It feels as though we are taking a flying leap into the unknown, and even though the present situation is destructive, the unknown can be very scary. When any change is well thought out and discerned as wise, the results are always positive, sometimes amazingly so.

> *When have you taken a flying leap, and how has it made*
> *your life fuller?*

Awakenings

13

Embracing Lessons of Motherhood

One of the most cherished gifts of my journey has been the growing awareness that as I learn and become free, my children are naturally affected. I know this to be true when they tell me about their own lives—their struggles and challenges—or the counsel they give to their friends. Sometimes I simply sit and wonder, amazed at their beauty and wisdom. I know I did many things as they were growing up that hurt them. We have had many conversations about those things, and I have had opportunities to apologize. But the awareness that I can be supportive now, or that my continued journey to be free is helping them, elicits deep gratitude in me. In a way it is my penance, not like the penance of my childhood when my knees bled, but the kind of penance in which something

I do that is beneficial wipes away some of the things that I did that were harmful. The gratitude I feel is toward God and my children for giving me this second chance.

Annie

When I first moved into the new house, Annie was the only one of my children living at home. Mark and Katie were very much on their own, although they often came to visit. Annie hated the new house. She said it was the ugliest thing she had ever seen. It was in a state of grave disrepair, and our previous house had been truly beautiful, redesigned after the fire by an architect who was a gifted artist and a friend.

Annie was thirteen at the time of the divorce, a very tender age. It was important to her that her home be as pretty as her friends' homes, and it wasn't. I wished I had kept the family home, but her father insisted we sell it. He was concerned that I couldn't keep it up and the value would depreciate. I didn't have the strength to argue, nor did either of us fully realize what it would have meant to Annie.

Annie's losses were significant that year. Toby, her beloved dog, had been run over and killed while she was away. She had also been away when Sean died. For a long time she feared leaving home, and, if she did go away, she would wonder what awful thing might be happening.

Then in September, Annie learned that Chloe, her closest girl-friend, was moving to Canada to go to a private boarding school near her father. It was too much. But by far the worst of Annie's suffering was the divorce. Not only did the divorce split the family but it sent me spiraling into a "discover yourself" mode. I, like many who repress themselves to fit into a mold, responded to a new-found freedom without appropriate balance. I burst forth with passion and enthusiasm towards my work, my friendships, travel and self-discovery, failing to remember that I had a daughter who needed me full time! In many ways I became like my mother as I ventured off into my own world. That fall, Annie developed what was diagnosed as scoliosis; she was stooped over and in pain.

Fear and Faith

I was in Peru that Christmas with Mark, who was spending his junior year of college studying Spanish language and culture. He and I were staying in a small hotel in Cusco, Peru, when we called my ex-husband so we could wish everyone a Merry Christmas.

He immediately reported news that was shocking. "The doctors told us that Annie doesn't have scoliosis, but that an MRI has revealed a tumor that might be malignant," he said. "They have scheduled her for surgery two weeks after Christmas. The doctors fear that a biopsy would spread cancer cells if the tumor is malignant. She has already given blood and packed her suitcase."

I stayed calm until I hung up the phone, and then my emotions erupted. I sat on the bed, crying uncontrollably and screaming as loud as I have ever screamed "No, no, no, no God, you will not, you will not, take another of my children."

That night, Mark and I sat in a restaurant trying to enjoy the evening while vacillating between shock and terror. At one point Mark suddenly interrupted me with a question. His face stricken with fear, he asked, "Mom, are all your children going to have to die?"

I calmed down. "No, Mark, all my children don't have to die. We have had enough. Annie will be fine."

I flew home and went into seclusion for three days to pray. The thought of an operation frightened me. The doctors said they would remove part of her spine and put her in a body brace for three to six months. Toward the end of my time in seclusion I had a vision of Annie after the operation. She could not walk. I called her father and told him that we had to cancel her surgery. Fortunately, he always trusted my intuition where the children were concerned. He checked with several surgeons, and we decided it would be safe to wait. I took Annie to lots of healers, and people came to the house to lay hands on her. Most of the time she resisted the "healing thing" as she called it. "It's weird, Mom," she would say. The women at La Casa gathered for healing circles, with me in place of Annie, and we prayed together often. One Sunday I asked Annie if she would do a meditation exercise with me and to my surprise she agreed. At thirteen, I am not sure she had any idea what we were about to do together but she trusted that it was for her benefit, so she said "yes." I asked her to lie on her bed. "Close your eyes and relax, breathe in and out slowly," I told her. When she was relaxed, I asked her "Can you visualize the tumor?" She nodded her head. "Tell me what it looks like."

"It is big and sort of round like a golf ball."

"What color is it?"

Without hesitation, Annie answered, "It's gold." That was all I needed to understand what was happening. Gold is precious. The gold tumor was Annie's ticket out of pain. She wanted to die. She had had enough disappointment. Like her brother, life was just too hard. "Annie," I said, "You have a choice. Would you be willing to take another chance on being happy?" I then told her that she had the power within her to shrink that tumor. She understood. To this day I can see her face as she looked at me, teary-eyed, and knowingly she nodded her head yes. I sat in church that day feeling filled with gratitude because I knew Annie had made a decision to let go of the pain and the gold tumor. Little by little, her tumor mysteriously disappeared, and with it went the pain and the stooping posture. The surgeon didn't understand what had happened. He could only say it was a mystery. He never could call it what it was: a miracle. Since then I have never approached healing without remembering Annie and the great lesson I learned: the person being healed is the healer. Annie healed herself. With the help of many people, she was able to bring to consciousness the hidden desire to die and release the gold tumor.

Annie's back is now straight. She walks with poise and graciousness, a very beautiful, intuitive, and creative woman. She is kind and very sweet. Her childhood experience has been her teacher. She shares generously what she has learned. Her wisdom is evident, and she is sought-after because of it.

As the children were growing up, I would share with them the wisdom I was learning. They almost always resisted, but then something would happen, and I would see that they were learning in spite of the resistance. A favorite thing of mine to do was to tell them about projection. When they would talk about "hating" or "admiring" something in another person, I would simply try to explain that their strong emotional response was most likely a sign that the person was reflecting back to them something hidden that they either hated or admired about themselves. It was something that they did not yet know about themselves, something they disowned and saw in another. One day Annie came home and told me a story. "One of my girlfriends at school asked me to help her because she had a really bad dream." She continued, "She had a dream about kissing a girl and wanted to know if that meant she was a lesbian."

Very curious I asked, "So, what did you say to her?"

"I told her that it is not a bad dream nor does it mean you are a lesbian... only that you are loving your feminine self. I told her that the girl in the dream is showing you how beautiful you are and that lots of people show us who we are." And she then asked "What do you think, Mom?" I was speechless. She was 14 years old and her wisdom floored me.

As a small child, Annie insisted on dressing herself. She loved color and every day wore as many plaids and stripes and checks as she could manage to put together. One day her nursery school teacher remarked to me in a snippy sort of voice, "Did you finally take Annie shopping for new clothes?" That was the day I had helped her dress in a party dress with white socks and her patent leather shoes without mixing all the plaids and stripes. Annie wasn't as pleased with her outfit that day, but clearly the teacher liked it.

From the time she was old enough to hold a crayon, Annie drew elegant dresses, mostly wedding and ball gowns. So it is no surprise that her first "real job" was with a top women's clothing designer in New York City. She courageously moved to Paris in March of 2004 in time to celebrate her thirtieth birthday and started her own fashion house. Her designs have been shown in the New York Times, worn in elegant fashion shows, at Emmy Awards, and by beautiful women and brides all over the world.

Annie lets her creativity flow with ease, not only in her exquisite dress designs, but in the way she dresses and the way she paints and decorates her home. She is her own person, and everything that she creates reflects that.

Katie

Of all my children, Katie was the easiest to raise. She followed two loud, rambunctious boys. She became agreeable and helpful. Actually, she was more than that. She was self-sufficient. There were many times that I would look for Katie and find her in her bed, her little red shoes neatly placed on the floor. She would be taking her afternoon nap. This was particularly startling, because getting her brothers to nap was a major event each day.

It wasn't until very recently that I learned the good girl was not quite so good. She revealed, somewhat gleefully, that she had done just as much rebelling in high school as Mark had done. She was smarter, she told me—she never got caught.

In the winter of 1991 when Katie introduced me to her boyfriend, Joe, I was thrilled. I could feel his goodness shining through his handsome, smiling face. And from the very first I quietly hoped they would marry. And in July of 1993 they did! It wasn't long before I began to love Joe, and even though he wasn't my son by birth, I felt as if he were. The feelings frightened and puzzled me until I realized that I hid a dark clump of fear that another of my children would die. And now with Joe came one more child to love and to worry about.

I embraced the fear with love, as I have had to do with all of my children, and prayed to be free, lest it cause havoc within and without. This fear comes and goes, but at least I am aware of it. I have learned to quiet myself with a few conscious deep breaths, as I remember to trust.

The fear rose again with Katie and Joe's first pregnancy, but, when Isabelle was born, there was no room for fear. She radiated love. Katie looked more beautiful than ever as she nursed her baby, and Joe shone as he gently stroked his baby's cheek or Katie's head. As I looked at them, I saw something that is difficult to express. I can only say that they shared one energy, one spirit, one breath. The moment was exquisite.

Two years later when Rosie came along, she moved right into the family and took her place next to Isabelle, as though she had been there all along. And then came Virginia, a little blond-haired, brown-eyed image of her Dad. The Morford girls are my joy and their parents' as well. I watch with awe as Katie and Joe parent together with such love and wisdom and with extraordinary awareness in the moments when they have failed. They are all blessed for they leave no time between impatience and apology. The love goes on. Now with the little girls there are three more to love, and when the worry comes, I breathe deeply and let it go. It's too precious a time to let fear get in the way. I welcome my newest teachers.

I watch Katie as she follows her heart. She has taken huge leaps of faith, leaving well-paying jobs, changing careers, choosing unfamiliar studies for her graduate work, and finally choosing to be married and have a family, even though the pain of death and divorce are part of her history.

Mark

Mark majored in art and philosophy in college and upon graduation went to work in a fancy San Francisco restaurant, earning minimum wage. The executive chef recognized something special in Mark and encouraged him to read her cookbooks, and later on to prepare the recipes that came to him in dreams. After a few years Mark went to Southern France and to Spain to learn from master chefs. Today he is a highly praised, award-winning, executive chef himself, with two very successful restaurants one in a small town near San Francisco and the other in the city of San Francisco. Along with his cooking, he continues to be an adventurer. I often hear his words, "Come on Mom, you can do it," when we're hiking on the edge of a mountain that is too scary for me. I watch him as he encourages everyone around him to trust and take another step forward. He does it without effort. But he met his match when Alison came to the restaurant to be his pastry chef! He wondered if he would ever meet his soul mate and was quite surprised to find himself making eyes at this pretty blonde woman as she baked her fancy tarts. This was a new adventure... no doubt more wondrous than rock climbing, surfing, or mountain biking, and one that decidedly took more courage. They married in September 2004 and are experiencing quite a new adventure together, an adventure that was especially heightened with the birth of Ezra, their first son and my first grandson. My family is growing more and more beautiful. I stand in awe!

The real truth we all live with is that we never know what the next moment will bring. I pray to be present so I can enjoy the moment I have when things are going well. I have learned to accept the things I cannot change and to trust the perfection of each moment, and for the days my family and friends are healthy and happy I'm very thankful.

I will always live with some fear, too, not only because two of my children died, but also because the lives of the others have been threatened. There was Annie's tumor. Katie almost died at seventeen from inhaling propane gas while asleep in a ski cabin. She was saved by her girlfriend, who dragged her out into the snow to breathe fresh air. And Mark was found unconscious in a pool of blood his sophomore year in college. He underwent emergency surgery, and the doctors discovered a blockage in his intestines. It was the enormity of the pain that caused him to pass out and cut his head on the bathtub.

Although I felt enormous gratitude each time Katie, Mark, and Annie recovered, I wondered why some children die and others live. It is a mystery that my children and I will always live with.

There is also the mystery concerning the whereabouts of my children, or anyone else, who dies. Whenever I think about Sean, I have a sense that he is in a wonderful place, and also that he has work to do in the world. He seems to be spiritually present for family members, especially the teens, during times of struggle. And there are times when I am hiking in the mountains, or on a bike ride, and just when I need it most, I feel a boost of energy. I know it is Sean. It's different with Maggie. I have been aware for a couple of years now of a struggle she is having.

One day while I was out walking, I had a very disturbing vision of Maggie.

> *I see a dimly lit room and several blurry figures. As I look at the image, one of the figures comes forth. She is a girl, about thirteen years old, with long, black hair, dark clothes, and a silver chain around her hips. She is angry, and I understand*

202

she is using her anger to cover a mountain of emotional pain. I realize instantly that she is Maggie. The other figures are her friends. They have taken drugs and are consuming large quantities of alcohol. They are also attempting to cover their rage and pain and fear with intoxicating substances.

Perhaps this is about Maggie's spirit re-incarnating. Perhaps not! I honestly don't know about the afterlife, other than that there is one. Whether we live many lives on earth or only one life is a mystery to me. I do know that our spiritual journey is ongoing, and whether it takes place on this earth or in another dimension, or in the spirit world, is of little consequence to me. The God I know will call our spirits to the fullness of life from the beginning to the end of time if it takes that long. Both Sean and Maggie have taught me that. They have also shown me how to be with them, and with others in the world of Spirit. Because of Sean and Maggie, I have come to understand that our personal spirits are ever present (always have been and always will be) whether we are embodied or not. So even if Maggie is in a new body, she and I are bonded with one another because I will always be her mother. The vision does remind me, however, to keep her close to my heart and in my prayers. But there is another possibility that is exciting to me, and that is that Maggie is showing me that there are teenagers who are in pain and in jeopardy who need prayers. I feel blessed to be reminded of this need and remember often to pray for young people.

Lessons and Memories

The most extraordinary challenge of my life has been motherhood. It has provided my greatest joy and my deepest sorrow. My children have taught me more than all my theology classes put together about God's presence and love. Sean and Maggie have invited me into the spirit world so that I could continue to be with them. They have appeared to me regularly over the years, in visions or dreams, or in a felt sense.

Although Sean and Maggie have been great teachers, Mark, Katie, and Annie have, and continue to be, my teachers, along with

Katie's husband Joe and Mark's wife, Alison. They acknowledge my gifts as mother and now grandmother, but they have also invited me to acknowledge my shortcomings. They are loving, and they are honest with me. Each of them has chosen to be in the world in ways that delight and challenge me.

When I am introduced at a workshop or lecture that I am presenting, it is my graduate studies and accomplishments as a teacher or spiritual director that are acknowledged as the fundamental source of my learning and teaching. But while I am grateful for my formal education, my spiritual directors, therapists and friends, the grist for the mill and my best teachers are my children.

Although I knew intuitively I would love my grandchildren, I never really understood how special a love that would be. I have begun to reflect on my own grandmothers, and to appreciate in new ways my relationship with them. But more than that, I feel deep sadness when I realize that I never acknowledged the pain that they felt at my children's deaths.

Maggie died at my mother-in-law's home. She watched as her son raised the very still baby from her cradle, and she was there when we left the house. As a grandmother, I now know that her pain must have been excruciating, but she remained stoic so she could be there for us. It was Maggie's grandmother who arranged most everything, even Maggie's burial and headstone. I never thanked her. I never realized that her pain was not just because her grandbaby was dead, but because her son and her daughter-in-law whom she loved were suffering. My grief was too great to reach out to more than my husband and children, and I doubt that I did that very well. It might be different now, but that's only because my experiences have taught me well.

I have learned that grief is an ordinary experience which, when fully embraced, creates extraordinary openings. Each of the tragedies in my life has left me feeling blessed, on the other side of the grief. The most significant blessing with each has been my deepening relationship with

Spirit... my spirit, and God's Spirit, allowing me to love more freely. Each tragedy has torn me open, allowing me to touch the darkness within me in which God secretly dwells. It is in that darkness that I see the truth most clearly. Sometimes the truth frightens me because it requires something of me that is challenging. ✳

Reflection Questions

Some of you have children who have died, and some of you have had other very significant losses. We learn that with time and faith, we can heal enough to go on with life and actually be happy again. But when we are in the midst of illness, with ourselves or loved one, when death is possible and hope is dwindling, we are in indescribable agony. The waiting can be hell. We pray. We adjust and smile some days, and on other days, we just cry.

> *As you reflect on your life, when have you had to wait*
> *and feel the fear and agony of not knowing the outcome*
> *of something very important to you?*

The death or serious illness of a loved one can shake a person's faith. I often hear "If God really loved me, he would have never given me this illness." Or "What kind of a God would take my child?" If our image of God is of a God who is in control of our lives, rather than a God who has graciously given us free will and walks along side of us as we make choices, then we will blame God for our suffering. When we blame God, we are left without the experience of God's love and protection. Although this can be a way we relate to God, it is lonely. Eventually, we discover a God who weeps as we weep, and who wants only the very best for us. We begin to trust again and our faith is deepened because we have stayed in relationship with God through the anger and the blame, rather than shutting the door and walking away.

> *Can you recall any experiences in which you felt angry with*
> *God and felt that God had let you down? What was this*
> *like for you?*

Healing is mysterious. We wonder why some are healed and some are not. We rarely are taught that what happens to us and our loved ones has at least some element of perfection about it, even though it may involve great pain. Rarely do we understand that someone is not healthy because the illness or death is consciously or unconsciously desired, as in the case of my daughter, Annie. I once had a spiritual directee who was ready to die. His cancer had progressed and he was in great pain. Without his consciously desiring it, he had a remission. Instead of rejoicing, he became outraged and then went into a great depression. It wasn't his time to die, even though he thought it was. On some level, unknown to him, he and God wanted the remission. When the anger and depression lifted, he had a full year to reconcile with his family. He died a very happy man.

Do you believe in praying for healing? Have you experienced healing? Has someone you love experienced healing?

14

Moving Toward Transformation

There was a time when I was as rigid as some of the hierarchy's dogma and held fast to every rule and principle I was taught. But this changed little by little as I became more conscious of my anger at the Church's exclusion of women, and as I discovered the voice of God's Spirit and my own spirit within me. One of the graces that flowed from the tragedies of my life has been the startling awareness that, although God has no gender, our image of God can be feminine as well as masculine. The feminine image of God was gracefully awakened in me, and with that I was able to see my own sacredness reflected back to me.

Longing for the Divine Feminine

Before I could experience my anger at the Church for excluding women, I first had to awaken to the repression of the feminine within myself. That began when I went to graduate school. It was grace alone that gave me the courage to hear God's voice that day and accept the invitation to study. That moment propelled me out of a darkness that was so familiar I could never have named it until I had moved beyond it. It was as though I had been drugged by my culture and my fear. I didn't see reality, nor did I live in it.

Another awareness came as I read Carol Christ's book, *Laughter of Aphrodite,* and experienced my repressed anger at the lack of a feminine image of God. It was an invitation into the communion of women and men who are generating an exhilarating wave of consciousness that is lifting the sacredness of the feminine into the light. There was nothing I wanted to do more than participate in this new wave. Although I didn't read the *Laughter of Aphrodite* until the fall of 1987, my friend Sharon and I had permission from our pastor to make changes in the scriptural readings for quite some time. Sharon and I would pencil over the pronouns in the scriptural readings in the lectionary in our parish, or wherever else I was given that freedom, changing he's, hims, and brothers to be more inclusive. Early in the 1980s I wrote an article for the church bulletin about the importance of the feminine image of God. It was a gentle invitation for parishioners to consider imaging God as feminine as well as masculine, and to imagine how that might affect our lives. The article was not well received. On the contrary, I was shunned. But that too was a gift, because it helped me understand how protective we are of our images of God. I was suggesting something that threatened others' faith, and that wasn't acceptable. But I didn't give up.

Back then people believed—and some still do—that words such as *mankind, men,* and *brothers,* do include women. I don't understand how this persists or why more people, especially women, don't realize how exclusive language implicitly supports the suppression of women, and why they don't resent the exclusion, except that it is intertwined with the masculine image of God. Could it be that we believe that masculine images and nouns and pronouns are more impressive—closer to the divine image? Or, even worse, that *men* are more impressive and closer to the divine image?

I tried to convince my friends, especially my friends in religious life with whom I studied and taught, of the importance of inclusive language. One morning at Mass I became unusually angry at the lack of inclusivity; but what I resented even more were the celebrant's words when he spoke of the sacrifice made by the apostles and disciples of Jesus and said, "The *men* of courage whom Jesus called then and whom the Spirit of Christ calls today," and so on (emphasis mine). I knew this priest well. He was intelligent and well educated. And although he knew better, or so I thought, he was tied to a system that protected its power through honoring the masculine and repressing the feminine.

I cried out to God in silent rage, "How do you expect me to continue to worship in this Church if you don't change these things?" And God immediately replied, *I can't change these things, but you can. All I can do is deepen your compassion.*

By this time I was well into my graduate studies in theology and especially interested in the mystics, but feminist theology had a strong grip on my heart. I felt acutely the dismissal and suppression of the feminine in the culture and in my own life, and I realized how much of the church encouraged this.

Even Mary Magdalene, whom I embraced as a child because her feast day is my birthday, was maligned. Mary, the Apostle to the Apostles, was viewed as a sinful woman rather than celebrated as the one whom Jesus loved, the one to whom he first appeared after his resurrection, the one he instructed to "go tell the others." As I have come to know Mary Magdalene through prayer and study, it seems apparent that Jesus appeared first to Mary Magdalene not only because he loved her, but because he trusted her. He knew she believed his most profound teaching: "I will rise in three days." The others were still too dense and frightened to comprehend and believe the mystery that was being revealed.

I sat in circles talking with women at La Casa de la Luz and discovering with my sisters feminine images of God. Eventually, men joined the circles, and the center grew even more.

I traveled to Greece and Turkey, Europe and Africa, to give retreats and to experience feminine images of God in cultures and traditions past and present. I met the Divine Feminine, the Goddess, in all her beauty and power and saw my reflection in her beauty, her body, and her power.

In the summer of 1993 I took a trip to Europe to discover Mary as Mother. I had already taken many trips to Europe to discover the image of the goddess. I now realized that Mary, the Mother of Jesus, that I had grown up with and whom I loved wholeheartedly, was the Mother I needed to pursue and the One I wanted to bring to the women at La Casa. Although Mary is not the goddess, she is the archetype and the image of the Great Mother that remains with us today in the western world.

I visited the famous images of Mary, most of which were in cathedrals dedicated to her. Whenever I encountered Mary, the question deep within my heart was always the same. "Who are you?" As the central image in a town square, the magnificent painting or sculpture in a 12th century cathedral, the grandiose presence in a chapel filled with icons representing peoples' prayers for healing answered, or the stories of the visions of Mary in small villages often to young children with messages of peace, of love, I asked, "Who are you, really?"

I took a train to Poland to visit Our Lady of Czestochowa, a stunning painting of the spiritual mother of all Polish people. She awaits her visitors at the front of the altar inside the church where she looks after her flock. She is daunting in her simplicity yet overwhelmingly powerful to behold. I felt her love and the grace flowing from her as I stood and prayed. I am blessed to have visited her. She is significant to me because she has taken the cup and has drunk deeply. Her beauty shines for all to see.

On the same day, I discovered that I wasn't far from the death camp at Auschwitz. It was here that I first felt evil in my bones. On a dim, rainy afternoon, I walked for about two hours through the camp, sometimes with a guide, sometimes alone. The experience was so oppressive and horrifying that when I got back on the train, I sat numbed as though in shock. Two days later I was in Germany, at Dachau, another internment camp. Here I made my way through the now familiar feel and smell of evil to the Carmelite Chapel at the far end of the camp. Alone in the chapel, I prayed for the souls that I still felt present, encouraging them to let go and journey home where they were being called. As I sat in the silence of the Chapel, a breeze brushed by and the candles went out. Just as suddenly the light returned, and I heard "Whenever blood flows, I bleed." Not only did I know it was Jesus who spoke, I understood that neither I nor anyone had to, or would, suffer alone. When I left the chapel I was filled with joy. I was not the only one who heard the message. Many spirits who were waiting to rise to the light were blessed by His visit and I could feel their joy as well.

In 1995 I dedicated myself to the Divine Feminine.

> *I created an altar outdoors on the earth. I lit candles and incense, and I sang to her. As I prayed I began to hear words that sprung joyfully from my heart:*
>
> *I dedicate myself to you my Mother*
> *To the wisdom and sacredness of the body*
> *To celebrating joyfully the abundance of beauty and love*
> *that is all around me*
> *To living in harmony and in love with everyone and*
> *everything in creation*
> *To honoring the circle...a gathering of all beings, inclusive*
> *of gender, color, race, and beliefs*
> *To celebrating creativity, art, movement, color, poetry,*
> *and all forms of expression which reveal your beauty,*
> *love, and truth*
> *To speaking the truth with love and compassion*
> *To seeking justice.*
>
> *I pray to dedicate myself in your name to serve all who*
> *seek freedom, most especially the freedom to feel all that*
> *is within*
> *To choose whatever is necessary so that I live fully and*
> *support the fullness of life in those who cross my path*
> *To honor the Christ within me and within all whom I meet*
> *To be the presence of the Divine Feminine in the world by*

the way I live my life in gratitude and joy even in the midst
of suffering
To honor the child-like qualities of life—play, curiosity,
openness and vulnerability— in seeing life anew each day.

After the morning Mass when I reacted so strongly to the priest who talked about "the men of courage who Jesus called," I went to Mass rarely—only for weddings, funerals, baptisms, or for holidays when the children were at home. I prayed for the compassion that the Spirit offered, but it took eight years before I felt a softening in my heart.

As I prayed for compassion, I was unknowingly praying for the purification necessary to free me from my harsh self-judgments and to invite self-forgiveness. Compassion came simultaneously with the release of unconsciously held beliefs about all the ways I had failed. The projections were strong. I could see the hierarchy's blindness, but not my own, the Church's lack of compassion, harshness, fundamentalism, lack of inclusiveness, but not my own. The softening was a gift of the Spirit; as I recognized my own failure and sinfulness and prayed for forgiveness, I slowly surrendered the unconscious self-hatred and anger that blocked the compassion. It was a long, hard, often very dark journey.

Awareness of the Everyday Mystic

Part of that journey was accepting the validity of some of my own experiences as being more than just my beliefs. As already related, many of my experiences were voices or visions. And when I began studying the mystics in graduate school, I learned that hearing voices and seeing visions did not mean that I was crazy, but that I was blessed. Even though I was riveted to the writings of the mystics and having many of the experiences they described, it never occurred to me that I might be a mystic. Then, somewhere along the way, I realized that being a mystic was normal. It simply meant one was consciously aware of God's presence and was responsive to God's love within oneself and one's neighbor and free to live in a loving relationship with a God who pervades all of life, even the parts we alienate and disown. We are all called to be mystics, but some of us take longer to wake up to what is so apparent to others: that God is ever-present, loving and blessing us. As we awaken to that all-pervasive love we can do little but love in response. Years of doing spiritual direction, keeping a journal, reflecting on my experience, and reading, helped me learn how to discern the truth of love's call and follow the Spirit of Christ rather than the false spirits and disordered voices within and around me. However, when I fail to let the Holy Spirit /the Spirit of Christ/ my own spirit guide my life and I wander off the path with anger or an unkind act, I experience pain. And the greater the trespass, the greater the pain. It is a pain of having separated myself from Love itself, and I am very unhappy until I make my way home again. The mystic is truly in a lively love relationship with God and God's creation. The richness of the mystical tradition within the Catholic Church is what has grounded my faith and made it possible for me to grow spiritually, to grow in Love.

I am opposed to the Church hierarchy's rigid exclusion of women from the ordained priesthood and deaconate, its exclusive language, and its exclusion of the image of God as Mother. I am especially opposed to the hierarchy's constant effort to overrule the voice of the mystic and the movement of love and compassion with laws that alienate and separate rather than create true Christian community. With all of this, I begin to wonder how I, as a member of the church, can reach out to those who feel alienated: those who have chosen abortion, those who are divorced, those who are in homosexual relationships, those who practice birth control and others who have been hurt by the laws of the church. I keep having this image of Jesus reaching out to "sinners" with love and compassion. If He gave Himself freely when He was alive, how could His Spirit ask anything less of us now?

My gratitude and love for the ways in which the Church has blessed me, keep me an active participant in the Church, although this was not always so. I am blessed personally in so many ways and am also very proud of the social justice teachings and actions of the Catholic Church, the concern for the poor, the oppressed and the alienated. As I have traveled in Third-World countries, I have seen a very generous outreach, most especially by Catholic religious women and men. These days, I am held fast to the fire that burns within me, as I struggle with issues within the Church especially regarding women...issues that are contrary to the inclusive teachings of Jesus and the early Church. I am refined by this fire, and as I struggle I grow in love and compassion. I am being taught to trust that we are all on a journey, growing in wisdom and in love, each at her or his own pace. The Church is an expression of our collective journey. The acceptance of the mystic in each of us helped me move from a faith in the institutional Church to the body of Christ which is the people of the Church. After all, the meaning of the word "catholic" (with a small c), as taken from the Greek, means whole or complete. In my mind, the word "catholic" then has to do with being inclusive and embracing all, especially when I experience my heart-felt sense of Christ's all-encompassing love, even His tough love. So the body of Christ is a call to all who are open to the wisdom of Christ's inclusive love. The wise ones know, however, that Christ's inclusive love calls us to intense purification, for His intention is for us to become one with love itself.

Letting Go of Guilt About Divorce

One of the dogmatic views that troubled me most strongly was the Church's view on divorce. I was profoundly affected one day when Frank, my spiritual director, said that the grace I had received that made it possible for me to leave my husband was the most significant grace God had ever given to me. He had watched over the years and seen me try everything I could think of to make my marriage work and no matter what I did, I couldn't, certainly not by myself. My husband and I were just too different!

Considering the Catholic Church's stand on divorce and the guilt I felt about my choice, his comment came as a huge surprise. His words were freeing, and I could feel my heart gently soften. It felt similar to the experience I had with the Franciscan priest who told me I was welcome to receive communion even though I was practicing birth control. I felt God's embrace and love in the midst of my difficult choices.

Four years after the divorce, my ex-husband requested an annulment so that he could be remarried in the Catholic Church. At first, I hoped that this was something we would participate in together, something that would help us accept our divorce and forgive one another for the pain both of us had suffered. I even had dreams of taking my engagement ring to a jeweler and designing a friendship ring. But although the marriage was annulled, the healing never happened, nor did the friendship ring. I am deeply sad that our friendship didn't survive the divorce. It has been a great loss.

Faith for the Journey

Another step in moving away from a dogmatic to a personal faith and a deepened awareness of the importance of my faith came in 1992, in a vision, which I have gradually over time integrated in deeper and deeper ways. It was like seeing a movie, but I wasn't in a theater. It was brief and powerful:

> *I see myself being taken by force from my home, a palatial mansion, someplace in Russia or Eastern Europe, probably in the 1920s or 30s. I am dressed in black, gagged and handcuffed, and struggling to be free from the military police on either side of me. They put me in an armored car, and as they drive away I see my beautiful children and beloved husband screaming in horror as they clutch one another. The police put me in a windowless, empty, gray room and tell me I have to stay there for the rest of my life.*
>
> *I do not know exactly what I have done, but whatever it is, it is an enormous threat to the government. Stripped of the family I so dearly love, and stripped as well of my life of power and wealth and social status and beauty, I have nothing to sustain me. I die of an irreparable broken heart shortly after being imprisoned.*

As I recall this vision, I feel a longing to take it seriously, as a gift from God to teach me something very important. I close my eyes and sink back down into the experience of the imprisoned woman in the vision as though it were taking place now. I allow the vision to become real and I become the imprisoned woman whose principal values are her power, beauty, and wealth. Although love is present, I realize it is self-serving, and her family, like everything else, is a possession. As I go deeper into the vision, I realize the great tragedy of her life is that she has no genuine generosity, and her heart is cold. She is unaware of her inner reality, her connection to the Holy Spirit, and to her own personal spirit. She has no faith in anything other than the material, superficial world that she has created. As I reflect further, I am struck by the way she is treated by many around her who say one thing and do another—who are inwardly resentful and envious, but outwardly display support and friendship. She is unwilling to acknowledge any disharmony even though much is present as a result of the pretense. I watch as the negativity within her and around her escalates, opening the doorway to demonic energy that eventually imprisons her. She is controlled by darkness well before she is incarcerated by the police.

The most insidious evil is the despair and terror that poisons her heart and mind as she lies in a darkened cell. She has lived her life with pride and selfishness, a need to possess and control, letting fear be her guide, and now she shivers, alone, entombed in four cold grey walls. Evil cloaks her in the terror of the empty blackness, and the last of the light is extinguished. She is completely lost. This vision reminded me of the woman who came to help me after Sean's death. Her son had died, but she never recovered. Like the Russian woman, she was disconnected from her spirit and got lost in her grief.

What she didn't have in this vision was an honest relationship with herself and God. She didn't have the freedom to be truthful, to see and discern and name what was real. She lived in fear. She was afraid to see. She pretended. She lied to herself and everyone around her. With that, she opened a doorway for the world of demons to enter and take control.

In the vision, she lacked the strength that would have come from being in communion with the Holy Spirit and her own spirit, her true inner knowing. That communion, which is always awake in early childhood, was soon buried under the need to conform. Her whole life was based on external realities, and so when she was left alone in solitary confinement there was nothing—nothing but fear and the bitterness and resentment that raged in her heart. She had lost touch with the "I" who was called to life by a God who could only love her; therefore she lost touch with reality, with God.

This was perhaps my second vision of Hell. I know that this vision was a moment of grace in which I was urged to pray, first for a deepened faith and communion with Spirit, and second for the strength to be truthful—to see, discern, and name what was going on in my life and around me. In communion with my spirit and the Spirit of God, and with the love that flows from that communion, I am free to risk living the truth.

Leaving Once Again

The compassion I sought in regard to the Church came slowly at first, but there was a period of time when it came like another volcanic eruption, when I was catapulted into a new life. It came when I heard the Spirit's call to leave everything behind and move to the mountains.

It was the same familiar voice, but this time I heard, *you aren't going to be here doing spiritual direction and teaching forever.* Then one day as I was returning from giving a women's retreat in Greece, I heard, *it's time to leave La Casa.*

It was an extraordinary experience to found and direct this sacred place in which many, including myself, awakened to the light of the Spirit within themselves and within the world. I initiated a discernment process to affirm that the call was from Spirit rather than from a disordered part of myself or a spirit whose interest was hostile. During my prayer, I heard the voice once again. *You have been with La Casa for sixteen years—one year of service in gratitude for each year of Sean's life. Now, it is time to go.* I knew I had heard the truth, even though I did not have a clear idea of what was next. This was the spring of 1997. It was only after I left that I realized the enormity of the gift and the charism that had been entrusted to me. Although many were interested in keeping La Casa alive, it literally dissolved when I left. Leaving La Casa was heart wrenching; it felt like another great loss, a death. It was also another experience of letting go and following my spirit.

I had prepared for a move without even knowing where I was going. The center had moved to its own facility, and I had sold my home. That happened in a humorous sort of way. One Friday night in the midst of cooking dinner, I felt a need to go outside and get my datebook from the car. To this day I can't recall why. A neighbor was passing by, walking his cocker spaniel and enjoying a glass of white wine. He stopped to chat, and he told me that he and his family were going to have to leave the neighborhood because the owner of the home he was renting was in Japan and wanted to return home. He commented that he loved this street, but there were no other houses to rent or buy. I heard the voice say, *Sell him your home.*

I responded silently, "What, are you nuts?"

No, the voice said emphatically. *Sell him your house.*

"But what about all my things?"

Give them away. Just sell him your house.

So I said to Phil, my neighbor, "Would you like to buy this house?"

"Oh, this is my favorite house. Are you serious?"

"Yes," I said, a bit nervously. So the next day Phil and Tracy came to look at the house and together with their son, Harry, and the dog, agreed to purchase it. I moved to an apartment in Alameda, on the water with San Francisco across the Bay. I swam every day, even throughout the winter, and waited for what was next.

One morning I awoke after having celebrated the Spring Equinox the night before. I was feeling joyful and exhilarated. I heard, *Go get the Sunday paper.* That was odd because I never read the paper. But I went out and bought the paper, turning quite naturally to the real estate section that had vacation spots, and found a small ad for five acres in the Sierras in Twain Harte, with a year-round stream and a lake and a cabin. I went to see the property and immediately recognized it. Though the cabin and land were in grave disrepair, ten years earlier I had drawn a picture of property in the forest where I would live and where people could come on retreat. This was it. It is where I now live and write.

The blessings that I received after leaving Las Casa and my home have been some of the best in my life! I am blessed with the beautiful property up in the Sierras where I now live with my husband and soul mate, Dave. Dave was the pro-bono lawyer for La Casa whom I knew of, but did not meet, for ten years. We finally met in person because he had been asked by our consensus board facilitator to help at the meetings. It seemed there were some difficulties around my level of involvement, which required his expertise. The problems resolved themselves when I realized I was being led to the mountains to write. Dave and I became friends and gently, over many months, fell in love. We were married in September of 2000. Now, God has given me the opportunity once again to be married. This time I am awake enough and mature enough to explore the possibilities of being in a sacred relationship, and I am with a man who is awake as well. We are open to learning what it means to live in mutual love and respect. We know that our relationship is given to help us grow in love, compassion, and acceptance, and to share what we learn with others. Blame and unhealthy fear or anger have no lasting place in our lives. When they or any other negative emotions surface (and they do), we are prepared to pray, trusting that God is there helping us to heal whatever is out of balance so we can love more freely. I believe that marriage is a big commitment, filled with challenges, and if those challenges are handled with care, our marriage is filled with joy. Over the years, I have experienced much suffering and loss; now I am experiencing much grace, love, and companionship.

Living in the forest and refurbishing the land and cabin was an enormous task, and there were days and days when I was completely alone. I had no ministry, no title, no reputation, no significance. I was nobody and I had an inordinate amount of time to feel the emptiness. In the midst of the beauty of the trees and the stream, I grieved the loss of La Casa, my ministry, and my companions. I had expected to begin writing this book as soon as I moved up here, but the only writing I did for three years was in my journal. I kept an office in the San Francisco Bay Area for about six months and went down weekly to see people for spiritual direction, but I did no retreat work or teaching. I even changed my name back to my maiden name. It was as though I had disappeared. I was taken into the most intense experience of purification I could ever have imagined. All of my spiritual friends and guides were far away. Except for my soon-to-be husband, Dave— who had not yet moved up and who came and went—and my spirit friends, the angels and saints who accompany me, I was alone.

For about two years, I experienced purification on every level. My emotions were unleashed, and their range was expansive. It was during this time that I had to face my deep, locked-away fears. Without warning or reason, I would go from dark despair to ecstatic joy, from gentle, sweet moments to tremendous rage. Sometimes I became physically ill. I vomited and had high fevers. I did not understand what was happening to me until later, when

I realized that the joy and the gentleness I felt was God loving me and holding me in the darkness as I acknowledged and released long-held, negative emotions. As fears were finally released, I would experience surges of joy. Bringing light into the darkness reveals unconscious beliefs, many of which are misconceptions and some of which are just plain lies. By pure grace, I burned up and vomited what was not true.

Although I managed my outward life reasonably well, there were many times when my mind felt empty. I couldn't think. Friends and family were unaware of what I was experiencing. I confided in Dave without reservation, but even he did not understand. His presence and support gave me the courage to surrender to a level of purification that was foreign and frightening. Most often there were no words, no way for me to understand or express what was happening. Dave just held me and helped me trust that God and I had not abandoned one another and that greater clarity and freedom were awaiting me on the other side of this physical and emotional upheaval. Of all the emotions that I released, fear was the deepest and most pervasive.

Letting Go

It was at this time I learned how profoundly affected I was by my birth story. As a result of being told the story that my birth had been so traumatic, I decided that I was destructive and that my power (being myself) was destructive as well. I was not at all aware of these beliefs, but they were apparent in most areas of my life. To reflect on the possibility that I might have done something to prevent the deaths of my children would have been normal, but the belief that hid within me for years was that it was my fault. I didn't need to reflect. I just "knew," somewhere inside me, deeply buried in the dark, that their deaths were my fault.

When the hidden guilt finally did emerge, I felt compassion for myself, sorrow that I had lived with this harsh judgment for so long, and gratitude to the Spirit for pushing this up into my awareness. It didn't mean that I was a flawless mother or that I could or should have been different, but I was freed from the belief that I had caused the deaths of my children.

I also feared that I had done, or not done, something that had caused every broken relationship, especially my marriage. Again, this erroneous belief was buried in my unconscious. The process of purification that happened while I was alone on the new property, brought this belief to the surface. These falsehoods are the things I vomited or burned up in the fire of high fevers. The weight of believing that whatever bad things happened were my fault was lifted, and with it the fear that kept me from speaking the truth, and of lovingly, yet strongly, admonishing those around me when it was needed. I no longer had to defend, protect, or hide myself. I was free to admit my failures and release what was untrue. I was becoming more myself.

I was also becoming more vulnerable. That may seem strange, because most of us think being vulnerable is being unprotected and open to injury. But the vulnerability I was feeling had to do with an openness. My heart had opened and therefore my capacity to give and receive love was rapidly expanding. I no longer have to protect myself from feeling the perceived guilt or fear or blame that stemmed from my birth trauma. It still amazes me how deeply that little baby girl's experience and the stories told to her over the years have impacted my life.

As I embraced myself with the newfound gift of compassion and learned to love myself as God loves me, as I am, I began to love others, including the Church hierarchy, in the same way. This awareness didn't mean that I was perfect or that the Church, the people, the priests, sisters and brothers, or the hierarchy, were perfect, but just that we were all in the process of remembering the truth, and becoming authentic.

The challenge I faced became clear when I recalled the words I'd heard that day in the church years earlier. *I can't change these things, but you can,* didn't mean that I could change the Church, but that I had something to contribute that was important. It also meant that what had to change was me. I've always loved the verse in John's Gospel when Jesus speaks to his disciples, and says, "You are called to do what I am doing and more." It appeared that I was being invited to participate in the "more."

It wasn't long after that that I heard the call in my heart to return to the Church. This time I understood that I was there for the people, people who were beginning to suffer from the difficulties of the Church... a growing priest shortage and the newly revealed abuses by priests. It wasn't that I would not be nurtured and blessed myself, but this time my perception would be more about serving than receiving. My issues with lack of inclusivity and the unjust treatment of women would take a back seat to the needs of the faithful. All of this I understood in a flash, and I knew it was a call to obedience that I dared not refuse. It has been, over and over, my joy to say, "yes."

There was a time when I believed that Jesus had not finished what he had come to do. I felt that part of his sadness as he approached the cross had to do with his belief that he had failed, and that if he had completed his work we would no longer suffer but be living in peace and love. Now I know that the gift of Jesus wasn't to free us magically from suffering or transform us instantly into peace-filled and loving people, but rather to bring the Spirit and to light the way for us to transform ourselves and support the transformations of our brothers and sisters. The journey isn't easy, but the rewards are extraordinary, and the gift of returning to others what we have been given is even moreso. Jesus came to awaken us, to set us on fire, so that each of us in our own way, using the talents given to us, can be free to work toward peace and love in our hearts and in the world.

The Gospel of John, the most mystical of all the gospels in the New Testament, communicates this with utter clarity:

> *Still, I must tell you the truth; it is for you that I am going because unless I go, the advocate (Jesus uses the word advocate and Spirit interchangeably here) will not come to you; but if I do go, I will send the Spirit to you.*

—*John 16:7*

Freedom to Let Go

The concept of letting Jesus go, as is suggested in the gospel reading above, seemed foreign and frightening to me. I didn't understand what it meant, but I wanted to receive the Spirit. As I reflected on the things my children had taught me, I recognized that letting go wasn't new. I had let Maggie go, and Sean as well. Had I held on to them, I would have died just as the woman dressed in black had died. I recalled the dream in which Sean came to me. When I reached out to touch him, he said, "No, I have to leave." And then I remembered my friend, Mary Magdalene, who with tears of joy reached out to Jesus when she recognized him at the tomb. And Jesus warned her, "Do not cling to me."

Holding onto the image or the person of Jesus, His teaching, and His power is always the way to something more, and stepping into the more is a huge leap for all of us. In letting go of the person of Jesus who dwells "out there," we open to His Spirit within us. We begin to take responsibility for our lives and our call to ministry because the Spirit of God dwells within us. We acknowledge that the gifts that we have come to know in Jesus are our gifts, and we grow into those gifts as our faith deepens.

The messages are all the same: *let go!* When the Spirit comes, it is because there is an acceptance of the present moment as it is. There is also an awareness that we do not have to be saints for the Spirit to dwell within us. We simply must accept ourselves as we are, with the awareness that our healing takes a lifetime at least. This does not mean that the present moment is all that God desires it to be, simply that it is what we have now... it is the gift we have been given to learn how to love. Acceptance of the moment and of ourselves as we are, opens our hearts for the Spirit to dwell within.

There is a familiar saying that God has dwelled in the past and will dwell in the future, but is with us now in the present. I often wonder if there is truly only a present moment. Perhaps the past and the future are also, in some mysterious way, in the present too. And even though we, in our little minds, live by the calendar, God knows no such thing as time. Everything is here and happening now.

Letting go didn't happen just with Sean and Maggie because they died, but with my other children and with my ex-husband as well. As each of my other children matured and sought independence, often before I was ready, I let them go as well. I learned that if they have the freedom to go, they also have the freedom to return whether, they are living in physical reality or in the world of Spirit.

I was being taught that for the Holy Spirit to rise up within me I could hold on to nothing, not even the person of Jesus. It was the message of the Dark Experience of Nothingness, the teachings of detachment, the Nada of St. John of the Cross, the vision of the abyss in the volcano, and of course the learning from my divorce and with the lives and the deaths of my children. I was learning that my life isn't about the terrible, tragic things that happen to me, but rather that it is a journey of awakening to Spirit. So I am free to share in the "more" that is requested of me. Everything that I experience is transforming me, freeing me to be myself.

Coming to Three Beliefs

Through the fire of purification I was being cleansed. I was experiencing the emptying out of my whole being. Enculturated religious and moral beliefs, false images of God and myself and the world, fear, shame, memories of abuse, and anything that kept the Spirit from moving freely within me were being exorcized. This meant one thing. I would no longer be able to expect "Jesus" or "God" to do it—whatever it was. God and Jesus had not disappeared. On the contrary, they were more present than ever, but they were asking me to be their eyes and ears, mouthpiece and hands in the world. How strange this seemed since I felt so unprepared and so unfinished. If the Spirit was awakening in me more fully, I would have thought that I'd be more unconditionally loving, and patient, never rude or judgmental, but I still struggled, and regularly failed to love with my whole heart.

Nonetheless, the call was clear. And the invitation to contribute to the "more" was also clear. It was an invitation to pass on three beliefs to others, whether in a class I was teaching in spiritual direction, retreats, or in the grocery store. The first and second beliefs are joyful and slip off my tongue effortlessly. They are challenging to live but easily shared and well received. The third belief is where I have to be more compassionate and patient because it is here that there is still much resistance in the Church and in the world, and even within myself.

The first is that **each of us is deeply and irresistibly loved by God** and in our very nature we long to become that love; that, when we

226

say "yes", whatever blocks the flow of love within us will be purified until we are at one with love. This is our life-long journey.

The second is that **'we are one body in Christ;'** that all of creation was spoken in the beginning of time by God's one Word and vibrates with love and breathes one breath. Creation quietly sings of Oneness, awaiting to hear and see and sing aloud the music that has been playing forever. **This is the gift of the Holy Spirit who dwells within every moment and every cell, communing with every spirit who is willing, weaving wholeness and holding all in love.**

The third is that **we must name and embrace the feminine as sacred** and include the feminine alongside the masculine in the Godhead, with inclusive language, in all forms of leadership, in every part of the world, in organizations, churches, families, marriages, and most especially in our hearts and minds, if we are to be free. It is urgent that we pray to put all fear aside and embrace Her with love and respect.

Over the years I have come to realize that being a Catholic is not a choice for me. It is simply who I am. It is similar to being English, Irish, and Native American. I was just born that way. The choice I do have is how I hold and practice my Catholicism. ✳

Reflection Questions

I was told by James Gill, SJ, a former director of Psychiatric Services at Harvard, that there was a study there some years ago that revealed that most freshmen come to Harvard with fairly fundamentalist thinking but leave with very open minds. An open and expansive mind, the university realized, is part of a maturing process which their education supported. Most of our world problems, our problems between countries and religions and within families, stem from narrow and discriminatory thinking. Some organizations actually support fundamentalist thinking, which keeps people from mature thinking and keeps the world in fear and at war. We are in great need of education to support the maturing of our world. I remember being very narrow-minded as an adolescent. Most of my narrow thinking had to do with the laws of the Church. I took them literally and insisted that my family and friends follow them verbatim. I once told a mother with ten children that practicing birth control was a mortal sin when I overheard a conversation about the use of condoms that she was having with my mother. My mother was visibly horrified and sent me out of the living room. I was sixteen years old.

> *Do you recall being narrow-minded or fundamentalist*
> *in your thinking?*
> *Has that changed? If so, how?*
> *If not, would you like it to change?*
>
> *Do you see the importance of being open to different ideas*
> *and ways of being?*

Every religion I am aware of is ultimately based on love, God's love for us and the call for us to love one another. The teachings of Jesus are filled with love and tell us over and over how we are loved by God. When we believe we are so loved we naturally overflow with love for others. God's love for us is a very important part of our faith life. It will eventually permeate our lives, and when this happens we will no longer have war, discrimination, hatred, poverty, oppression, or any of the things that cause imbalance and distress. This will be the fulfillment of the Reign of God.

> *When you hear that each of us is irresistibly loved by God,*
> *what do you feel or think?*
>
> *Do you feel irresistibly loved by God?*

The story about the Russian woman taught me that when we are not in communion with the Spirit of God (the Divine Energy which dwells in the center of each of God's creations), or our essential self, we are also not in communion with our own personal spirit or our higher self. We then lack the necessary strength to live our lives with courage and integrity. The woman in the story was disconnected from the spirit world, her inner world, and therefore not in touch with her deepest reality or truth and had little personal freedom.

> *Do you believe that the Spirit of God really dwells within*
> *you and within everyone in creation?*
>
> *If so, what feelings arise within you as you rest in this*
> *awareness?*
>
> *If not, what feelings arise when you contemplate this idea?*

15

Resurrecting the Divine Feminine

There is an immense collection of images of the Mother God or the Goddess in museums all over the world, many of which were dug up from ancient ruins and pieced together so that we can remember that She was once revered. The groundbreaking archeological work of Maria Gimbutas sheds light on the presence of the Mother God, as far back as the Paleolithic era, 25,000 years ago, when the earliest image, the Goddess of Laussel, was discovered in a cave in southern France. In ancient times, religion was a matriarchy, which was disallowed and finally destroyed as the patriarchy took hold some 5,000 years ago.

The image of the Sacred Feminine that I am slowly uncovering and piecing together isn't interested in domination, but egalitarianism.

She longs for partnership and mutuality. To do this, we must first resurrect Her. I am challenged today by the invitation to embrace God as both Mother and Father, so that balance, respect, communion, and cooperation will bring peace at long last.

I am terribly saddened that many religious denominations, including the Roman Catholic Church, continue to repress the feminine and the feminine image of God. How often have I sat in spiritual direction with women who ached in every cell of their bodies because they couldn't bond with their mothers. That pain lasts their entire lives, and the impact is enormous.

It is clear that the desire of every child to bond with its mother is very strong. This is also a reflection of our desire to bond with the Mother God. We are grieving. It is not the grief over a mother who abandons us, or hurts us, or ignores us. We're not even dealing with the death of the Mother God. No one ever said she died; they never even told us she lived. There is no mention of the Mother God in most Christian texts and traditions. I have no memory of hearing about God as Mother until I was an adult and even then the idea was absurd and simply not allowed. Jesus alludes to Her in the New Testament when He refers to God as a mother hen who gathers her chicks under her wings. I was told this passage was only a metaphor. There is also the Book of Wisdom in the Old Testament which, although it is present in the Catholic versions of the Bible, is excluded in most others. In this Scripture Wisdom—Sophia is seen as "the mother of all good things" and "the breath of the power of God," "whose radiance never ceases." It is here that I began to get a very slight sense of the Mother God or at least of the possibility that God had a co-creative aspect that was feminine. I didn't fully encounter Wisdom—Sophia until my mid-sixties, as you will see in the following chapter. She is still deeply hidden from most of us today. The notion that God is Mother as well as Father is considered by many to be an unwelcome thought which rests precariously on the outer edge of Christian teachings.

In the Catholic Church, Mary is honored as the Mother of God but is not to be prayed to or seen as the Mother God. For me, Mary has become a pathway to experiencing God as Mother in the sense that she is completely transformed and made one with God by the presence of God within her. As St. John of the Cross writes, "We become God through participation in God."

It's all very confusing not to have an image of God as Mother, because we know that every human being that has ever been born has come from a mother, yet we are taught that the Godhead, the creative force of the entire universe, is solely male.

Sometimes it feels to me, as hopeless and dark as the *Dark Experience of Nothingness*. But I know in my heart there is a Mother God. She was held sacred in prehistory and has re-emerged for many to stand beside Father God, to recognize and empower the feminine, and to establish a holy partnership. In such a partnership, God is experienced and embraced as both Mother and Father, with the qualities of each gender acknowledged as sacred. This partnership naturally reflects the sacredness and equality of both genders in the workplace, in church leadership, in marriages, and in families throughout the world. This integration is happening now, but slowly. We are familiar with the qualities that we traditionally call masculine, qualities such as power, strength, protection, intellectual knowledge, independence, etc., and we are seeing that unless they are integrated with qualities deemed feminine such as nurturance, intuition, the capacity to feel deeply, compassion, a desire for community and connection, etc., neither men nor women will be complete or spiritually healthy. Truly, all of these qualities are inherent in men and women alike, though some may lie dormant. We live in a world in which most people in powerful positions are men, and many of those men have not awakened to the qualities within which are traditionally considered feminine.

The integration that is taking place is at the grass roots level. I see this especially in the ways my children and my friends' children relate to their spouses, their children, and their work. Partnership is replacing ownership, and subservience is shifting to a long-awaited egalitarianism. The qualities we label as feminine are absent in our patriarchies and hierarchies, and as women and men throughout the world accept and fully integrate their feminine gifts—gentleness and care of others, heartfelt nurturing and intuitive wisdom, the interior world of Spirit and her guidance, willingness to be open and vulnerable—the longing in our hearts for peace and love is slowly being fulfilled. But, we cannot overlook the importance of the other, the qualities we call masculine, which we are more familiar with. As we are willing to think for ourselves, search for and risk seeing the truth, we awaken the courage to speak out and stand up for what we see and believe to be true. Using our power and strength in harmony with our hearts, each of us can participate in creating a loving and peaceful world.

Rediscovering Mary

Even though I grew up without ever hearing about the Mother God, I have a Sacred Mother figure in my life; I have Mary. As a child, I wasn't taught to pray to her as if she were divine. I just did. I pray to Mary as wise, confident, gentle, compassionate and powerful, and I love her as I feel loved by her. The Church rules about her went over my head as they go over the heads of most everyone who is devoted to her. There are words, phrases, and dogmas that define Mary in Catholic theology which I never knew until I was an adult. My heart has yet to limit the way I relate to Mary. Only God can do that. After years of traveling to cathedrals and chapels dedicated to her, asking to understand who she is, I realized that though she is not the Mother God that I long for, she is in our unconscious minds the archetype of Mother that some of us search for in the Christian world. I believe this is why she is honored all over the world and central to the faith, especially for Christian women.

There is something else that I will try to articulate here. Just as images are stepping stones, which we need, but which we leave behind, as we enter into a pure experience of God, who is ultimately nameless, I sense that whatever we call ourselves or others is only our temporary means of identification—a stepping stone to our true selves. The Bible tells us that we are made in God's image and likeness. Mystics tell us we are made to be at one with God, and we long for that moment. The truth is, we are already one, except in our conscious minds. Our spirit selves, while maintaining a personal quality, will, in this life or the next, eventually make us conscious of our oneness with God. When I bring that thought to Mary, it really no longer matters, to me, whether we call her the Mother of God or God the Mother. More than anything, I am called to enter into oneness with her, as I am called to enter into oneness with all creation. Titles, names, positions, gender, nationality, skin color become inconsequential. All that is of concern, is the desire placed in all of us, by our Creator, to return to the place from which we have come. But, for now, in our human condition, most of us struggle to understand and categorize using names and titles! These are our steppingstones. They are the steppingstones that lead us, one at a time, to the Divine Feminine. She is the vibration of light within the hearts of all women and men. Most essentially, she is present in the heart of Mary, the Mother of God, as a pathway to the Mother God.

Recently Dave and I were on the Baja peninsula of Mexico in the small artists' town of Todos Santos. We went to the Catholic Church on Sunday for Mass. I gasped with wonder as I looked up at the altar. "There you are Mi Madre," I heard myself say with gentle tears wetting my eyes. There, in a niche just above the altar, sat Our Lady of the Pillar, a beautiful Mother and Child perched humbly, yet powerfully on a pillar, with a magnificent sunburst behind her. She and her Child are the central focus of this old Mexican church. I was entranced and sat through Mass with my heart beating softly in her presence.

Women came to La Casa to seek spirituality and self-discovery. As they worked up the courage to see and speak the truth and to be true to themselves, they needed to be supported by images that portrayed feminine strength and wisdom. Many women who came to La Casa had never been able to relate to Mary. Their notion of a meek and mild servant didn't fit their idea of a desirable feminine role model. This was at a time when women were remembering the Goddess, and although I sought out the ancient goddess through reading and travel, Mary remained the feminine strength with whom I most resonated.

It became a challenge to bring a new image of Mary into the hearts of those who came together to pray on Wednesday mornings at La Casa. "But she is meek and mild," the women would say. "How can we identify with her if we are to be strong and stand up for ourselves?" I often think of Carmen, a participant at the Wednesday morning prayer circles, whose mother died when she was a child. She longed for a mother figure and often articulated her desire. Her longing had taken her to a group of women who were studying the Goddess. "I can't make an intimate enough connection with images that are so far back in history. I was not brought up Catholic, but I am fascinated with Mary. I know she is real and alive because she appears today in many places all over the world. I want to get to know her and see if she won't be my mother." There were many gatherings for people like Carmen, in which Mary was the focus. Statues of Mary, which I brought from pilgrimage sites all over Europe and South America, took turns being the centerpiece. Mary would sit proudly or humbly or powerfully (depending on the statue's demeanor) on the altar cloth spread on the carpet, along with flowers and candles. Using Scripture, and visualization, we prayed and dialogued our way into experiences of Mary, the Mother of God—a woman of strength and beauty, wisdom and warmth, vulnerability, courage, and faith. It was Mary, who many eventually accepted as "Our Mother," whose heart merged with our hearts as the mother of Jesus, the one who birthed the Light of Christ and brought forth the Word...for us! I believe there will be confusion about who Mary is until we fully acknowledge the presence of the feminine counterpart to God the Father.

There is a wonderful piece of art in the Musee de Cluny in Paris entitled *The Mother of God*. It is a sculpture of Mary made out of wood. It looks like many images of Mary until you notice the hinges on her side and the small latch in front. Her dress opens, as if it were a little cabinet, to reveal God the Father on a throne, God the Son, and all people in creation. This is the Theotokos, the Mother of God, raised to the heights of the Goddess archetype.

Perhaps Mary and Jesus long for us to reunite our consciousness with God the Mother, with Mary pointing to the Divine Feminine, an image which was buried alive a long time ago but who never died—and to place her Spirit in our hearts along with God the Father so that we regain balance and full respect for both genders.

"The Mother of God,"
Musee de Cluny, Paris

It was at the Church's Council of Ephesus in 444 A.D. that the title Theotokos was given to Mary. It was debated whether to call Mary, Theotokos or Christotokos (the Mother of God or the Mother of Christ). For me, she is both. For many others, even the unknown artist of the fifteenth century sculpture at the Musee de Cluny in France, the title Theotokos represents more. It represents Mary as the quintessential, Great Mother, much the same as the Goddess of ancient religions prior to the patriarchy. This concept is in total opposition to Catholic teaching, yet one cannot help noticing how more and more people of all religions are drawn to Mary, especially as her appearances increase all over the world. I smile as I recall even some stirrings on EBAY when someone tried to sell a piece of bread with Mary's image on it. This seems a bit ridiculous, but since many responded, I believe, it points more to our desire to make contact with her than to the greed or silliness of the one who tried to sell the bread.

This is all mystery, and in fact all images of God are just that. Each image eventually disappears, if we are free to let go, leaving us with the awareness of Presence, a Divine Presence, which is neither masculine nor feminine, but simply Spirit. That is true for us as well. Eventually, if we are willing, we will become conscious of the Divine reality within us, and with God's grace we fall in love and surrender to that Presence. That is what St. Paul says in the letter to the Galatians 2:20, " It is no longer I who live, but Christ who lives in me." Once that surrender happens, we are truly awakening, being freed from every negativity that has ever bound us, and in a way that is mystery, tasting our oneness with God and with all that is, was or ever will be. I experience this as coming home—like ET who says, "ET phone home," to let us know that he has made arrangements to go home. Did you cry when you saw the part of the movie when ET boarded the space ship to go home? We are all waiting to go home but we do not have to leave home—home is here right now, we just have to say, "yes," as Mary did!

The essential reason for acknowledging the Divine Feminine is to bring balance to the image of the Godhead in our consciousness. For women to fully accept themselves as co-creators with the Divine Creator, we need to experience God as feminine as well as masculine.

La Casa drew women and men of all faith traditions and some who had no tradition at all. Those who came were searching for a deeper meaning in their life. They had had some awakening, some inkling, that there was more to their life, and that faith had something to do with it. They wanted "the more." They were often confused, and they had questions.

Veronica was a young mother with two daughters. She was not raised in any faith tradition, but wanted one now for herself and her children. She struggled because no matter what church she went to she couldn't find any mention of a Mother God. She couldn't understand this. It confused her and it made her angry. "Why is this so?" she asked in an annoyed voice. "How will my girls ever come to see themselves as powerful, wise, and loving women without a Mother God to reflect to them who they are? How can I belong to a church that disowns the feminine?" I don't think I will ever forget her, because, as she spoke that Wednesday morning in the women's circle, there was utter silence. Veronica's anger turned to tears as she looked at the women around her and asked, "How have you been able to see yourselves when all you have is the image of a male God, or have you simply given up trying?"

We have called forth the image of the Divine Feminine in our world. She comes in many forms. Today, many people, both Christian and non-Christian, recognize her in the courage and the strength, the faith, the power, and the gentleness of Mary. Mary said "yes" to God and brought forth Christ into the world, and so we have hope. Christ is the embodiment of love, and love changes everything. Love even can soften the hearts of our patriarchal world and melt their fear of the Divine Feminine.

While I feel Mary is not the Mother God I seek, she is my Spiritual Mother and she opens the way for me, and others to find the Divine Feminine both within ourselves and out in the world. She, like us, is human but she has been filled with God and transformed. In this, she is our hope. I searched to understand who she is for years, and I taught class after class about her, but the question continued, "Who are you?" I had all the information but was blinded by years of being told, "No, she isn't who in your heart you feel she is. She is not the archetype of the Great Mother. She is a simple Nazarene woman who said "yes" to God." What I feel in my heart is the way she has loved, embraced, and nurtured me as Mother. She has been present for us for 2000 years and is present today, most especially in Third World countries where people are especially open and who know they need the nurturance of a Mother. She is more than a simple Nazarene woman who said "yes" and teaches us to say "yes."

All those years of being told "no" went flying out the window when I read Charlene Spretnak's book, *Missing Mary* in the fall of 2006. Every time I tried to talk to my husband about what I was reading, I would cry. And when I finished the book, I cried for two days whenever I saw something beautiful, which was often. *Missing Mary* expressed clearly, with excellent scholarship, research, and passion, the very beliefs that lay tucked away in my heart. No longer hidden, I felt as though the fullness of the Mother I was denied was returned to me. I shared this as best I could with my husband, "Dave," I said with tears and a shaky voice, "I have my Mother back, the one who was lost to me, the one who was there but hidden is fully in the light, and I am overjoyed." But still I could not really articulate what that meant.

I prayed to understand what I had felt in reading *Missing Mary*. Soon after, while in church, I asked Jesus to help me. For me, this is entering into mystery and although I received an instant knowing, it is difficult to put into words. It was something like this: we know that sometimes when people are in the presence of an enlightened being and are totally open, they become enlightened. I saw how this was for Mary. She was a simple woman but she was open and she said "yes." That is all God needs. It was the Christ Light within her and with her throughout her life that awakened her to the truth of who she was. She did not become God but she became one with God. In some mysterious way, Mary became one with the Trinity. In that moment, she expanded Trinitarian theology to potentially include all of us. She encourages us to come to inner peace, to carry the Christ Light within us and to manifest that Light in the world. We can, if we are open and say "yes." Being open and saying "yes" is not so easy, because we are different than Mary. Scripture tells us that she was born without sin. We are not born without sin. We have the sins of our ancestors to contend with. Most of us are born into families that love as best they can but which have many dysfunctions, and we learn much that keeps us closed and in turmoil. We have much purification to tend to before we are open as Mary was. This is our work and why we must have gratitude for our teachers, those who are in our lives as spouses, children, friends, strangers, etc. who help awaken us to the beliefs and fears that cover the Light. It seems that the more a person has to teach us, the more difficult the encounter, but the reward is nothing less than eventually coming to the realization that we are one with God. My connection with Mary opened me to the connection with the Divine Feminine. While Mary is not the Mother God who creates the Light, she is the

Mother of God, who brings forth the Light and in so doing becomes Light itself. This connection makes it possible to step into our power and stand up against imbalances in the world.

As we see ourselves as bearers of the Light and made in the image of the Divine Feminine, we present this image in the world, and we stand together saying, "No more." With that united front, based on love, power and the heart will be reunited. Abuse of the feminine, women, children, the earth, and all creation will slowly cease. Pornography will be replaced by honoring the body as sacred, and sex as a divine co-creative act will once again be connected to the heart. We will create a world that is safe for our children. I believe we are striving for the awareness that each of us is a beloved daughter/son of our Mother and Father God.

For as long as I can recall, I have prayed to be at one with God. I believe that this is already so, but it is through the purification of my beliefs and habits and in the healing of my wounds that I am more and more able to experience this truth. One day the truth that I am at one with God will be realized in my every cell. I will know this has happened when I experience everything in creation as beloved. Whether I meet friends or enemies, a bag lady or a queen, I meet God. I will be present and accepting of the moment as it is. I will live in a family, community, and a church which I love in the midst of its flaws, because I have grown to love myself that way. I'm not there yet. I still catch myself judging or wishing that things or people, or I, were different. I'm learning to acknowledge that whatever or whoever I pass along the way is an Image of the Divine who, like me, is gradually remembering the Truth.

As I continue to pray to Mary and realize that it is she who awakened the Mother in me, I realize that Mary's place in the Catholic Church is an extraordinary gift. The Catholic Church unknowingly preserved the image of the Sacred Feminine in Mary, the Mother of God, well after the demise of the Goddess and fall of the matriarchy in other cultures. Although the Catholic Church consistently represses the feminine, it leaves a door open with its love for Mary. Because of this, it is possible for us to find and honor the feminine. As the feminine Spirit emerges within the Body of Christ, the Church, its hierarchy, and its people, Christ's love is freed.

I believe I was drawn to Mary so that through her I could feel the embrace and love of the Mother God in my suffering and my joy. I am blessed to know her and I give thanks for her love and presence. I delight in sharing the importance of her love and presence with those I meet.

It is she who has birthed and nurtured my spirit, because of who she is and the guidance she offers. In her embrace I am brought to the light and moved beyond the images of Mother God and Father God to the experience of Pure Creative Presence, which I find deepest in my heart.

I give thanks for all of the images of God that have brought me to the Spirit within, both my own personal spirit and the Holy Spirit. My spirit is my essential self, my true self. It is me, without ego drive or unhealthy needs, judgments or resentments. When I am engaged with my spirit, I am free to be what I am created to be. I am free because my spirit is at one with the Holy Spirit, the primordial, eternal spark of life. I am at home, in love and peace. Although this state is a place beyond images, it is through sacred images that I arrive here. My home is filled with images and pictures of Mary that I have gathered in my pilgrimages to shrines and cathedrals dedicated to her. I love each one, because each one encourages me as a woman to let go of shoulds, oughts, and all judgments—of being liked or right, important or not—so in the quiet of a peaceful mind, I can feel the embrace of the Holy Spirit within my heart. And, as Mary did, I can bring the light and the peace of Christ into the world. As I live this, I am given the courage and wisdom to more fully discover my spirit, my truth, and to live in harmony with the Spirit of God. I feel abundantly blessed and joyful when I am surrendered to this mystery.

The realization that the experience of God as Mother or Father is only an image is a significant awakening. Images of God are stepping stones to the experience of God as a benign and beneficent infinite presence—the Great I Am, the Alpha and Omega, or whatever name you may call this Divine Energy that inspires and sustains all life with love. With this in mind, I believe that the only reason to image God is so that we can begin to grasp the ineffable in a world that needs to see God reflected in everyday life.

The image of God the Mother woven with God the Father reflects for us the wholeness of the family, the sacredness of the Mother as well as the Father. It is the balance the world needs so desperately if it is ever going to honor fully women, men, and families. It certainly was the image I needed personally to raise my self-image and discover a way to be in healthy and mutual relationships. And it was what I needed to take seriously as a woman, without apology or shame—the call to priestly ministry that found its way into my life and was the source of the energy out of which I ministered and encouraged many women and men to do the same.

Over time, Mary has come to symbolize for many women the Mother of all Creation, since she brings forth the Light, the Fire of the Holy Spirit. This parallels the original spark that ignited life, the mysterious brilliant energy that exploded in space, creating the universe. It isn't just Mary, the innocent and faith-filled maiden who rode on a donkey to Bethlehem, that I hold dear to my heart, but the Mary whose purity of heart, whose faith and freedom led her to surrender to the Divine within her and bring the Light of Christ back into a world that had been lost in the darkness for many centuries.

A sense of Mary's significance and the significance of the Mother of God continues to grow within me. As my heart expands to accept her creative power, her strength, peace, love, joy, and suffering, a wondrous shift has taken place in me. I am more in touch with the sacredness of all creation, which not only includes the earth, with its animals, birds, insects, trees, flowers, and little people, but also the sky, with its stars, moon, sun, and planets, and, of course, human beings of every gender and race.

Acknowledging the Damage

When I was young, I didn't understand that the gift of Jesus was to bring the Light back into the world. Nor did I recognize the importance of Mary as the Mother of the Light. The Light was hidden, as a result of the destruction over many years of images of the Mother God as the creative force, and with it, the denial of the sacredness of the earth and the body. In its place there came a warrior, male God who was controlling and jealous, and a society built on competition, power, and material wealth.

The dishonoring of the feminine, the earth, and the body, left women with shame about our femininity and our sexuality, and men with the belief that they have the right to possess and control all of creation, including women.

As a result of the dishonoring of the feminine in my own life, I lost touch with my body, as did all my sisters. It was safer to be in my head with my thoughts, rationalizing everything, than to stay tuned to my body and all the emotions, dreams, desires, and heartaches or heart throbs that ran through me. Our Wednesday morning prayer circle at La Casa always had a theme, which I would write creatively on a large piece of newsprint that hung on an easel. Using colored chalks, I would display the theme that we would be focusing on that morning. One Wednesday morning I wrote:

> *Our Needs, Desires, Dreams and feelings are Holy—They*
> *Guide us to our Deepest Selves and Ultimately to God*

And on the pages that followed, I wrote each of these questions:

> *Are your Needs, Desires, Dreams and feelings Conscious or*
> *Are They Buried Beneath the Needs, Desires, Dreams and*
> *feelings of Others?*
> *Are They a Blessing or a Burden?*
>
> *Do They Liberate or Imprison You?*
> *Are they Expressed, Realized,*
> *Embraced and Celebrated by You? By Others?*

One woman who was in her seventies said, "I know what my dream was when I was young, but I buried it years ago because there was no place for it within my culture or even my family. As a child, I loved classical music and I wanted to be a conductor for an orchestra. Whenever I would say this, people would laugh at me and tell me "do not to be ridiculous, only men are conductors." One day I decided I couldn't say it anymore. It hurt too much. From then on I have monitored my desires and my dreams and have only allowed myself to express the ones that were acceptable. There is a deep sorrow in my heart because of this and I have kept it to myself until now."

Another woman burst forth with, "I don't even know my desires or dreams or needs. They are truly buried, and even though I try and try to find them, I can't. I feel so ashamed."

Then a third woman added, "Until this discussion, I had not even thought about this." Then she started to cry.

These responses resonated deeply within me. They had been my responses a few years before and became the underpinnings of La Casa. As I awakened to my own repressed dreams, I longed to support the awakening of my sisters and brothers.

These women were becoming aware of the blocks that prevented them from being whole, from being who they truly were. The period of purification had begun for them and would be followed by illumination, and then union—the second and third stages of the mystical journey. Illumination is the "aha," the inner knowing of God and the self and the determination to be oneself. Union is coming home to be at one with self and with God.

This journey isn't linear, but rather a spiral, which takes us down into the depths of ourselves, to God. It begins anew each time we find something that blocks our progression into wholeness or holiness. It is a most challenging and joyous journey, and once begun, one must not turn back. It is often said that once we consciously say "yes" to the invitation to walk the spiritual path, we enter into God's reality. To close the door at this point is to choose the darkness.

Needs, dreams, desires, and feelings that have to do with our bodies are often the very things that we want to forget, have learned to put last, or are a source of embarrassment. For example, through the centuries, the wonder of the menstrual cycle became a painful monthly intrusion that I learned to call "the curse." Breasts became symbols of desirability, often used to allure and keep men. Many women, like myself, hid their breasts for fear of creating unwanted attention. Addictions to drugs or alcohol or food (food was my choice) can still numb the pain and try to compensate for the unconscious pain of the loss of innocence and honor.

When Maggie died, I wondered how a woman or a couple could abort a baby. I wanted mine so badly. Today I've met enough women who have aborted their babies to know that there are many reasons. I am thankful that I never have to stand in judgment of this choice. Sitting in judgment is God's domain. I stand with compassion and love alongside the people who make this choice, for, although I cannot imagine taking the life of a baby in utero, I also know this choice has never been a part of my life. I cannot even imagine what it would be like to walk in their shoes. Although some people seem to abort without concern, most grieve deeply the choice they feel they have to make. I believe that the essential reason for abortion is the imbalance within the Godhead, and therefore in the world. How can we fully celebrate and respect the sacredness of being women and hold sacred the gift of our womb if we are not taught to sit in reverence and awe of the Mother God and Her creation? In denying the Mother God's reality, we end up denying the beauty and sacredness of the feminine aspects of all life. It is understandable then that we have lost both the sense of wonder for the magnificence of creation and the sense of awe for a mother's capacity to do the work of God...to birth new life. Since the Mother God has and continues to be denied and therefore violated, we, Her offspring, will feel the effects and respond accordingly. Abuse follows abuse. It is impossible for the male who has no understanding of the sacred feminine within him or before him, to keep his heart open and make love with reverence and gentleness. He guards his heart with a need to be powerful and successful. He is cut off from love and left with a need to control the world around him. He takes what he wants, when he wants it, believing it is his right. Likewise, it is impossible for the woman to feel safe, to access her wise self and to trust herself while the truth of her power and beauty lies hidden in the darkness.

Most people give a gender to God because it makes God more approachable, but how sad it is that most Christians are enculturated to say God can only be masculine! Since we know that each of us has come from our mother's womb, we must know in some deep place within us that it is the Mother God who is the creative force; the One who metaphorically brings forth all life from her sacred womb. What happened to the image of God as Mother? Why have we dismissed this image of God as Mother? We live as though She never even existed. Father God stands alone, a single parent, having been alienated from His beloved, as though it does not matter or isn't really happening. She is kept hidden, as a secret, and in this secret lies a grave violation.

More than one woman has come to me in tears because her sexual life with her husband was so emotionally painful. "I long for my husband to come to me with an open heart, with words of love and gentleness, instead of a need to pleasure himself with my body," was one woman's cry. They had been married for twenty years.

Jane told me she was relieved that her husband had suddenly become impotent. She said, "I have never felt safe saying 'no' to his sexual advances because he would become angry. I tried so many times to talk to him, but it was always the same response—he would laugh and tell me, 'Don't be so emotional—it is only sex.' That is the issue in a nutshell. It was only sex, and I wanted us to make love."

The problem and the pain that these women faced is not uncommon. Our society fails to teach us how to love each other in an intimate and sacred way. In these cases the women were not seen as beautiful images of the Divine Feminine, because, sadly, their husbands had not learned to see beyond their own needs in this area of sexual intimacy. Nor had the men come to understand that the Divine dwelt within themselves. The men did not see their own sacredness, reflected in their wives. They saw their wives only as sources of pleasure. Unfortunately, this is a greater problem than we want to admit. Most do not want to know about it... another secret in our society!

The power of the Divine Feminine, which we see in the Mother God, lies in vulnerability, compassion, love, truth, and reverence for the body. She is present in the moment, in our bodies, the earth, the trees, the water, and all that is manifest. Without the awareness of her presence, we destroy the sacred. When we deny the Mother God, we trample her creation.

Without the feminine dimension, the sexual drive is disconnected from the heart and there is tremendous fear that compels us to control everything and everyone. There is rape with little remorse. There are also unwanted and unsupported pregnancies.

Because most women believe that our bodies are burdens rather than temples, we no longer have the awareness of ovulation, and therefore little choice in when we might or might not conceive. We rely on artificial means of birth control because we've lost connection with our own bodies. We live in a world where all too often violence and fear, rather than love, begets new life, and so, sadly, we choose abortions. We women and men have lost the sense of how beautiful and holy we are, and of the indwelling of the Spirit of God. Rather than calling this sin, we must call it tragedy, and grieve, for when women are unconscious, we prostitute ourselves, and when men coerce or rape, it is because they have lost touch with the sacredness of life and the sacredness of our creative potential.

The Spirit Still Dwells in the Darkness of our Hearts

Women are still oppressed by the government, by the Church hierarchy, by big and small businesses who fear their power, and by other women who are not ready to take responsibility for their lives. I remember well the fear of my own power as a woman, and how I hid behind a powerful father, and then a dominant husband, for years. It terrified me, unconsciously of course, to imagine myself fully empowered. What I didn't know then, but understand now, is that being powerful is synonymous with being myself. I am coming to understand just how much of a challenge that is for me and for all of us. It means being willing to see what is real, and to articulate what I see, regardless of how I might be perceived—no easy task, especially for those of us who like to be liked.

As the patriarchal system continues to dominate society and religion, it protects its power with inquisitions and witch-hunts. The inquisitions are ongoing and occur whenever someone significant speaks out against a particular teaching.

In the mid 90's I found a book at the Graduate Theological Union bookstore entitled, *Eunuchs for the Kingdom of Heaven: Women, Sexuality and the Catholic Church,* by Uta Renke-Heinemann. I couldn't put the book down. I was fascinated by all of her research about the early Church fathers and how they influenced our present- day views on women and sexuality. Her research is impeccable, and her viewpoints made me reflect on the ways in which I viewed sexuality. Uta is the world's first woman who received a PhD in Theology to become a professor of Theology, and was the first woman given a Church-appointed chair at the University of Essen in Germany. She had been removed from her teaching position by the time I read this book because she declared the virgin birth to be a theological belief and not a biological fact. In the book, Uta discusses at length how the belief in the virgin birth impacts the ways in which women are regarded or disregarded. I began to understand that the idea of the virgin birth separates us from Mary and takes away from the innate beauty and sacredness of conception and birth. This is a very controversial subject, not only in the circles of hierarchs, theologians, and priests, but also among Catholic lay people. Uta's brilliant research perhaps came too close to a truth the Church hierarchy is not ready to accept—that Jesus' birth was a normal, healthy, sacred, human event that does not in any way demean his Divinity. I can't imagine anything more sacred or co-creative than the conception and birth of a child. The belief that Mary's hymen was never broken is truly something we need to leave behind.

The removal of Uta from her teaching position was meant to preserve the unity and teaching of the Church. Sometimes these decisions become destructive, and sometimes, years later, they are rescinded, as with the writings of Teilhard de Chardin, a Jesuit priest, mystic and scientist. Teilhard saw the divine in all of creation at a time when this was not yet accepted teaching. His theology was rejected, and he was consistently denied permission to publish. His writings were passed to fellow Jesuits and friends who then published them on his death in 1955, at which time his theology was finally recognized.

Teilhard de Chardin is one among many. The Church, in its attempt to preserve its teachings, has a long history of enforcing orthodoxy. The Papal Inquisition began around 1233 with the campaign by the Church to annihilate the Cathars, a Gnostic, heretical sect which, among other things, held women to be equal to their male counterparts. The witch-hunts in Europe first began in the Middle Ages, about 1450, and lasted more than three hundred years. They are a tragic example of patriarchal fear of the feminine and the subsequent need to suppress and dominate. Tens of thousands of victims, mostly women, were unfairly tried, tortured, and executed because their gifts as healers threatened the power of the Christian hierarchy. These "witches" used herbs, prayer, music, and ritual to cure the sick, birth babies, soothe the grief stricken, and comfort the dying. They could not be usurped, owned, bought, or controlled so they had to be destroyed. In the famous book about this atrocity, Malleus Maleficarum, published in 1485-86, we have a detailed description of misogyny (the hatred of women by men). "All wickedness is but little to the wickedness of a woman. Women are by nature instruments of Satan. They are by nature carnal, a structural defect rooted in the original creation."

(Quoted in Katz "The Holocaust in Historical Context" VOL.1, PP.438-439). These witch-hunts are in the past, but the memory lingers on.

Women and men whose feminine spirit is awakening within them, fear using their power and speaking the truth, and are besieged with shame for holding back. Is it safe, we wonder, to speak what we see and feel or will there be an inquisition, or worse, a witch-hunt? And so the truth and the power hidden deep within us often remains in the dark of the abyss, along with the Light of Christ.

Uncovering Hidden Treasure

With an awakening of Spirit, many women are freeing themselves and living more fully with the wisdom, courage, and power that are ours as beloved daughters of the Mother/Father God. We risk being empowered by God and find within ourselves a desire to express what is in our hearts. But we also live with enormous criticism and are often called names, such as "angry feminists." In 1998, I wrote a letter to my bishop in response to his homily at Mass. I admire this man and believe he is a person of fine integrity. In his homily he encouraged us to speak up as Jesus did, regardless of the consequences. I wrote, "Dear Bishop, I was again reminded of the dreadful inequity in our church regarding women's ordination today at Mass as I watched the two adult women serve you at the altar. It would not have bothered me if they could also be served by you as they celebrated the Mass as ordained priests." The letter continued, making the same point clearer, and I enclosed a picture I had drawn of the bishop as the altar-server and the women in vestments. I mailed the letter. A few days later, a woman came to La Casa and told a group of us about a meeting she had just come from at the bishop's office. She said, "The bishop read a letter written by a woman who he called "another angry feminist." It was about ordaining women, and he said she even drew a picture." She said that the bishop was really angry and could hardly hold himself together for the meeting. So much for risking the truth of how you feel! My father said often, "if you don't like someone, you had better get to know them better." I decided that I had better get to know the Bishop better. I made an appointment to meet with him a few weeks later and visited him many times after that to talk about my ministry. He never mentioned my letter, nor did I. About three years after the letter, I was invited to accompany a friend to one of the bishop's parties for generous donors. He greeted me warmly and about half way through the party, he made an announcement. Everyone turned as he said, "I want you to meet a friend of mine. She has come to visit me over the years to tell me about her ministry. There is one thing that has always impressed me about her visits; she always asks me how I am doing. And I always tell her, because I know she really cares. This is very unusual for me and I just want to thank her." Perhaps he forgot about my letter, or perhaps it was a gift that took a while to unwrap. In any case we found a way to be in harmony, and with that, God can work wonders for both of us.

As our Divine Mother reemerges in our minds and hearts, her presence empowers us, giving us courage to continue on, and little by little we find ourselves coming back into balance.

My entrance into the terrible *Dark Experience of Nothingness* when I was twenty-nine years old was a powerful initiation, a moment in time, which I now recognize as an opening. In that experience I saw and felt a reality in which the feminine spirit, the force that creates life, was in fact totally annihilated. I saw that I could not exist if this were so, nor could anyone or anything in creation. It was the annihilation of life. It is my most profound religious experience.

Jesus brought a new way of thinking into the world. He brought the light of the Spirit, a heart overflowing with love and compassion, a longing for justice, a sense of egalitarianism, and respect for women. He appeared first to Mary Magdalene after the resurrection and chose her to be the one to preach the good news to the others. He showed intense anger when he saw behavior, especially in the temple, which was oppressive, controlling, and hypocritical. He instructed us to love with our whole hearts and to speak the truth. He called Satan the father of lies and showed us how to exorcize evil. His gift, the Spirit of Love, is our salvation, and, when fully awakened within us, can do no less than what it did in Jesus.

The truth is simple, and in its simplicity it provides the most challenging and adventuresome experiences imaginable. Although it is simple, the courage it demands is extraordinary. *Be yourself!* it commands. The ancient oracle of Delphi, sought out by kings and queens and ordinary folk alike, repeatedly revealed its wisdom in the words, *Be true to yourself.* I have heard the words of Shakespeare spoken to me many, many times by my mother, *To thine own self be true.* These sayings ring loudly in my ears!

Until voices of women are heard, respected, and integrated in every home, church, and governing situation, the world will suffer. The voices of women and men, together, have the power to bring about peace and harmony in our communities and in our world, but we must be true to *ourselves,* and speak out with love, regardless of what others may think or say.

Jesus' call to me is clear. I am to follow in his footsteps by being myself, my deepest, truest self, and by using the gifts I have been given as He used His, with all my heart. The only way that is possible is if I am open to my spirit and the guidance of the Spirit of God, who enlightens, nurtures, supports, and embraces me, as I accept and live the challenges that come my way. Sean shed his blood, and it wasn't wasted. Sean's death was violent, and it woke me up. It didn't feel like that at first, but, as I began to heal, I realized that the blessings that were emerging, and that have continued to emerge, have to do with raising my awareness of the indwelling presence of Spirit and the truth of who I am.

With the intensification of the light of the Holy Spirit through purification, I was able to see the ways in which I was not true to myself or faithful to the gifts that were mine. My need for approval and my fear of expressing myself were more apparent than ever.

Even the disciples of Jesus were not always truthful or free to be themselves. That is most evident with Peter, who not only doubted Jesus but denied that he knew him. I am fascinated by theologians and scholars who today are uncovering truths and possibilities about Mary Magdalene. Ramon K. Justino, who is teaching at Notre Dame Academy High School and Rev. Ester de Boer, author of *The Gospel of Mary: Beyond a Gnostic and Biblical Mary Magdalene,* are speculating that Mary Magdalene, the first one to whom Jesus appeared after his death, might have been the beloved disciple. Ramon also suggests that she is the author of the fourth Gospel, rather than John, and that she was the recipient of the most mystical teaching of Jesus concerning the Spirit. I begin to wonder if perhaps she was even the one Jesus chose to lead the community after his death. Jane Schaberg, a professor at the University of Detroit, Mercy, suggests in her book *The Resurrection of Mary Magdalene,* that Mary Magdalene was a significant contributor to the faith which revolves around the Easter story and a woman whose importance was not just downplayed but murdered. The Second Vatican Council sanctioned her title as "The Apostle to the Apostles," a title and place of leadership which the disciples did not have the courage or humility to acknowledge, simply because she was a woman. So she was suppressed and, with her, the feminine presence in the Church. I was born on July 22, the feast day of Mary Magdalene, and feel blessed by her Spirit and her guidance, especially as I struggle to speak out against the cultural and institutional problems regarding the liberation of women.

I often wonder if perhaps the greatest pain of Jesus' life was the awareness that his message would be carried forth *only in part.* Continuing to free the Feminine to take its rightful place would have to wait. Until that happens, the world will continue to suffer great imbalance and enormous power struggles. I feel a sorrow as war, hunger, and greed continue to flourish, because the Light is so dim and Wisdom is so suppressed. Our fear to speak out what we know in our hearts to be true is the demon that awaits transformation. ✳

Reflection Questions

When we welcome women as we do men in all areas of life, there will be a very positive shift in our world. Areas such as government and church leadership are still predominately, and sometimes exclusively, in the hands of men. I believe part of our healing as a planet requires that we include and celebrate women's gifts, and that means first of all including and celebrating our Mother God who is the bearer of all life.

How comfortable are you with the image of God as mother?
Have you incorporated Mother God into your prayer, and
if so, what is that like for you?
If not, would you be open to the possibility of a Mother God?

Is it possible for you to name and embrace the feminine
as sacred?

If you are a woman, do you feel it is important to have an
image of God as Mother for you or your daughters to feel
sacred? Why? Why not?

Have you ever felt excluded because language used was
not inclusive of the feminine pronouns or because the word
"men" was used as an inclusive word?
If so, please explain. If not, please explain.

If you are a man, do you feel a desire to embrace God
as Mother?

Would anything change in your faith life or the way you are
in the world, if you prayed to God imaged as feminine?

16

Embracing Wisdom-Sophia

My search for the Mother God has been going on for thirty years. In October of 2006, she awakened anew in my heart in the magnificent basilica of Hagia Sophia in Turkey.

I had searched for her among the Goddesses of long ago. I read books by feminist scholars like Vicki Noble and Eleanor Gadon, hoping to discover Her in the ancient matriarchal cultures. When I read about the preserved sites where the Goddesses had been worshipped, I knew I had to visit them personally and experience the Goddess for myself.

I first went to meet Aphrodite, the Goddess of Beauty. I flew to Cypress, where the books told me she mythically emerged from the sea.

Myth became reality as I swam in that sea and asked to know and to feel the beautiful Aphrodite. Sometimes I swam underwater, sometimes I floated, letting the waves rock me and the sunshine warm my face, and sometimes I would be still; all the while I was praying to feel her energy, her spirit, her presence, and be filled.

I met Ixchel in Mexico, near the Mayan pyramids. As a moon goddess who protects birthing mothers and newborns, I resonated with her. I carried a large statue of Ixchel home on one of my trips to Mexico. She sits in an alcove in our sunroom and reminds me of my search. She is dark-skinned, peaceful, strong, and beautiful.

I discovered Minerva, the goddess of Wisdom, when I went to Rome. I was later surprised to learn that Minerva, and her owl, are on the Prime family crest. I am intrigued by her because of that and wonder who in my family chose that image and why!

But the one with whom I resonated most was Isis. When I visited Egypt, I discovered that she is present still in her ancient Egyptian temple, sitting proudly with her son, Horus, on her lap. She reminds me of Mary, as Mary sits with Jesus on her lap. Centuries apart but with sons who are called God, these blessed, strong, holy women are called Star of the Sea and Queen of Heaven. I have a statue of each, both about the same size, and both with their sons sitting proudly on their laps. I place them together on my altar so they can be together, as mothers and children are drawn to do.

I found many Goddesses in my reading and travels, communed with them and discovered the importance of what is today called "pre-"history. This is the story in which God was a woman and women were honored because they could do what the Goddess did—they could create new life, and they could feed and nourish the new life they created. Unlike early Christianity, when St. Augustine believed and taught that women were only receptacles of the man's sperm and had nothing to contribute to the life of a child, the people of early matriarchal times believed that the woman was totally responsible for the creation of a child. Hopefully, most of us today know it takes both male and female to create a child and both to raise a child.

Although I delighted in knowing about the Goddess and felt the memory of her ancient feminine energy and strength empowering me, I never felt called to worship any of the goddesses I met. They are extremely significant in history and in my life, but they never felt alive to me. As much as I wanted to, I was unable to call any of the goddesses "my Mother God."

As I searched the goddess sites I also visited the shrines, basilicas, and cathedrals dedicated to Mary, the mother of Jesus.

The question that haunted me was, is Mary my Mother God? Throughout my life, Mary has been a loving presence, a guide, and a companion. Even though I pray to her daily and love her as a mother, I have always been hesitant to worship her as "my Mother God." I tried to call her Mother God as a child might pretend that a loving mother was her birth mother, but I couldn't.

Although Mary is called Theotokos, the Mother of God, a mighty title, she is not the Goddess. Many have taken her role as Mother of God, born without sin and assumed into heaven, and made her not only into the archetype of the Goddess, but into the Goddess herself, because we so desperately need that divine feminine presence in the Christian tradition and in our world. Women search to find themselves made in the image of God when God is only God the Father, and men long for the gentle, compassionate, feminine side of God to reflect their own feminine qualities.

But Mary is not the Divine Feminine Presence for whom I searched. I know and accept her as beautiful, faith-filled, surrendered, humble, obedient, and powerful. I watch how she stands tall in the face of her son's torture and death, supporting Him with her love as He takes in and holds with love the sins of greed and fear, transforming them by His unconditional love. I am in awe of what she graciously "holds in her heart." She is celebrated, honored, and respected, a gentle yet powerful presence as a reminder and supporter of who each of us is called to be. She is my Spiritual Mother but not my Mother God.

I knew I would find my Mother God. I just didn't know where or when.

In 1989 I was given a holy card of an icon called "Christ Sophia," painted by my friend, Franciscan friar, Robert Lentz. The image was of a dark-skinned woman with piercing, inviting eyes, holding a small statue of a goddess. She is held in an egg-shaped mandala, and there are Greek inscriptions (which I could not read.) Mesmerized by this image I longed to know "Christ Sophia" and prayed to find her.

I sent for a large plaque of the icon and asked for some information about it. I learned that the Greek inscription written in her halo reads, "I am who am," and the inscriptions on either side of her are the abbreviations for Jesus Christ. Robert Lentz writes, "She holds the 'Venus of Wallendorf' and points to herself as if to say, 'I am she. Know me now more fully.'"

I so wanted to know her. The description of the icon resonated deeply within me. Robert writes, "In the Byzantine Church, these references to Wisdom are considered references to Christ."

In the spring of the same year, I flew to Istanbul to meet Sophia. I thought if I went to Hagia Sophia, which I learned meant Holy Wisdom, She would reveal herself to me. I loved the Old Testament Book of Wisdom and had memorized some of it but I had not really understood what I read or felt the longing for Wisdom-Sophia until I saw Robert's icon. And now, I stood in the doorway of the Basilica and I prayed to find her, not in my head but in my heart. I recalled some of the Scripture:

> *Wisdom is bright and does not grow dim*
> *By those who love Her She is readily seen,*
> *And found by those who look for her.*
> *Quick to anticipate those who desire her,*
> *She makes herself known to them.*
> *Watch for her early and you will have no trouble;*
> *You will see her sitting at your gate.*
> *Even to think about her is understanding fully grown;*
> *Be on the alert for her and anxiety will quickly leave you.*
> *She walks about looking for those who are worthy of her*
> *And graciously shows herself to them as they go,*
> *In every thought of theirs coming to meet them.*

> *Wisdom 6:12-16*

The magnificent 6th-century Byzantine cathedral, dedicated to Jesus Christ, was originally built over the site of a pagan temple in the year 360 AD but was destroyed by fire. The present Hagia Sophia was built in the year 532, after twice being burned to the ground. It was turned into a Mosque in the mid 1400s and remained as such until 1935 when it was dedicated as a museum. Though still beautiful, I found it empty of Her

Presence, except in my longing, and I returned home empty of my hope of ever finding her.

Although my search ceased, the longing to find my Mother God never did. There was a constant, gently burning desire that I felt, sometimes with tears and sometimes with a painful hopelessness.

In the fall of 2006 I traveled to Turkey once again, this time with Dave, my husband. Our four-week trip would begin and end in Istanbul. I anxiously awaited another experience of Hagia Sophia, not really expecting, but hoping that I would find Her this time. We arrived in Istanbul too late in the day to visit the cathedral, and the next day it was closed. Sad but determined, I waited.

With a population of over 17 million, Istanbul is bursting with activity, sidewalks overcrowded, public transportation filled way beyond capacity, and the Imams, the mosque's spiritual leaders, calling people to prayer over loudspeakers day and night. It was Ramadan. People were sitting in restaurants and parks waiting for sundown. At 6:10 the feeding frenzy began, with the children playing as the parents finished off their fasts with feasts. Unlike the previous trip where I found a Catholic Church and friars to converse with, this time I found none. No one at the hotel, our driver, our guide, nor anyone else we asked, knew of a Catholic or Christian Church. For the first time in my life, I felt the fragility of Christianity. The area which we now call Turkey and surrounding areas were all Christianized by St. Paul shortly after Jesus' death, and now there was little or no sign of living Christianity. Most of the cathedrals and churches had been destroyed and turned into mosques. The sadness I felt was all encompassing. I entered Hagia Sophia, a museum under restoration, with these feelings of loss, and I prayed to Holy Wisdom for guidance.

The mosaics within the cathedral are magnificent. I felt held by them; their beauty shone brilliantly, even after all these years. I left feeling somewhat calmed, and although I firmly believed, I walked away without a felt sense of Sophia's Presence.

It was on a Turkish gullet, an 80-foot schooner, sailing along the beautiful Emerald Coast, that I began reading Sue Monk Kidd's book, *The Dance of the Dissident Daughter.* I felt I was walking with a kindred spirit as I read her journey toward discovering the Divine Feminine, and I would sit for long hours on the deck of the yacht, reading, pondering, and recalling my own journey. Then I arrived at Page 146, "Herself as Sophia," was the sub-heading. Fascinated and excited, I read the next pages as fast as I could, and then I read them again and again. For the next couple of days I sat by myself on the bow of the boat, gently rocked by the sea, and felt Sophia emerging from deep within, where for centuries she had been buried. I had no words for what was happening, but I had some deeper intellectual understanding, and I had a heart swelling with love.

I read the prayer of Solomon in the Book of Wisdom as he addressed God:

> *Now with you is Wisdom,*
> *who knows your works*
> *And was present when you made the world;*
> *Who understands what is pleasing in your eyes*
> *And what is comfortable with your commands.*

> *Wisdom 9:9*

And then I prayed the prayer with Solomon, *"Send her forth from your holy heavens."* Wisdom 10:1

I sat quietly in the warm, Turkish sun, water lapping the sides of the yacht, wind blowing in my face, and the words of Wisdom resting in my heart, I felt the same heart-opening ecstasy as when I had read St. John of the Cross so many years ago.

Every once in a while, my husband would come and sit beside me. He knew something important was happening and wanted to share in the sacredness of the moment. Then, there were the meal times or times to swim, and I would re-enter life playfully, as though I were having a very normal day, after which I'd return to my quiet, warm and ecstatic inner journey with Sophia.

Some of what I pondered brought up anger and confusion. Why, I wondered, did the church patriarchs of our contemporary religions bury her? In reflecting on how the female image had been hidden or changed, Sue Monk Kidd writes in *The Dance of the Dissident Daughter,*

> *In Deuteronomy 32:18 the Revised Standard Version read,*
> *"You forgot the God who gave you birth." But actually the*

words in the verses about giving birth are the Hebrew words
for "writhing in labor," which makes "giving birth" a re-
markably subdued translation. Even more interesting, the
Jerusalem Bible translates the verse "You forgot the God who
fathered you."

Dance of the Dissident Daughter, p. 147

Sophia is very present and revered in the Old Testament, but she certainly is lost in the New Testament. Her importance is obvious.

Theologian Elisabeth Schussler Fiorenza has suggested that
Wisdom is the God of Israel expressed in language and im-
agery of Goddess. C. G. Jung referred to her as "God's self-re-
flection." Indeed, if you highlighted all the references to her
acts in the Bible, they would far exceed references to the Old
Testament giants we are so familiar with — Abraham, Isaac,
Jacob, Moses, Isaiah. Yet we have scarcely heard of her.

Dance of the Dissident Daughter, p. 148

Why did the early church fathers want to separate us from the Feminine Image of God? Was it to move us away from the ancient matriarchal religions where God was Mother? Did it have to do with fear that we would be confused by knowing that Christ is the incarnation of Wisdom? Is gender so significant that they couldn't allow Wisdom, the Logos, to be feminine and embody or bring forth the Man/God, Jesus? And are women barred from the priesthood or deaconate because we are a reminder of Sophia in our feminine beauty, wisdom and light? Do we reflect too much the injustice done to the Feminine Image of God, to Sophia, God's very breath?

She is a breath of the power of God, pure emanation of the
glory of the Almighty; hence nothing impure can find a way
into her. She is a reflection of the eternal light, untarnished
mirror of God's active power, image of his goodness.

Wisdom, 7:25-26.

For years I have prayed on these passages in the book of Wisdom. I have memorized them. I hold them in my heart, but until this trip to Turkey, they did not awaken me.

Sophia!
You are the whirling wings,
Circling, encompassing energy of God;
You quicken the world on your clasp.
One wing soars in heaven,
One wing sweeps the earth,
And the third flies all around us.
Praise to Sophia!
Let all the Earth praise Her.

Hildegard of Bingen

I have fallen head over heels in love with Sophia, and I wait impatiently to commune with her fully.

After eight days of sailing we arrived at our port and were driven to a lovely hotel on the outskirts of Ephesus. The following day we had a guide and driver take us to see the ancient ruins, one of the Seven Wonders of the World. Although I was interested in the temple dedicated to Artemis and the history of the site, my heart was set on Mother Mary's House. This is the little house discovered through the writings of Sister Anna Katherina, a German mystic. She had never been to Ephesus, but in a vision was told that Mary had gone to live in Ephesus with John the Evangelist and given the exact whereabouts of Mary's House. Following her information, the house was discovered in 1896.

As the guide left us off to explore Mary's House, she said, "You have 15 minutes." We both just shook our heads in disbelief and ambled joyfully along the narrow cobblestones path to the shrine. As we rounded the corner we were elated to see a small gathering of tourists up on a platform with a priest vested for Mass. We motioned to our guide and told her we would be at least an hour and fifteen minutes. Still somewhat stunned by our good fortune, we seated ourselves with the others. We had missed only the opening prayers and the first reading. Father Tarcy, an Indian priest who lived at the friary nearby which dedicated itself to caring for Mother Mary's House, was a delight. His homily was riveting, but when he began to speak of wisdom, my eyes widened. Sure enough, the first reading had been from the Book of Wisdom. To say I was speechless would be an understatement... I was breathless! Now I knew that Sophia was just as interested in revealing herself to me as I was in finding Her!

I talked to Her, prayed to Her, and I asked to understand more of who She is.

On returning to Istanbul at the end of our trip, I tried to make arrangements to visit Hagia Sophia one more time. It was the last day of Ramadan and the streets were packed with people, young and old, celebrating the end of their sacred time of prayer. The museums were closed, but by chance we discovered that Hagia Sophia would open at 1:30. The line to enter was long, but I had to go one more time. Again I entered the massive cathedral, hoping and praying to meet Sophia, but my heart felt empty.

As soon as I was inside under the main dome, I felt huge rushes of energy warming and expanding my heart. My feet firmly planted on the ground, I walked to the apse and found myself drawn to Mary, the Mother of God holding the child Jesus, the son of God. The image is breathtakingly beautiful. They came to life for me and flooded me with compassion. Humbled by love, I prayed to Sophia, "Fill my heart with your love. Take me to yourself as you did for Mary."

I felt tears rimming my eyes. Relishing the tears that were evoked by this sacred meeting with Sophia and feeling blessed, I walked through the enormous cathedral/ mosque/museum, aware of its magnificence. Wandering amidst the many images and icons which had been covered over with plaster by Mehmet the Conqueror which are now being brought back to life—the huge shields with Islamic inscriptions and large circular pieces of wood with Allah written in gold, I felt the weave of basilica and mosque coming together as museum. I began to pray for this weave in our world... that we could all live together in peace and gratitude. Robert Lentz, my Franciscan friend, painted the Icon of St. Francis and the Sultan together as friends, to remind us of this possibility. After I had returned in 2006 from my trip to Turkey, Robert told me that the only mosaic that was left fully visible is the one of Mary and Jesus in the half-dome of the apse where people exit the museum. He said that because Muslims consider Jesus to be a prophet and revere Mary as His mother and because it was out of the main area of prayer, they left this mosaic intact.

Trusting that someday my prayer would be answered and feeling blessed even in the waiting, I walked toward the exit. I was aware of a sadness because of the many transformations of Hagia Sophia as well as an appreciation of the beauty that had been. I was also aware of the potential gift of the museum, not simply as a museum but as an agent for healing our differences. I had not yet really felt it, but I believed in the presence and the power of Sophia in that Basilica. I felt a fullness in my heart alongside a longing for more... a longing for Sophia.

As we exited, I saw before me the image of Mary reflected in a mirror. I turned to see the image behind and above me in the half-dome above the apse, and as I communed with her, I found myself focusing on her eyes. Then, it happened. It was as though I was assumed into her and through her to another dimension. I heard the question I had been hearing throughout the entire trip, but this time I really heard because it was She who spoke, my Mother God, Sophia, Holy Wisdom. *Are you going to follow the way of Jesus, the wisdom and the light, or are you going to be like a sheep, fearful of voicing the things you have been shown?*

Suddenly I felt and saw the hypocrisy of "making myself fit" and I was horrified. I sobbed right there in the small round room with the image of Mary above me, the exit sign flashing and people milling about.

Dave held me, tourists passing on either side of me, as a watershed burst the bubble of the "Good Catholic girl" who wanted to remain a part of the church she loved. Shaking, I could hear Sophia's call from deep within me heart and soul to Come forth. She pleads, *Be a Catholic woman who will stand powerfully with grace and truth, regardless of the consequences.* Tears of gratitude flowed and a knowing that the One who had called me to life and who had awakened me time after time had finally broken through and amidst my tears loved me as the veils of hypocrisy were falling from my shoulders. I had awakened to my Mother God embracing me, and I was ecstatic.

Later in the day Dave asked, "Why did Sophia come to you through Mary?" I recalled her eyes and felt the ecstasy of being assumed into her. I wasn't sure why, but then, I remembered being in a chapel in Germany... the chapel is exquisitely decorated in black marble and silver and holds the magnificent Black Madonna of Altotting. I had knelt before her silently in prayer for quite some time when a large and noisy crowd entered. I left the tiny chapel and gently closed the doors behind me. On my way out of the vestibule, my eyes were drawn to a life-size statue of Jesus, resting, battered and lifeless on Mary's lap. The statue was beautiful. I knelt down and looking at Mary. I asked, "Why is it that so many people come to visit your shrines? Who are you that this is so?" Without a moment's pause, I heard, *I am the Mother of God. I brought forth the Christ, and you are to do the same.* I sat there stunned by the power and simplicity of the revelation. Now I understand, almost fifteen years later, that Mary is the passageway for all of us to bring forth our God. She shows us the way. Hail Mary full of Grace, thank you for your gift, your "yes" and for your reminder that my role, and the role of each one, is to bring forth the Christ. In so doing we find Wisdom and are claimed as hers... one with the Mother, the very breath of God. ✷

Reflection Questions

We often confuse our image of God with who God truly is. Our image of God is a tiny fraction of God's reality, and if we are maturing, our image of God is changing. As children, we might see God as an old man in the sky. As my daughter Annie once cried, "If you think I believe in a white-haired, bearded man in the sky, you are wrong. There is no such thing." Her old image was gone but her new image had not yet come into focus. She was angry, confused and rebellious. She was also only thirteen years old.

> *What is your image of God now? Has your image of God changed over the years?*
>
> *How does your image of God change as you read this book?*
>
> *How do you feel about what I have written in this book? Are there things that have frightened you or things that have supported you? Have I written things that have made you angry or that have given you a sense of peace about yourself and God?*

Remember all emotions will lead you to God if you stay with them. I invite you now to place your hands over your heart and take a few deep breaths. Invite your strongest feeling into your heart. Be with that feeling for a few minutes, focusing on your heart. Keep breathing deeply and watch what happens. Do this every night before you fall asleep. Love, gratitude and joy will soon fill your life.

Epilogue

New Life

The Dark Experience of Nothingness is like a cloudy night sky when the moon is dark—terrifying because momentarily there is no light! A total eclipse! I know now that even in the midst of the darkest night, if I am faithful and courageous, I will find the light—a light more brilliant than ever before.

It is also like the dark and terrifying moments when I heard the words, "Your daughter is dead," and then later, "Your son is dead," and still later, "Your marriage is dead." Finally, being in the darkness is like the moment of realizing that the hierarchy of the Church that I love represses the feminine spirit along with the gifts women offer. And finally, the darkness is like the moment I heard the call to speak the truth even if it means I lose my place in the Church I love.

Of these moments, the only one I can do anything to change is the repression of the feminine. I am challenged by my spirit and the Spirit of God to work toward reconciliation so that the feminine image of God is acknowledged and celebrated, alongside the image of God the Father. I have never wanted to return to the matriarchy as it had been, nor do I believe that the patriarchy, as it is, is even remotely healthy. The inclusion of both, the balance of the masculine and the feminine is what I believe will transform our Church and our world. I envision a world and a Church in which women are welcomed and invited to all positions, whether pope or president, to work alongside their brothers as partners in creating healthy, loving, and safe environments. For this to happen, fear of the feminine, especially fear of the Mother God, must give way to a love that espouses mutuality, egalitarianism, and the original teachings of Jesus. The resistance to this is enormous since men fear losing their power and women have been taught to fear and disown their power.

In the midst of this fear and darkness, I am led to trust, to stay awake, to be present to the moment, and to know that I will be lead to the light. If I am faithful to my spirit, my truth, my emotions, doing what I am called to do, I know now that sacred winds will rise, sometimes gently and at other times with ferocity, to move aside the clouds of fear and pain—to reach beyond the darkness to the brilliance that lies waiting in the abyss. I know this is true because I have seen the stars light up the sky when the moon is dark, and I have felt the Spirit's powerful force moving on the earth and in the heavens within myself—and within the many who seek the truth.

Suffering, loss, and pain brought me to the depths of the volcano, to the *Dark Experience of Nothingness*. And when the sun rose, I climbed to the top of the mountain, and I saw that the volcano, its eruptions, the darkness, and fire, the pool of clear water, and the reflections, are all within me, and I am within all I see. We are never separate from God—never, never, never—nor are we separate from one another, or any of creation. That which is real is the Divine Presence. All else is given as a gift to awaken each of us to that truth... to enlighten our minds, and ultimately to free us to embrace the sacredness of each moment with gratitude.

Our capacity for awareness is like a beautiful garden whose potential for beauty and expansion is limitless. My journey continues. I grow in my relationship with Sophia and am learning to see her in the Wisdom of Christ in whom She manifested her light. I awaken to new dimensions of darkness and light daily, but I remain open to the "more." There will always be some trepidation, since the birthing process is painful, but the joy that the new awareness brings quickly obliterates the suffering. All that is left is gratitude for the privilege of living in the light—even when the moon is dark.

The day is coming to a close as I write these last words. Snow is falling and the trees are glistening with white crystals. It is the Spring Equinox. My husband is sitting on the couch reading, with Emma, our little white dog, sitting beside him. It is peaceful here and a wonderful place to write. I am blessed. ✳

About the Author

Pamela Prime is a teacher, spiritual director and writer. She received a Masters in Systematic Theology in 1984 from the Graduate Theological Union in Berkeley Ca. and was adjunct faculty at the Jesuit School of Theology and core faculty at the School of Applied Theology, G.T.U. graduate schools. Pamela founded La Casa de la Luz, a spirituality center for women and men, and currently runs a spiritual direction training program. She lives in the sierra foothills of California with her husband where together they run a small retreat center. Pamela enjoys nothing more than being in nature and spending time with her children and grandchildren. ✳

The following organizations will each receive 5% of the profits from this book:

Dawn's Light in Sonora,Ca, which offers support to people who grieve the loss of their loved ones.This center has an emphasis on group support for grieving parents and offers classes at the schools on the prevention of teen suicide.

The Center for the Divine Feminine at the Institute of Transpersonal Psychology is a resource to ITP students, alumni, staff, and faculty, as well as to the local and global communities. Its mission is to support the exploration, education, and embodiment of the Feminine face of the divine in women's and men's lives.

Future Church, a national organization dedicated to the renewal of the Catholic Church with special emphasis on full participation of all people in ministry.

The Printed *Voice*

The Printed Voice is dedicated to publishing books that transform our world. Its mission is to help authors find their readers through direct access. For more information and for a list of our other books, please look us up on the web at:

www.printedvoice.com